The unexpected
Artists' Ceramics of the 20th Century

Janet Koplos
Max Borka
Willemijn Stokvis
Jos Poodt

The Kruithuis
Museums Collection

Distributed by
Harry N. Abrams, Inc., Publishers

Lucio Fontana
untitled 1959
vase; 19 x 14 cm
collection Museum Het Kruithuis

The unexpected
Artists' Ceramics of the 20th Century

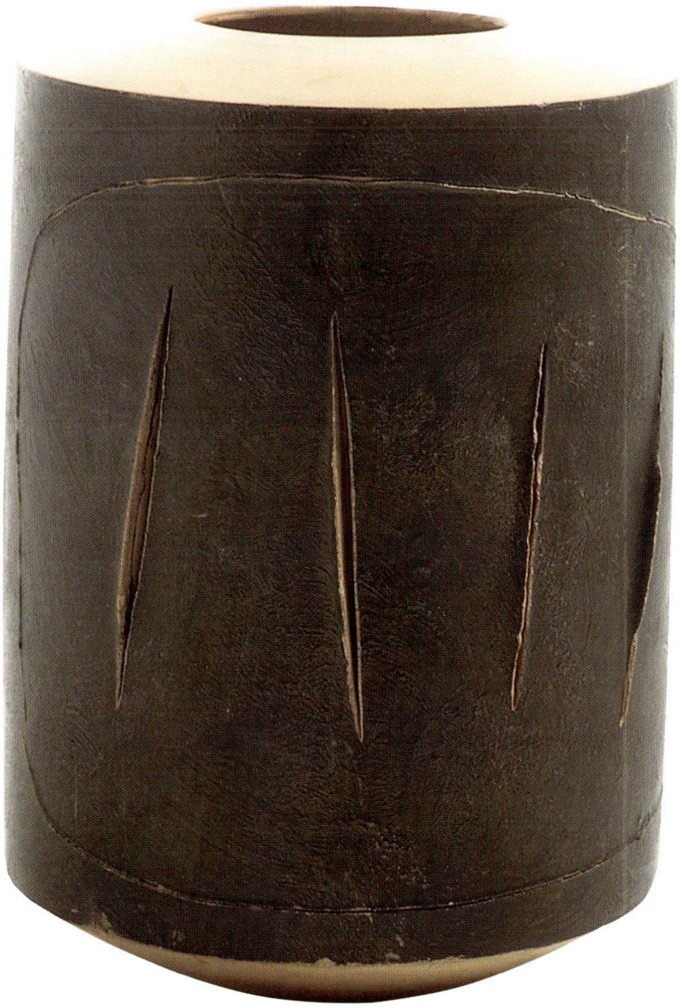

Contents

Foreword

by Yvònne G.J.M. Joris
Director Museum Het Kruithuis

During the mid eighties, Museum Het Kruithuis in 's-Hertogenbosch purchased Pablo Picasso's *Vase Femme* from 1954, produced in the studio of Georges and Suzanne Ramié in Vallauris. This formed the start of what is now known as its collection of "artists' ceramics". The work was among the most beautiful pieces of an extensive exhibition of Picasso's ceramics, organized by the museum in 1985. The selection of the ceramic work produced by Picasso, shed light on a relatively unknown aspect of his wide-ranging and versatile oeuvre. The presentation clearly showed that working in clay and painting clay meant more to Picasso than an impromptu broadening of his expressive means. He turned it into a discipline in itself, one which goes far beyond the craftsmanship traditionally associated with ceramics. He used clay to produce works that could not be realized in any other medium. Ceramics provided him with the opportunity to fulfill his sculptural and his pictorial ambitions at the same time. Whereas, on the flat surface, illusion must generally be created with the aid of painterly artifice, it is immediately and concretely present in the sculptural nature of clay. Picasso exploited this in an unparalleled manner and with almost palpable delight. His *Vase Femme* from 1954 is a brilliant demonstration of this.

Picasso's ceramic work set us off in search of countless other prominent artists who employ the medium of ceramics as an adequate expressive means, along with and in equivalence to other disciplines. Here it seems that the map of modern art history unjustly contains a number of blank spots, and these deserve to be "colored in" with the ceramic work of twentieth-century painters. Museum Het Kruithuis aims to achieve this objective by way of research and exhibitions and - not least - by building a high-quality collection in this field. Over the past fifteen years, exhibitions have been organized including ones devoted to the ceramic oeuvres of the classical moderns in "Terra Sculptura, Terra Pictura" (1992), the COBRA group in "Everything Valuable is Defenceless" (1993) and contemporary artists in "An Extra Dimension" (1994). Each time one sees how unknown and how surprising the ceramic work of the artists is. Each time one also sees the extent to which this work forms an integral part of their oeuvre. Considering the intensity and conviction with which artists work in this medium, and considering the strength of the results, it continually suprises us that their ceramics are so poorly represented in large public collections.

Since the purchase of Picasso's *Vase Femme*, more than seventy ceramic works of historically important artists, young and old, have been acquired. Every one of these artists can be said to have played an important role. The collection has been compiled in this book in such a way that each artist's ceramic work is considered, partly by way of written contributions, from the perspective of the individual oeuvre as well as from that of the history of twentieth-century art.

The collection has grown into one of the largest and most specialized of its kind in the world. We are proud of that. But what pleases us most is the fact that, with this work and this book, we can present a little-known and unexpected facet of many highly respected artists.

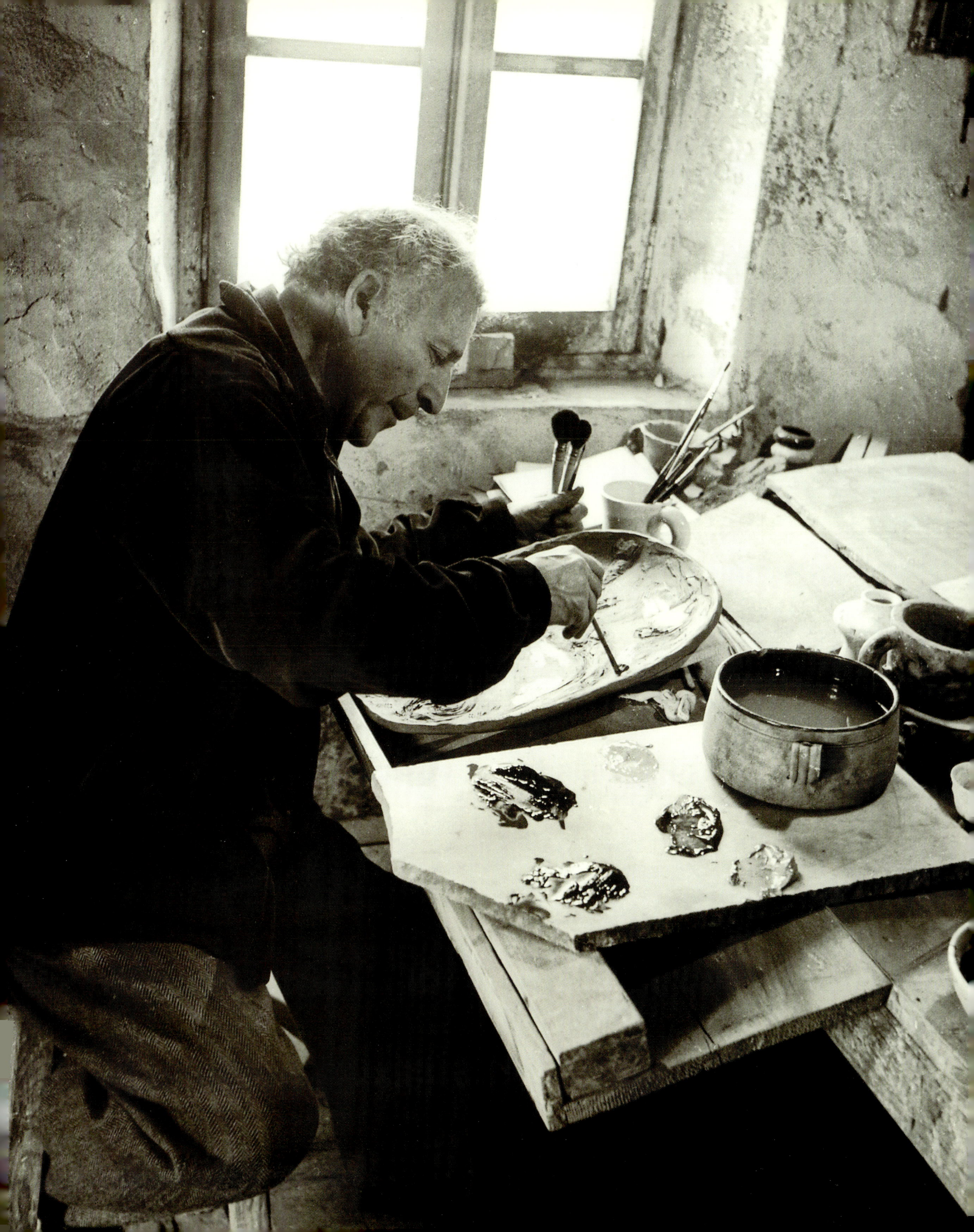

From Picasso to Penck: Playing With Clay

by Janet Koplos

It's a pitcher with a pear-shaped contour and a thick, hollow handle. Something has happened to the spout, and the distortion probably makes it unusable, but there's no question about this being an ample and attractive pitcher form.

She's a young woman with round cheeks and dark, flashing eyes. Her soft black hair hangs in a braid down her back, and glossy yellow flowers and shiny green foliage crown her forehead. Something is not quite right about her jawline, which flares in a most unusual manner, but her face is cheerfully plump and she's lively and charming.

"It" and "she" are one and the same in a work of art created by **Pablo Picasso** (1881-1973 – fig.48). Picasso, known for his artistic invention and fecundity, his willingness to try anything and his ability to make art of disparate and unlikely materials, is one of the many artists of the 20th century who at one time or another has made artworks in clay. He manipulated pottery forms made for him by others and worked directly with slabs or lumps of clay to make whatever sculptural shape he wished.

Picasso's little pitcher is part of the collection of Het Kruithuis, a Dutch art museum that takes a special interest in 20th-century ceramics. The museum's collection of more than 5,000 ceramic works includes a substantial and constantly growing number by painters and sculptors. It is this work, by what are sometimes called "visitors to clay," that is the subject of this book.

With this pitcher, Picasso gives living reality to one of the truths about functional pots: that their forms echo aspects of the human body. We use body terms for pots every day, hardly thinking of what that implies: we speak of the lip or neck of a vase, for example. Ceramics terminology carries this analogy even further: a pot also has a shoulder, a belly, a foot. And the identification also travels in reverse, since we speak of a pot belly on a person.

Just as he saw a bull in a bicycle seat and handlebars (1942) and a baboon's face in a toy car (fig. 1), Picasso responded to the human qualities in the curves of the pitcher, and from that observation he let his imagination run free. He was not limited by the necessity of creating a realistic resemblance to a young woman. A likeness in manner or spirit was enough. The flowers across her brow are sufficient to distract attention from the real hole in her cranium. What's more, with this association of a pitcher and a woman, Picasso has made a little joke on art-history conventions, from the "women at the well" image in 19th-century art to Ingres's famous *The source* (1820-1856), a painting of a placid, naked young woman pouring water from a jar on her shoulder. Picasso not only conflates a pitcher and a head, but a modern art image with an old one.

FIG.1 PABLO PICASSO
BABOON AND YOUNG 1951
sculpture bronze; 53.3 X 33.3 X 52.7 cm
COLLECTION THE MUSEUM OF MODERN ART, NEW YORK

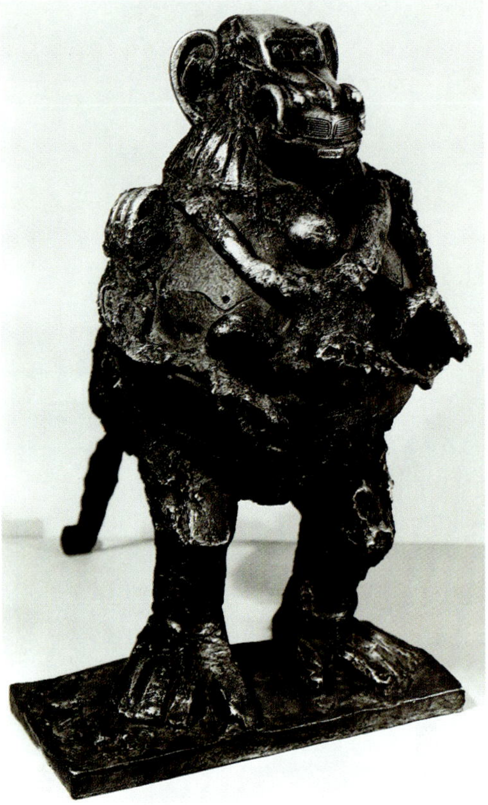

FIG.1

Inextricably tangled up in the meaning of his work is the history and purpose of the familiar genre of ceramics. Ceramics is as old as civilization, and in all times and cultures it has been used for both functional and expressive purposes. Picasso could have modeled the little head out of a lump of clay, shaping the soft material into a likeness. He could then have fired his sculpture in a kiln to vitrify it and render it more or less permanent, or he could have used the clay as the preparatory stage for casting in bronze or another material. But in this work he started instead from an existing form – the pitcher was prepared by someone trained in ceramic techniques – and he took it from there. His imagination was applied to the pot as to the handlebars, the toy car, or objects welded together in his assembled sculptures, many of which take a whimsical tone. Viewers can simultaneously see, as if in an optical illusion, the difference between what the work is and what it looks like. It is a handlebar and seat, but it looks like a bull; the disparity is amusing. Here is a kitchen vessel that looks like a girl, which introduces the funny thought of kitchen cupboards crowded with partial people.

There is richness in that association. Functional ceramic objects are in multiple ways related to the human body – in scale, sometimes in form, and metaphorically in material (the earth of which Adam was made). We may kinesthetically respond to ceramic volumes because they evoke interior spaces in our own bodies. This human metaphor gives ceramics a deep potential for artistic meaning. Yet ceramics as an aesthetic category, and especially functional ceramics, occupies a peripheral position in the official art world today, exhibited and written about in different contexts from painting and sculpture. Appreciators of ceramics often blame this separation on Modernism and its ostensible notion of purity that separates art from life. However, as the many examples in this book will show, that is hardly the case. In the late 19th century Gauguin worked extensively in clay to make vessels and sculptures, and many of the most important 20th-century Modernist artists also responded to opportunities to work with clay. Matisse, Rouault, De Vlaminck, Redon, Renoir, Bonnard, Derain, Maillol and other major artists were exposed to ceramics in the early years of this century – and that's citing only France.

Throughout the 20th century, painters and sculptors have at various times experimented with ceramics, and many of them have had a long and devoted involvement with it. This was particularly so just after World War II. Interestingly, that was also the time that the studio clay movement began to flourish in the U.S., when veterans flocking to college art departments wanted to work with real and direct and expressive materials. Whether a similar feeling may have affected the Modernists would be an interesting subject for research. That is, in fact, the assertion of some European historians, who suggest that the displacement of war took the artists out of the cities and into simpler and even preindustrial cultures, and also fostered in them the desire to escape established cultural hierarchies.[1] The entire avant-garde tradition in modern art has pushed at boundaries, chafed at the modesty and propriety of

1. Gérard Monnier, "À Le Rencontre Du Métier et du Dialecte," L'Art En Europe, Les années décisives 1945-1953, Saint-Étienne: Musée d'art moderne, 1987, p. 54.

easel painting and debated the line between art and life.

Working with ceramics, for some artists, is just a momentary adventure with new shapes, colors and surfaces. The ones whose engagement with clay has been deeper are those who have found a particular meaning in the substances and processes (the primordiality of earth, the unpredictable test of the fire) or those who have embraced multiple forms of creative expression (not just painting but sculpture, stage design, stained glass, prints, textiles, etc.)

Obviously, a distinction between clay and other art materials is not an issue or an obstacle for all artists. More likely the explanation for the marginal position of ceramics is the departmentalization of art museums and the specialization of art critics. Ceramics, being three-dimensional, is closer to sculpture than to painting, but it's the two-dimensional arts of painting and photography that have inspired the growth of art criticism as well as its increasingly theoretical language in this century. Artists become prominent because of their paintings, and when they have retrospective exhibitions the paintings and supplementary two-dimensional work are emphasized; their work in clay may be included in an exhibition and/or pictured in a catalogue, but it is rarely given a substantial analysis.

This book attempts to look closely and think carefully about work in this particular medium by a number of major artists – much of which has not been discussed elsewhere. We face a new set of questions. Picasso used clay, and anything that Picasso did is of interest just because he did it. But faced with these sometimes-familiar objects and their sometimes-unfamiliar surface treatments, how are we to understand them? What do we see? Are these things to be regarded as sculptures? How do they relate to the painting or other sculpture of these artists? What is specifically "ceramic" in the character of these artworks? What makes them interesting? What makes them good?

Classical Modernists

That Picasso's pitcher-woman formulation is not the only way to merge a ceramic vessel and a head can be seen in a work by **Jean Cocteau** (1889-1963 – fig. 4). Cocteau and Picasso were friends, of the same generation, and almost equally broad in their range of interests. Cocteau was a novelist, a playwright, a filmmaker, an artist, a dandy and a celebrity who has been described as "the first self-promoter of this century, and among the greatest."[2] He used his skill of hand to design posters for Diaghilev's *Ballets Russes*, as well as for witty sketches of Diaghilev himself, and he wrote essays for the fashion magazines of the 1930s and '40s illustrated with his fluent line drawings (fig 2). In his ceramics, as in his life, Cocteau has been accused of being "merely" decorative and preferring arabesques to "content."[3] Perhaps that accusation of a light approach is accurate in the case of his ceramics, which are editions rather than unique products of his hand.

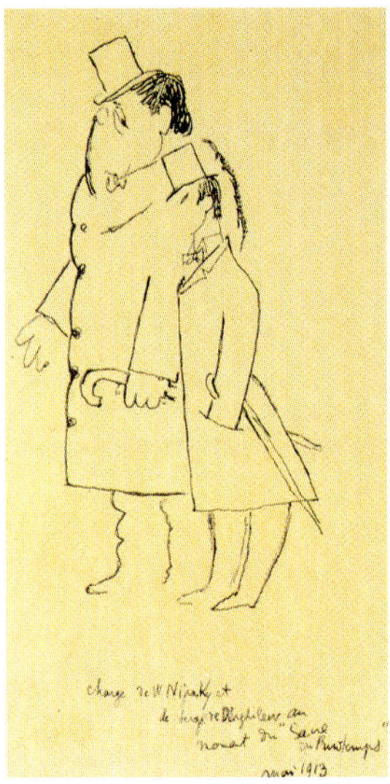

FIG. 2

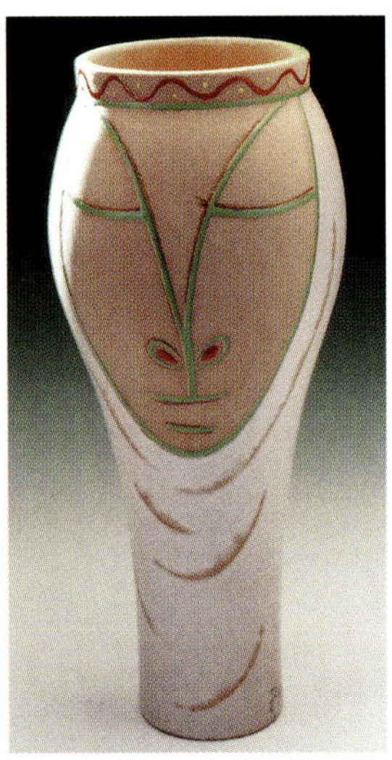

FIG.3

Cocteau designed a head on a crisp, modern, uncontoured pitcher (fig. 5). The face painted onto this near-cylinder lacks any sense of fleshy contours. His approach to defining the head is essentially two-dimensional: it is painted on the vase. The only incursions into the third dimension result from his positioning of the features to make use of the handle as hair and the spout as a nose – although the upward flare of the spout is an exact inversion of the downward flare of a nose. The sharpness and clarity of Cocteau's pitcher are graphic, whereas Picasso's is more naturalistic and sensual. (Considering the English potter and aesthetician Bernard Leach's assertion that "the pot's the man," one might note here that Cocteau had a distinctive appearance, with a narrow, handsome face, long nose and prominent jaw; his sharp features have a certain relationship to the hard forms of this pitcher!)

Even though both artists treat a pitcher as a head, the results reflect their entirely different approaches.

FIG. 2 JEAN COCTEAU 1913
DIAGHILEV ET NIJINSKY (LE SACRE DU PRINTEMPS)
India ink on paper

FIG.3 JEAN COCTEAU
MÉDIÉVALE (ED. 1/50) 1958
vase; 29 cm

FIG. 4 JEAN COCTEAU

2. Julie Saul, "Introduction," in Jean Cocteau: The Mirror and the Mask," Boston: David R. Bodine, Publisher, 1992, p. 5.
3. François Mathey, "But This Is Another Story," Terra Sculptura, Terra Pictura, 's-Hertogenbosch: Museum Het Kruithuis, 1992, p. 36.

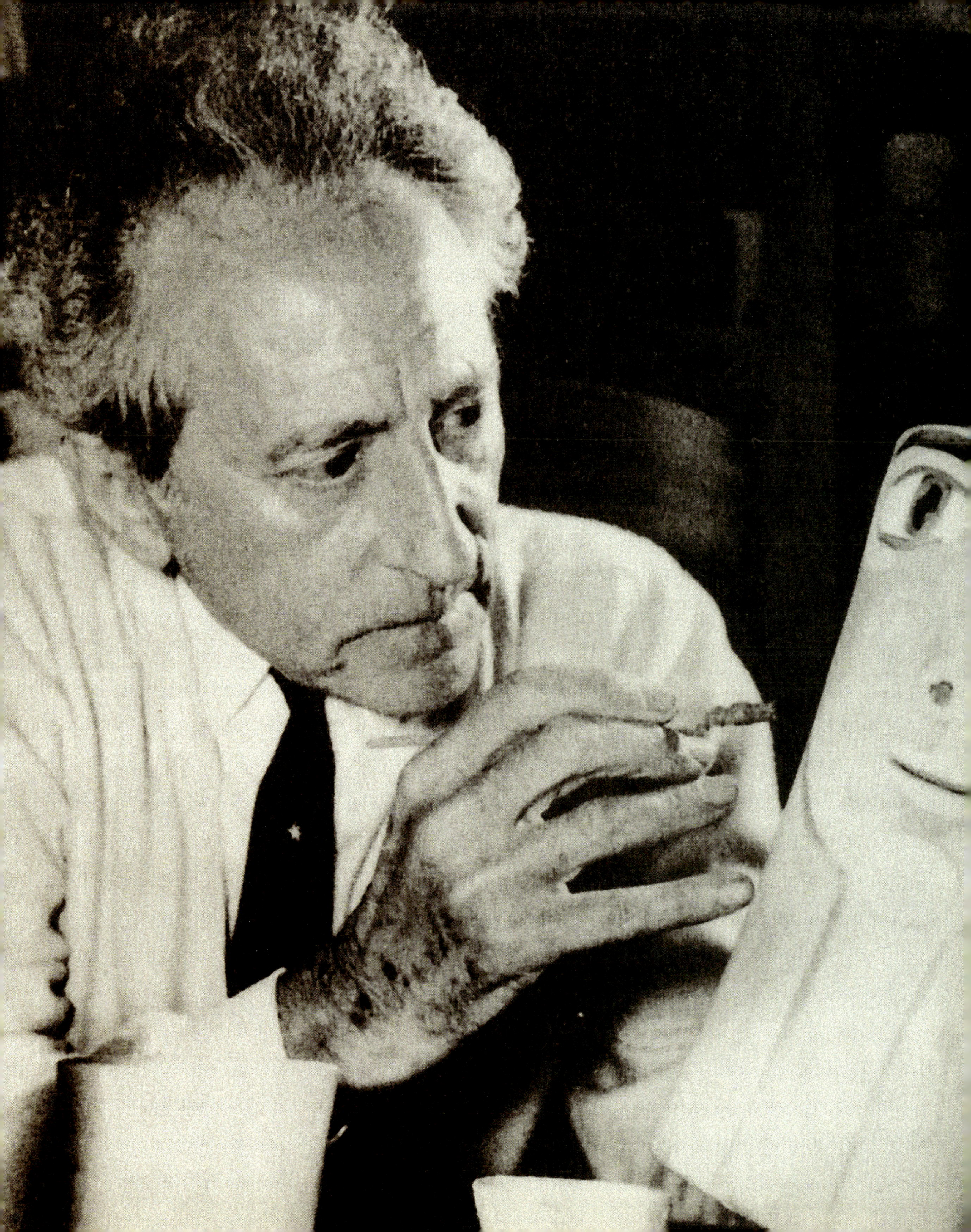

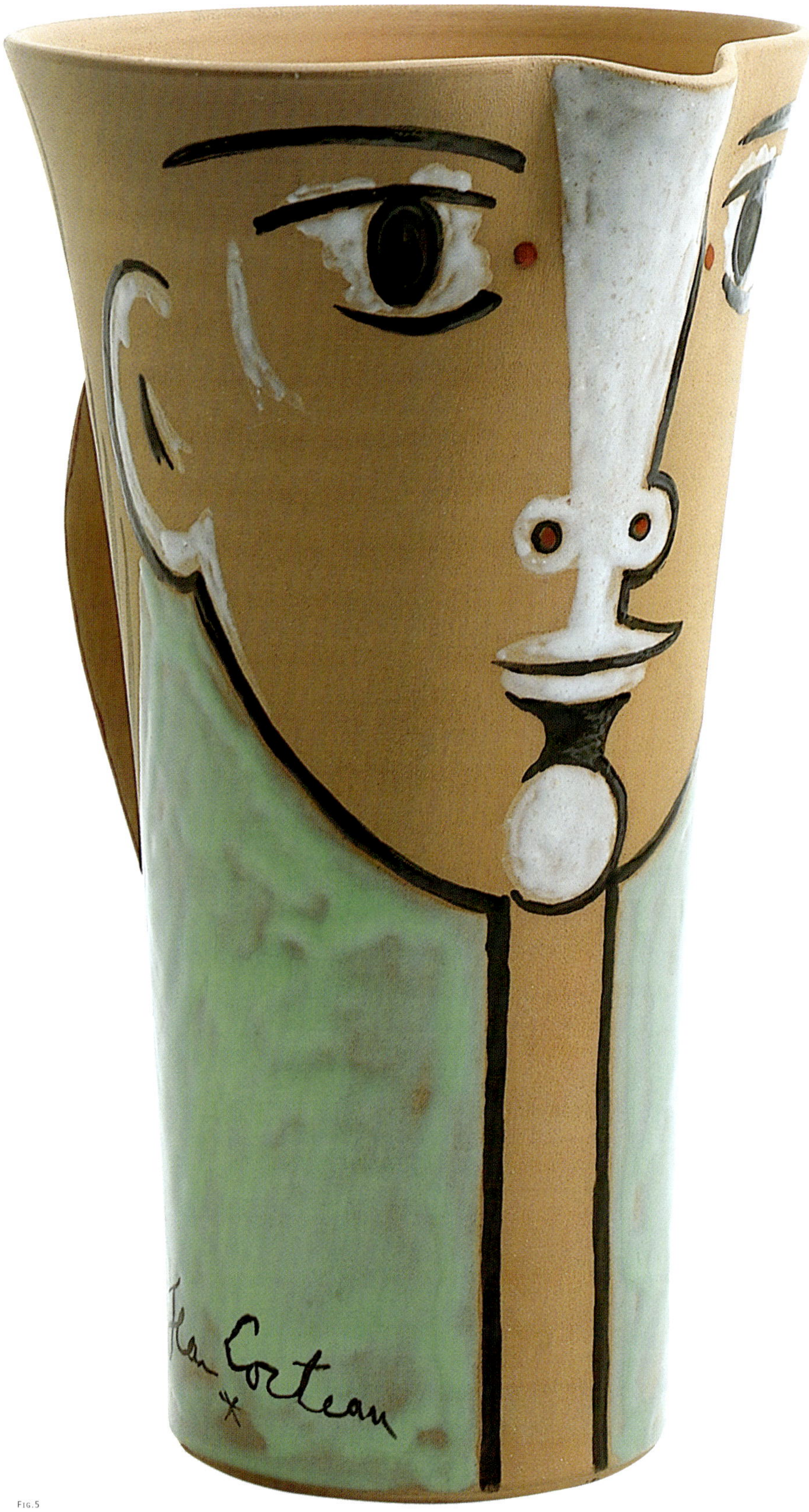

Fig.5

Fig.5 JEAN COCTEAU
VISAGE (ED. 29/30) 1968
vase; 27 X 21.5 cm
COLLECTION MUSEUM HET KRUITHUIS

Cocteau has decorated the object with a human image, and all the distortion is to the image. Probably he hardly thought of it as distortion: he also designed a vase called *Médiévale* (fig. 3) that depicts a wimpled woman in the same degree of stylization, and he made a cup and a wide two-handled goblet in which the foot/stem of the vessel is equated with the neck of a simple head, and the container itself is the jaw.

The plates Cocteau created show a consistent flattening and clarity. He is not known for sculpture but for drawing, so his usual style of work transfers much more naturally to the plate. Plates may be slightly concave or entirely flat, but even when they have a raised rim, their depth is modest, so they can usually be treated like a tondo (a round painting). This simplicity and flatness suit the many "visitors to clay" whose usual work is two-dimensional, allowing them to extend familiar imagery and treatment within the particularities of a new medium. Painters often respond to the color possibilities of ceramic stains, underglazes and glazes, as well as to varieties of texture, but Cocteau's ceramic works, like his drawings (fig. 6), find their strength in line rather than color.

In the 1950s Cocteau made a number of plates with iconic or medallion-like female profiles (fig. 7, 8 and 9). He employs the wide rim of the dish to isolate or to visually compress the image, which increases its focus and visual force. These evoke the late-19th-century drawings of Aubrey Beardsley. In other plates, Cocteau cuts into the clay, carving lines of emphasis or radiance around the faces. The softness of clay before it is fired makes it receptive to such gouging, as thick paint or a block of wood would be. The energy of this accenting also brings to mind the fact that fired clay is rigid and breakable (although fragility does not mean ephemerality; what we know of ancient civilizations is often based largely on

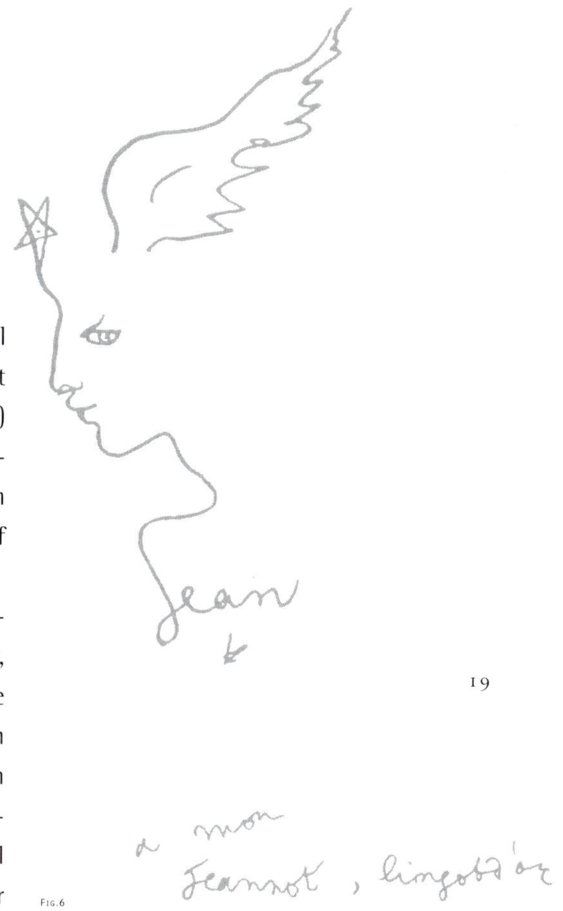

Fig.6

Fig.6 Jean Cocteau
A mon Jeannot 1939
portrait of Jean Marais
drawing

Fig.7 Jean Cocteau
Jeune-fille Florentine (ed. 22/25) 1957
plate; ø 18 cm
collection Museum Het Kruithuis

Fig.8 Jean Cocteau
La Femme au chignon (ed. 5/15) 1957
plate; ø 31 cm
collection Museum Het Kruithuis

Fig.9 Jean Cocteau
Béatrice (ed. 12/25) 1957
plate; ø 31 cm
collection Museum Het Kruithuis

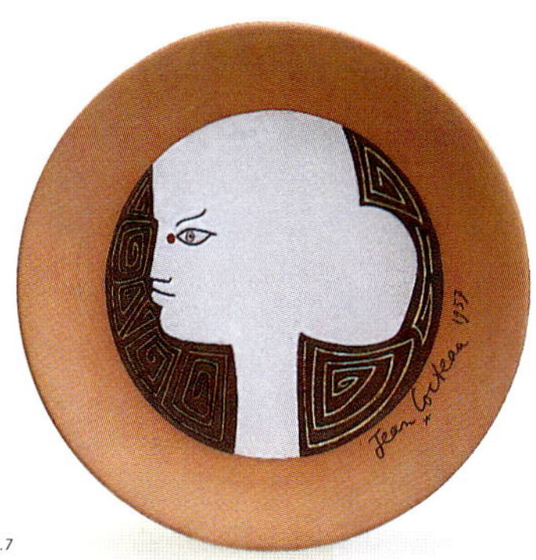

Fig.7

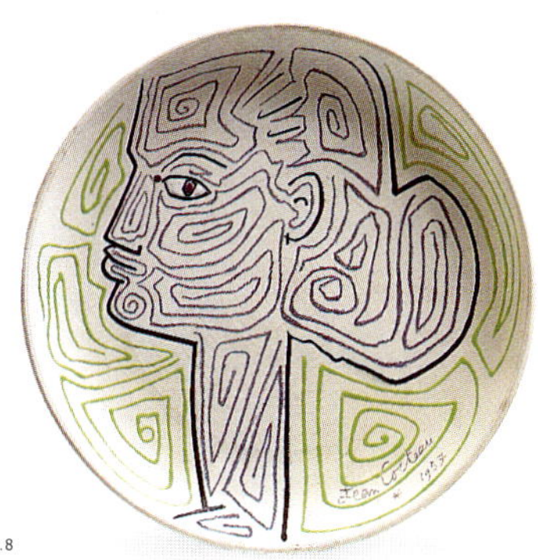

Fig.8

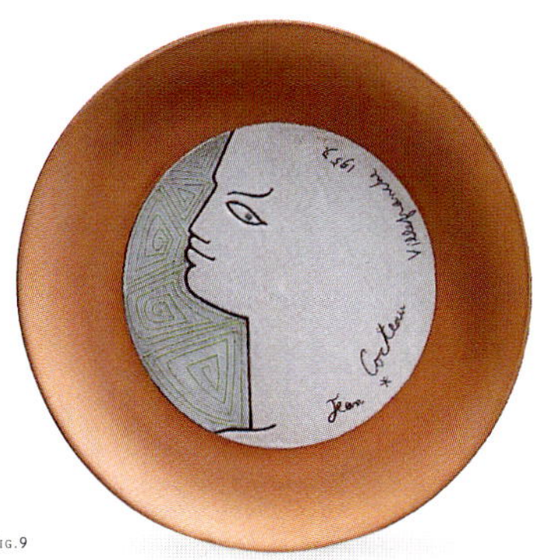

Fig.9

the persistence of broken bits of clay). The qualities of force and fragility combine with the female image in an unexpected and exciting way in these plates. On another plate (fig. 140), Cocteau has depicted an athlete in silhouette. There is probably some homoerotic appeal in this work, since the outline of the figure calls attention to nipples as well as underarm and pubic hair. The neutral, gently curving surface and shape of the plate frame the figure.

Joan Miró (1893-1983 – fig. 10) worked with clay extensively in the '40s and '50s. Among his works are two heads of clay (fig. 11 and 12) that are quite different from the pitcher-heads of Picasso and Cocteau, without any of the associations of water, use, domesticity, femaleness, or even art history except to the degree that they relate to his earlier Surrealist paintings. His heads are dream-creatures, or perhaps nightmares. They are built of rolled and cut slabs of clay, and are essentially shallow boxes standing on edge. The most pot-like thing about either of them is the handles on *Tête multicolore* (1946). In both these heads, the artificial roundness of the ears is echoed in the roundness of the applied eyes and other cylindrical elements – all of which contrast with the sharp rectilinearness of the heads themselves.

FIG. 10 JOAN MIRÓ

The heads are primitive or monstrous beings, and the strong tactile contrasts Miró has exploited in the ceramic materials add to the impact. *Tête carrée* (1955-56) is a complex, playful form with one round ear, one square one, and a cylindrical protrusion at the center of the forehead that brings to mind Buddha's *urna*, the mark of an extraordinary person. Miró has used a very rough clay and left the surface dry and unprettified. Four real rocks occupy the mouth like fearsome teeth. The eyes are painted in flat black, but over them are wide circular outlines of slightly glossy glaze – green for one eye and yellow for another – in a syrupy, dimensional application. Dribbles of thick white glaze mark the face like some kind of ritual scarification, and there's a dot on one ear. The eyes and mouth seem to drip like a sad clown's tears. An orange blush that flares across the clay is probably caused by the flames of the wood-fueled firing. This face is not just geometry and not just primitivism but a creative combination of the two, the new and the old. The rectangle at the top of the head, even more than the cylinder in the forehead, is inexplicable except as a sophisticated Brutalism.

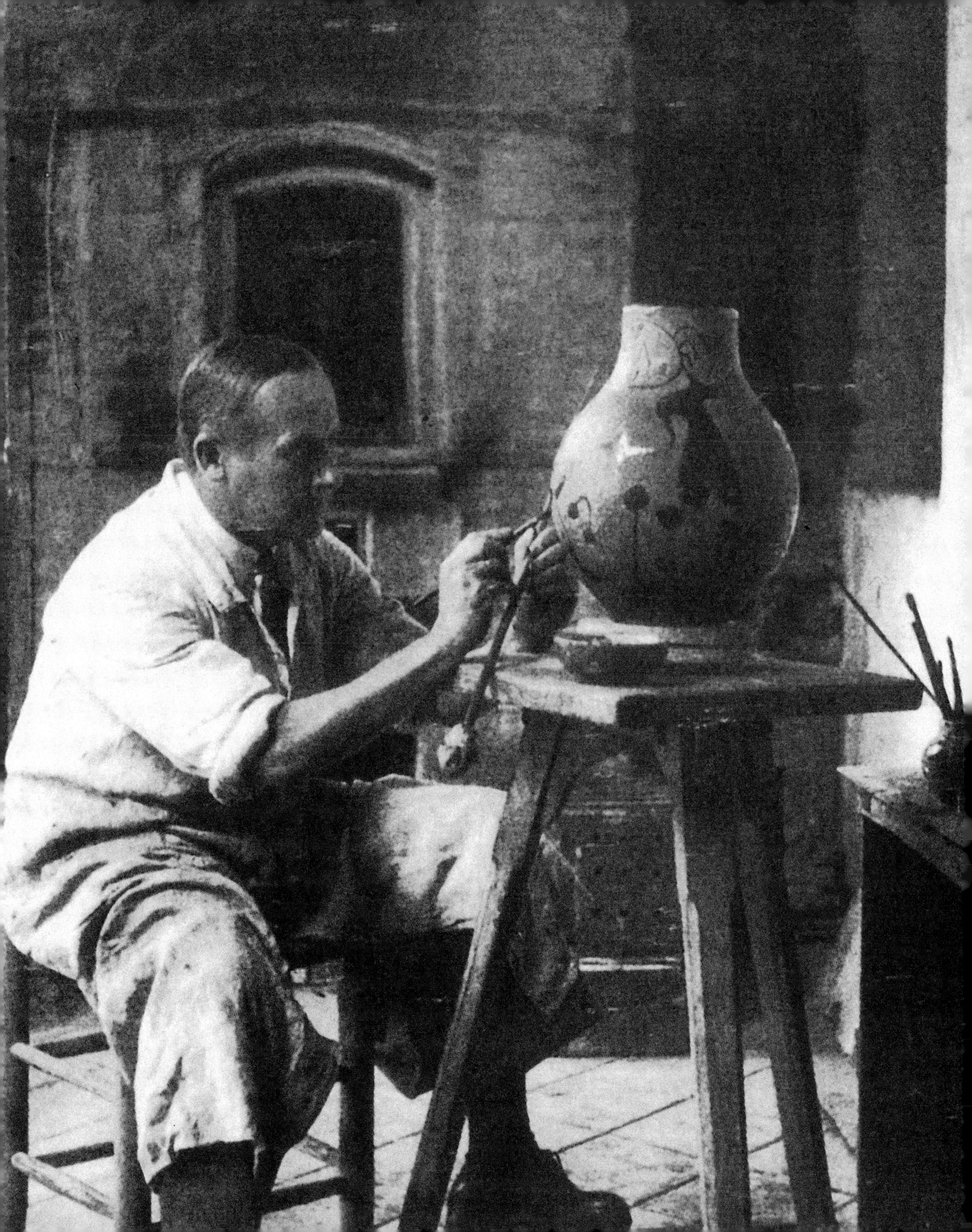

These works bear many relationships to Miró's paintings. One is the figurative subject matter itself (his work has been called "a long rumination on the ubiquity of the body in space"[4]). In addition, the heads show a familiar reduction to the basics of identification such as eyes and mouths, and the use of brilliant color and undulating line (the almost hand-shaped dribble on *Tête carrée*). As always with Miró, the heads are abstracted, but he always insisted his work was not abstract; he wanted to retain "the imagistic force" of representation.[5]

In a painting he could scatter the parts of a figure around the canvas and ignore the laws of gravity, but in his sculptures like these, the features must remain within the limits of a physical frame, for practical reasons. Another difference between these works and his painting is the boxiness of these ceramic heads. Miró is known for his curving, involuted or eruptive organic shapes. In most of his paintings, the only rectangles are passages of color in backgrounds or occasional more positive and aggressive foreground color elements. Block heads appear in his later sculptural works in bronze, such as a 1968 figure consisting of a flat, square head with eyes and meandering lines gouged out of the face and the impressed shapes of bare feet symbolizing the rest of the body (the prints of bare feet are also a traditional way to symbolize the Buddha – a coincidence?). A catalogue for a 1994 exhibition of Miró's bronzes includes 1967 and '68 preparatory drawings that show square heads, and a studio photograph in the catalogue (regrettably undated and uncredited) has the artist sitting before a wall on which is drawn a rectangular head.[6] Thus one might wonder if the ceramic box heads of '46 and '56, forms so simple that Miró could have constructed them with his own hands without training in ceramic techniques, introduced the idea of a rectilinear head.

A life-long friend of Miró's was the Catalan ceramist Joseph Llorens Artigas. In 1944, as Miró waited out the war in Barcelona, he first began experimenting with ceramics, with Artigas's aid. He produced objects for several years, and returned to this medium again in 1954-59.[7] He always credited Artigas as a collaborator. The ceramic work exemplifies

4. Carolyn Lanchner, Joan Miró, New York: Museum of Modern Art, 1993, p. 18.
5. Lanchner, p. 18.
6. See photograph on p. 20 of Miró: Matter and Color, Lausanne, Musée Olympique, 1994.
7. Roland Penrose, Miró, New York: Thames and Hudson, 1985 (1970), pp. 108, 123.

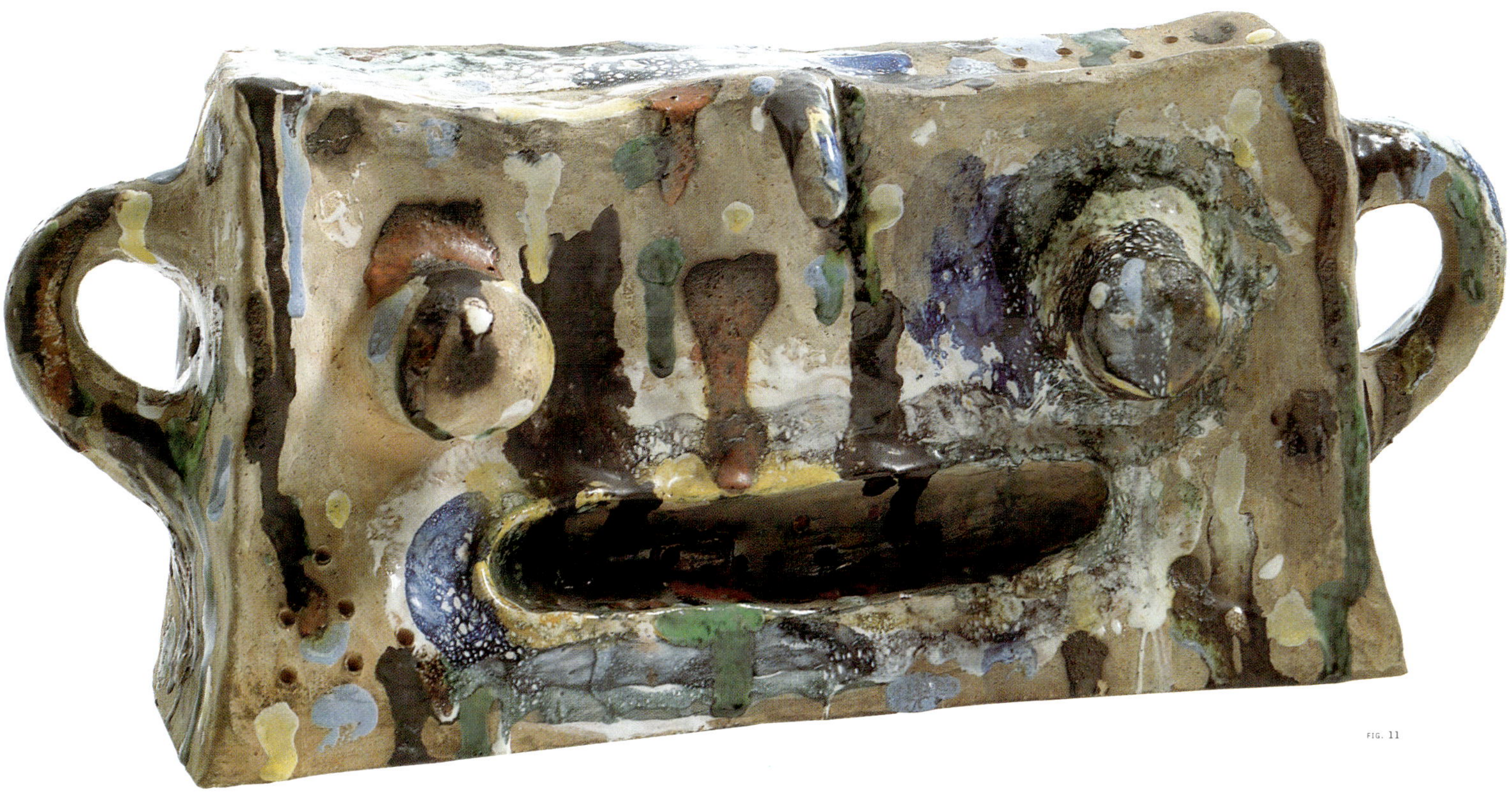

FIG. 11

FIG. 11 JOAN MIRÓ

TÊTE MULTICOLORE 1946

object; 17.5 x 44 x 10 cm

COLLECTION MUSEUM HET KRUITHUIS

[ACQUIRED WITH SUPPORT OF STICHTING VSB FONDS, UTRECHT & VERENIGING REMBRANDT, AMSTERDAM]

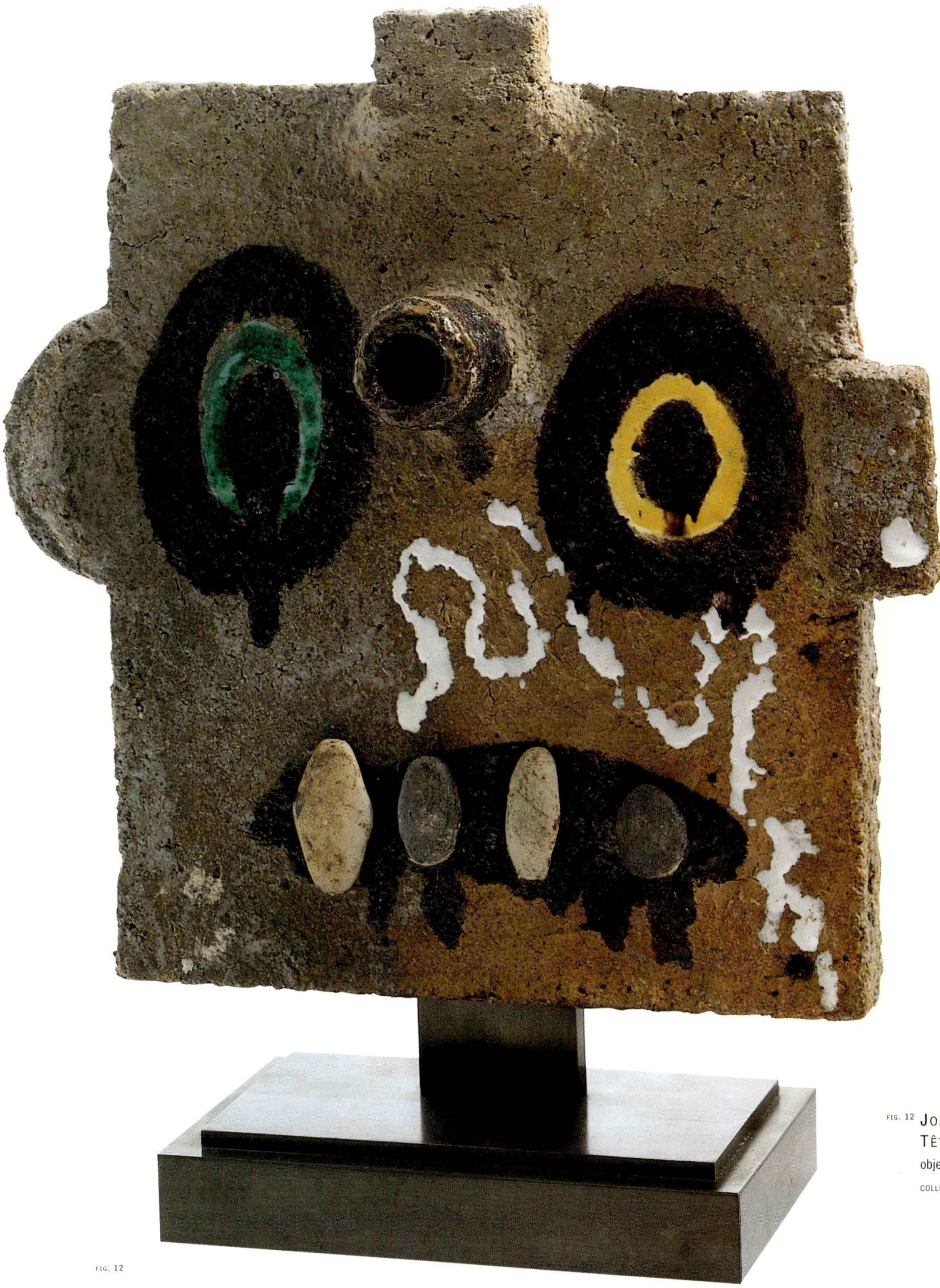

FIG. 12

FIG. 12 JOAN MIRÓ
TÊTE CARRÉE 1955-56
object; 30 x 30 cm
COLLECTION MUSEUM HET KRUITHUIS

Miró's well-known interest in materials and in mediums other than painting. As a young man, in the 1920s and '30s, he made collages as well as art objects of found materials. He has been quoted as saying "To me, rich and vigorous material seems necessary to give the spectator a blow between the eyes at first sight, which must hit him before other thought can intervene. In this way poetry expressed visually speaks its own language."[8] This is a surprisingly sculptural sensibility for someone known first and best as a painter! Among his uses of "the real" are the incorporation of postcards into paintings or drawings, and collages that include some of his most Surreal and poetic combinations. For instance, the 1928 *Spanish dancer* consists solely of a hatpin and a feather attached to a canvas. "Materials," he wrote, "always excite me and give me points of departure of great richness."[9] All his works, in every medium (fig. 13), are "a constant attempt to surprise meaning from matter... In whatever medium he worked, Miró's intent was... 'to rediscover the sources of human feeling.'"[10] Some of his sensitivity to materials and the third dimension may have resulted from his family history: his father was a goldsmith and his father's father a blacksmith, while his mother's father was a cabinetmaker.

In the war years, Miró grew closer to nature,[11] and he himself said that his interest in sculpture was renewed when he made ceramics with Artigas.[12] His ceramics are straightforward; even when they are painted with imagery, the material is undisguised. Someone observed that for Miró, ceramics is an extension of both painting and sculpture, in which many of his discoveries in both arts can be combined. There is everything in this art to enchant him. It begins with the earth, the clay which can be modelled in the hands, pressed against an object or a surface so as to receive its imprint, thrown on a wheel so that it has both an exterior

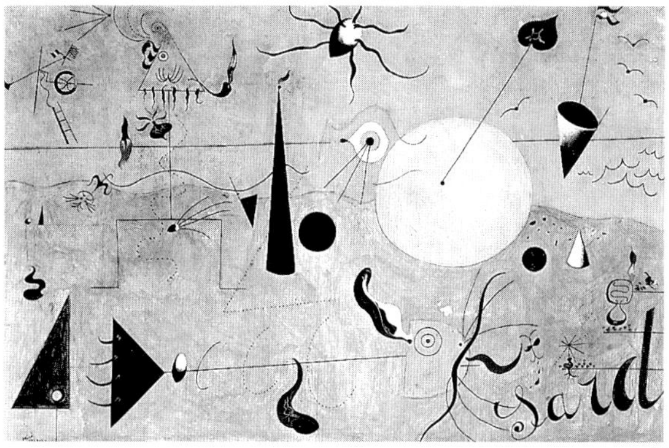

FIG. 13

FIG. 13 JOAN MIRÓ
THE HUNTER 1923-24
oil on canvas; 64.8 x 100.3 cm
COLLECTION THE MUSEUM OF MODERN ART, NEW YORK

8. Georges Duthuit, "Où allez-vous, Miró?," Cahiers d'Art, vo. XI, nos. 8-10, 1936, p. 261, quoted in Roland Penrose, Miró, New York: Thames and Hudson, Inc. (1970), p. 69.
9. Penrose, p. 69.
10. Miró quote from Francis Lee, "Interview with Miró," Possibilities (New York), no. 1, Winter 1947-48, pp. 66-67, quoted in Lanchner, p. 74.
11. William Jeffett, "Metamorphosis in Metal; Joan Miró: Sculptor," in Miró: Matter and Colour, p. 23.
12. Quoted in Jeffett, p. 22.

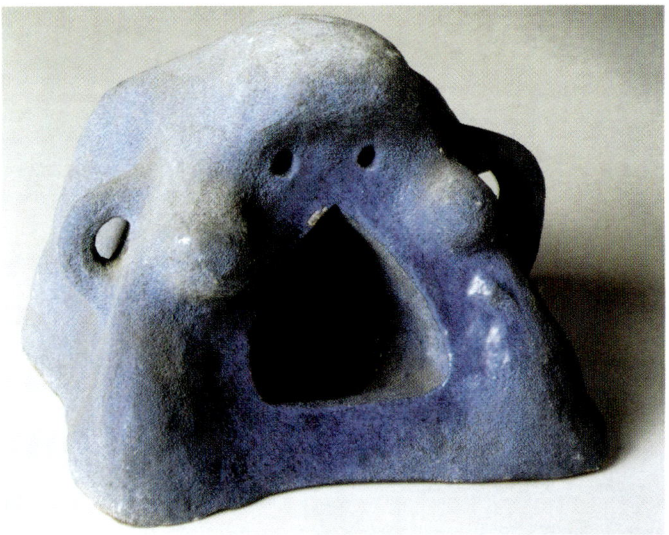

FIG. 14

FIG. 14 JOAN MIRÓ
TÊTE 1944-46
object; 25 x 18.5 cm

and an empty space within: its surface can be embellished with colour, texture and signs. The next stage is more dramatic. Fire now takes all into its control, and artist and craftsman stand aside, imposing their will only in so far as they are able. Miró is undismayed: the firing may by some unaccountable freak produce a result which was unexpected, but he is prepared, as in his paintings, to find ways of taking advantage of such happenings. [13] Both directness and acceptance of accidents were consistent with his general artistic approach.

Clay was appealing to him because of its earthy nature. The dramatic landscape of his native Catalonia was for him "an essential element in my plastic and poetic conception"; he saw ceramic forms as like the rocks of the mountain landscape and was pleased that fired ceramic sculptures could be shown outdoors, in natural surroundings.[14] These natural possibilities excited Miró. He "possessed the earth by choosing it as a vehicle" and found ceramic colorations "subtly mixed of a thousand tints, as the earth itself is."[15]

Clay can be used at any scale from the domestic to the monumental, and Miró, with his prodigious creative energy, seems to have worked at most scales, making an enormous ceramic mural as a public-art commission for the Barcelona airport and also painting on vases and plates with "primitive" or child-like figures that communicate a euphoric innocence. Among his early clay works were small, hand-modeled biomorphic forms in which the mouth that usually gives access to a vase's interior at the top, appears instead on the front as a more human mouth for a rudimentary figure (fig.14). He had no concern for the requirements of function or even of self-support: he made forms that had to be suspended or held up

13. Penrose, pp. 144-45.
14. Penrose, p. 150.
15. Dore Ashton, "Miró/Artigas – Their New Ceramics," Craft Horizons 24, January 1964, p. 54.

by a rod, such as mask-like fragments. In addition, he made various "personage" sculptures two or three feet tall, as opportunities to present many of his familiar motifs through the manipulation and glazing of the ceramic material. The rectilinear heads in the Kruithuis collection are strong examples of his range and of the strange, mesmerizing power of his figures.

Miró's sculptures "often depict near-totemic figures and embody a symbolism rooted in archetypes of the female and the male, the telluric and the celestial, matter and spirit, nature and intellect, as if the figures depicted in his sculpture are mediators between these two realms."[16] Among his ceramic works are objects to which this description could apply, including a 1962 *Tête de femme* (fig.15) that consists of a weathered wooden beam on which are stacked bricks with glaze poured over them, and above that an irregularly octagonal plate with a very stony surface, at the center of which eyes, nose and mouth have been cut. Of equal interest is a small (about a foot wide) blue-glazed ceramic sculpture that is closely related to such non-ceramic sculptures as his *Lunar bird* and *Solar bird*, as well as with the monumental cement gate he made for the Fondation Maeght in St.-Paul-de-Vence. Another suggestive abstraction, called *Femme*, is a three-foot-tall unglazed ceramic form, the curves, dimples and tactile skin of which allude to a female body. Two flaring legs that seem to have small crescent moons (or horns? or smiles?) emerging from their outside edges are joined by a thick crosspiece with several breast-like protrusions. This piece is dated 1944-46, so it must have been one of the earliest works Miró did with Artigas. Miró also made what he called *steles* – irregularly shaped ceramic slab painted with scenes or symbols that look like they have broken off some larger wall – as well as gourd-shaped bottles symbolic of wombs and fecundity. Miró (as well as Picasso and Chagall) had a dealer, Aimé Maeght, who was enthusiastic about ceramics.

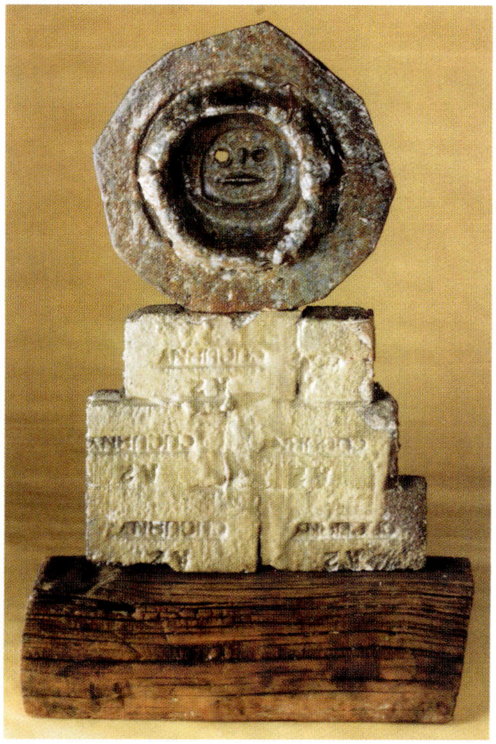

FIG. 15

FIG. 15 JOAN MIRÓ
TÊTE DE FEMME 1962
object; 85 x 60 x 24 cm

16. Jeffett, p. 22.

The common way to create a figure in ceramics is not through the geometric construction Miró used for these heads, but by means of drawing, painting or scratching the figure on a ceramic surface, as in Cocteau's plates. Delightful realizations of this more usual surface procedure, the success of which take them out of the ordinary, are the many figure-decorated vases by **Raoul Dufy** (1877-1953 – fig.17) in the Kruithuis collection. They show a curving, fluent line of the type we may associate with Picasso rather than the lighter, sketchier touch for which Dufy is best known.

The *Vase aux baigneuses* (fig. 16) is a pink color that seems to make a romantic overstatement in its association with flesh. Nobody is that rosy! But every bit as effusive as the color are the forms of the curvy nudes, roly-poly and ribbed with belts of flesh. They're not identical – they are individually scribed into the clay – but they are all loose, easy, free, generous in gesture and proportion, the classical body relaxed. All are seen from the back, and only hair provides a clue as to whether they're male or female. Although the bodies are elongated and thus adult-looking, one might almost expect to see sturdy wings, for this cheerful, innocent corpulence seems to belong on cherubs.

FIG. 16 RAOUL DUFY
VASE AU BEIGNEUSES 1926
vase; 34 x 27.5 cm
COLLECTION MUSEUM HET KRUITHUIS

FIG. 17 RAOUL DUFY

Dufy's drawings often have a lolling, Mediterranean, hedonistic character. The figures' appearance on this full-formed vase is particularly happy because its shape suits them so well, and even gives them an extra curve as they swim/float, untroubled by gravity (or, apparently, calorie count) along its spatial contours, on an indefinite plane that cuts through space. The figures derive something extra from their depiction on the curving surface.

This capability of ceramics has attracted artists from China to Crete: it is possible to bring "intimately together the imaginative reality of the painted figure and the actual reality of the world which the pot inhabits as object," notes the British art historian Philip Rawson.[17] This spatial doubleness can cause a sense of dislocation. The pot defines its own terms of reference: "we are ourselves virtually transported and located into a world whose scale is determined by the images on the pot. We do not – and this is important – adapt the scale of the images to the scale of our surrounding real world, but the other way

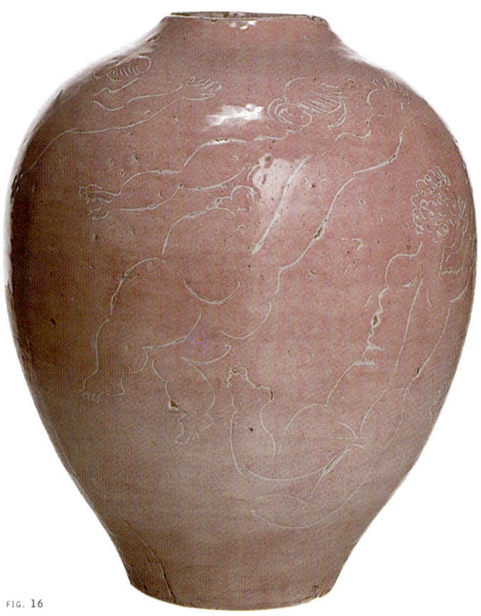

FIG. 16

17. Philip Rawson, Ceramics," London: Oxford University Press, 1971, p. 187.

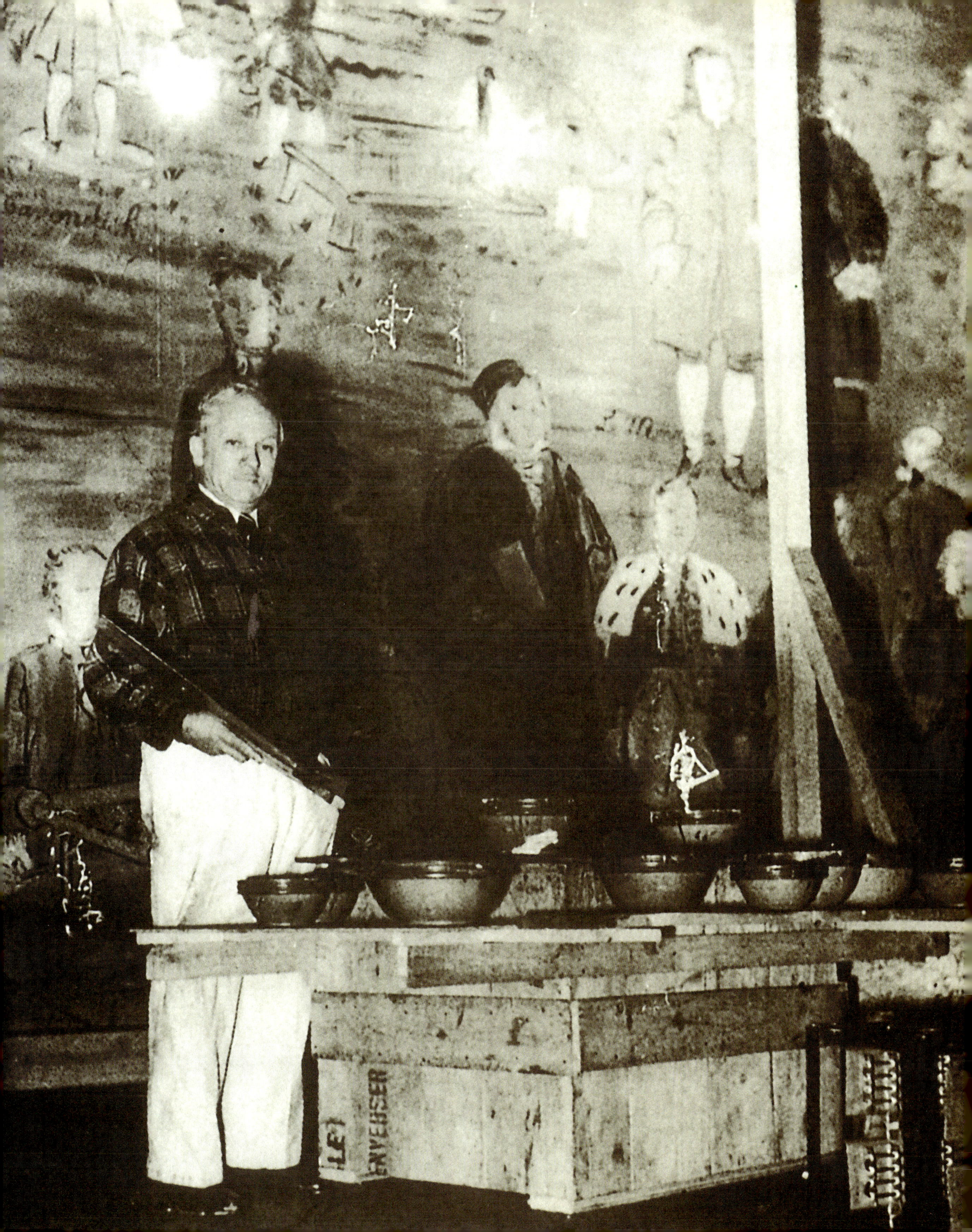

round," Rawson writes.[18] Dufy's vase also furnishes an instance to test another of Rawson's observations: "More, perhaps, than with any other art will the actual sexual and culturally endorsed erotic attitudes of the spectator condition his or her approach to a pot. Whereas a woman may identify, a man will appreciate..."[19]

As the figures gain dimension from the reiterating curves of the vase form, Dufy seems to make reference to ceramics in his composition: the figures move in the same direction, diagonally upward to the right, so that one thinks of rotation and the vase's forming process on the potter's wheel. Another delight of this work is the way the white line of Dufy's inscription of the bodies sometimes penetrates the pink underglaze to reveal a darker fleck, particularly where lines intersect. These are not flaws but punctuation. They are realizations of the ceramic substance and, more than that, they are dimples that augment the sense of flesh. Other odd marks suggest bubbles rising.

Other Dufy vases are consistent in character with this one. Though they are not so spectacularly euphoric, they have their own appeal. *Vase bleu aux femmes* (fig. 18) is a heavier form and more open at the top. The blue color is less voluptuous than pink – its association is with water rather than flesh – so these bathers are somewhat less erotic and become more of a pattern. The curves of their hair echo the curves of the waves which echo the curves of their muscles and fat rolls (maybe here the contemporary term "love handles" is appropriate, since these bodies look slightly harder and more mature than those on the vase just discussed). The flaring base is embellished with an appropriate shell motif. One of the most enticing features of this pot is the interior glaze, which is quite visible because of the openness of the form. It recalls raspberry sorbet, a luscious summery association that suits the sensuality of the bathers.

In another type of ceramic work, Dufy exploits an entirely different association which is also native to ceramics: he adopts architectural configurations. Clay, of course, is an architectural material – bricks can be constructive elements or decorative facing. The Mediterranean style of Dufy's little ceramic walled villa called *Jardin des papillons* (fig. 21), with its

18. Rawson, p. 188.
19. Rawson, p. 101.

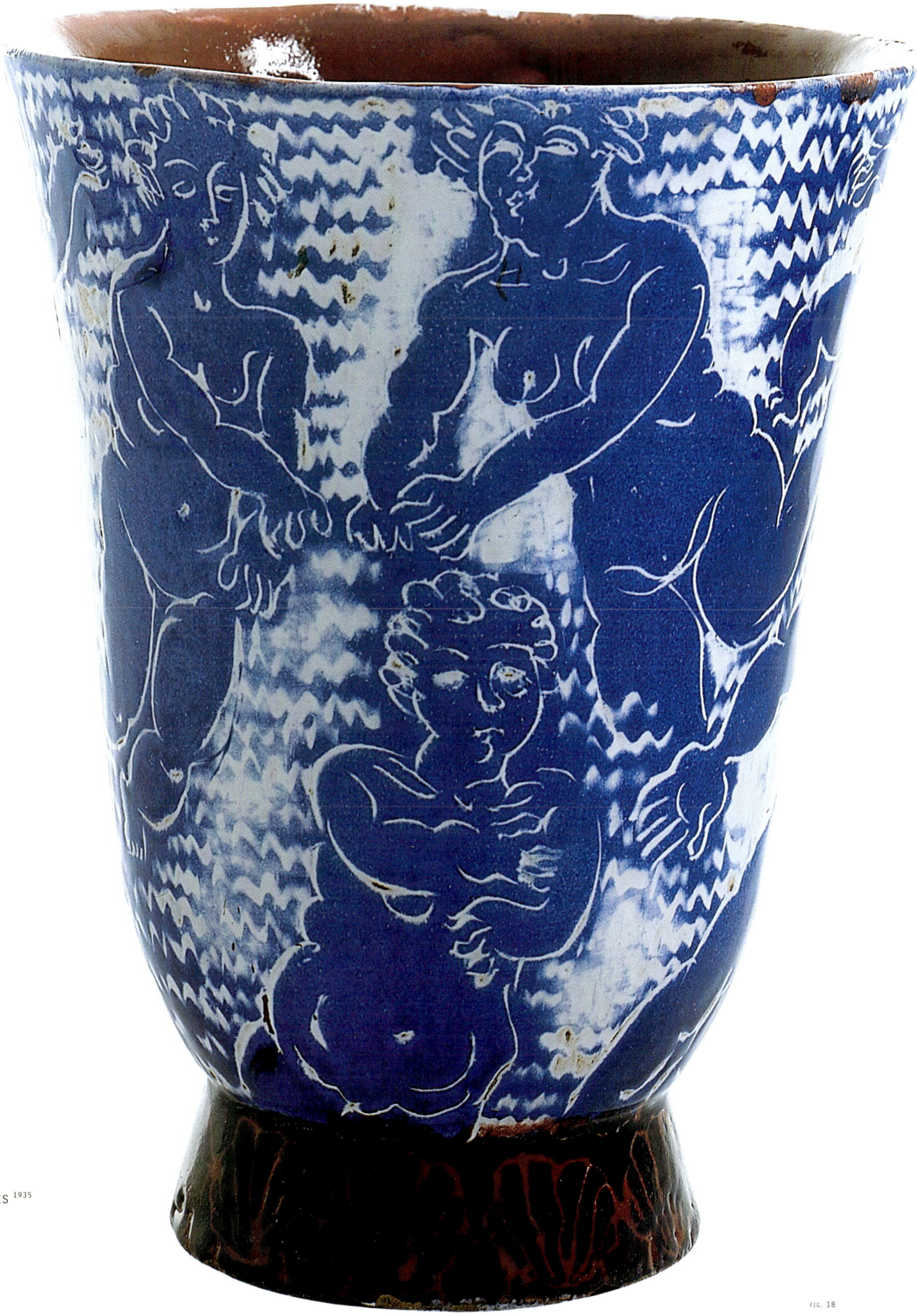

FIG. 18 RAOUL DUFY
VASE BLEU AUX FEMMES 1935
vase; 27 x 21 cm
COLLECTION MUSEUM HET KRUITHUIS

FIG. 18

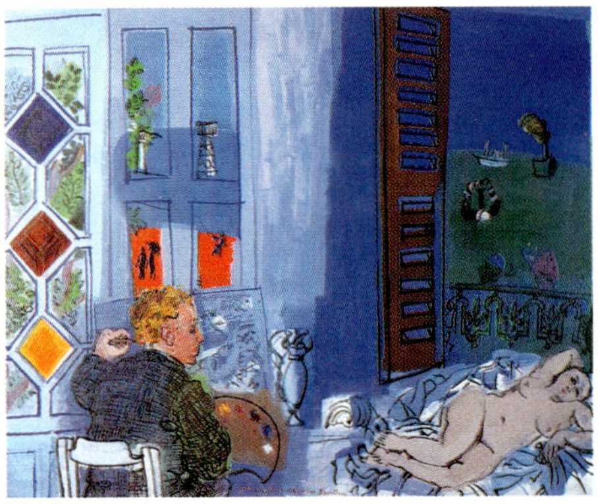

FIG. 19

blue roof, its whitened windows, its symmetrical steps and fountain, invokes dazzling sun-swept villages before seas as blue and sparkling as that roof. Not content with simple sculptural suggestiveness, Dufy has fantastically painted the walls of the courtyard and the house itself. Some of his depictions set the scene of this place: fountain, water, sailing ships. But the piece gets its name from his proportionately enormous renderings of butterflies, all seen from the side, depicted in greens, blues and pinks. Like his bathers, they are captured in spirit rather than scientific detail. Dufy has a light touch here, confining himself mostly to outlines and shading. At the back of the house, where his signature appears on the work, he has quickly sketched the form of a vase and flowers, and loosely filled in the brown outlines with yellow and pink.

Dufy made other building-like objects, as well as constructing decorated boxy structures to serve as water gardens. His architectural pieces were made in collaboration with the Catalan potter Artigas, whose later work with Miró has already

FIG. 19 RAOUL DUFY
L'ARTISTE ET SON MODÈLE 1929
oil on canvas; 130 x 165 cm

FIG. 20 RAOUL DUFY
NU ACCOUDE 1925
tile; 15.5 x 15.5 cm
COLLECTION MUSEUM HET KRUITHUIS

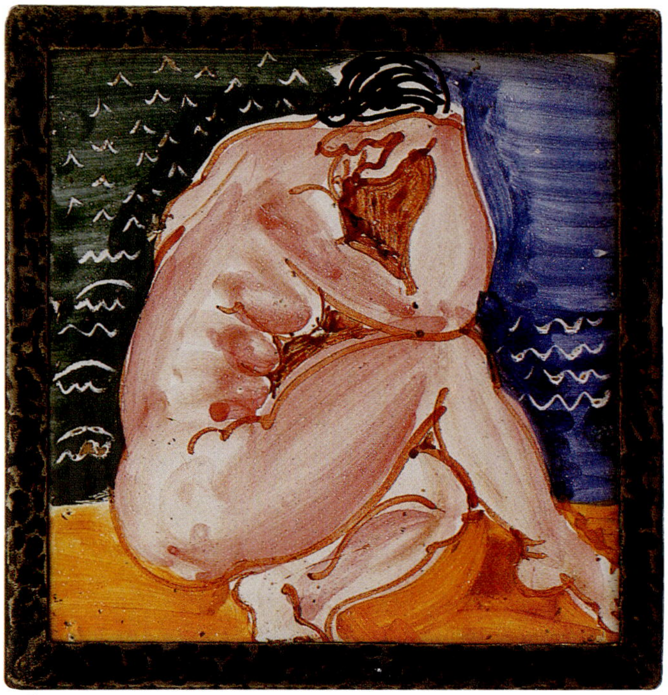

FIG. 20

20. Raymond Cogniat, Raoul Dufy, New York: Crown Publishers, 1978 (translated from the French by Thomas L. Callow), p. 89.

FIG. 21 RAOUL DUFY
JARDIN DES PAPILLONS 1926-27
object; 26 x 23 x 42 cm
COLLECTION MUSEUM HET KRUITHUIS

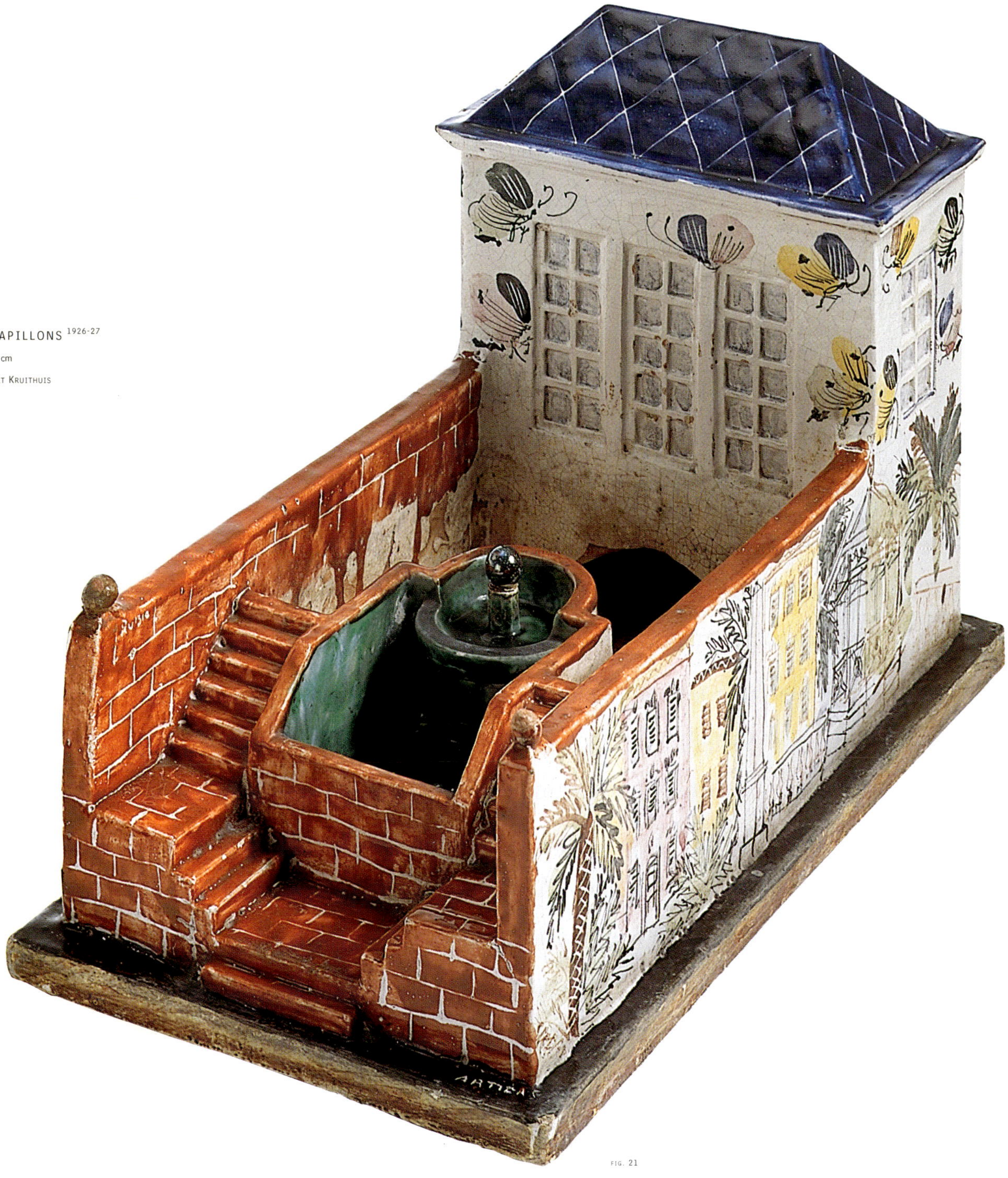

FIG. 21

been mentioned (Artigas's signature is visible on the work along with Dufy's). They worked together between 1923 and 1930, and again from 1937 until the war. They referred to these boxy pieces as "apartment gardens."[20]

Architectural associations are less common in ceramics than references to the body or organic motifs. On the other hand, Dufy also made tiles, a format which is as common as the plate, and as receptive to painterly activities. The tile puts no restrictions on a painter, not even the distraction that the rim or the slight concavity of a plate may present. In the tile illustrated here (fig. 20) Dufy has painted a nude against a tricolor background that schematically represents shore vegetation, sand and sea. Breasts disclose that she is female, but her musculature makes her as androgynous as Michelangelo's female sculptures. The angles of the figure are reminiscent of Braque's early Cubist painting *Grand nu* (1907-08) and seem to rhyme with the square corners of the tile. The tile is blunt, balanced, unambiguous; the figure is firm, concentrated, intense.

In his paintings, Dufy frequently used the patch-of-color background seen on this tile; one of his most distinctive aesthetic characteristics is the independence of the linear description of a scene or a figure from his free-floating and emotionally suggestive color. "Dufy's characteristic use of a compact, tersely eloquent calligraphy and pure, clean, unfussed, fast-flowing line is perhaps the most radical extension in the first half of the twentieth century of Van Gogh's passionately forceful and explosive handling of line and color in his own later paintings... The colour in Dufy is never more than approximately contained by the form and sometimes it is set against the form in abstractly emotive counterpoint."[21] (fig. 23) Because line and color were not superimposed "volumes had no real density: they were transparent and immaterial..."[22] Dufy often worked with a certain impersonality; he was more interested in humanity than in individuals and "did not intend to crowd his canvas with individuals, with particular cases which would spoil the order of his composition and would emphasize details too much."[23] One can see that the nude in this tile is a type, a design, rather than a personality.

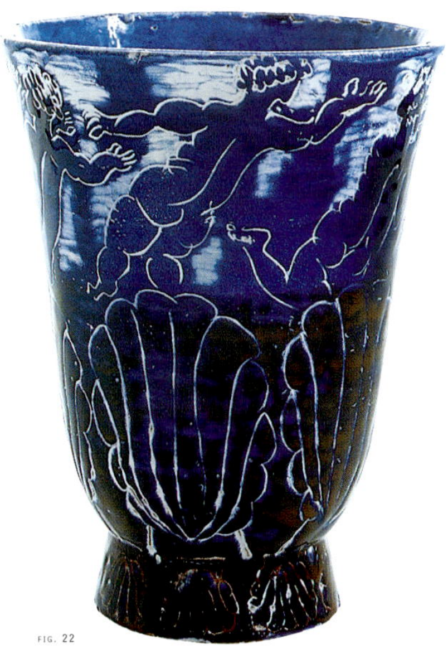

FIG. 22

FIG. 22 RAOUL DUFY
VASE AU BAIGNEUSES BLEU MARINE CA. 1930
vase; 26.5 x 19 cm
COLLECTION MUSEUM HET KRUITHUIS

21. Robertson, p. 18.
22. Cogniat, p. 64.
23. Cogniat, p. 71.

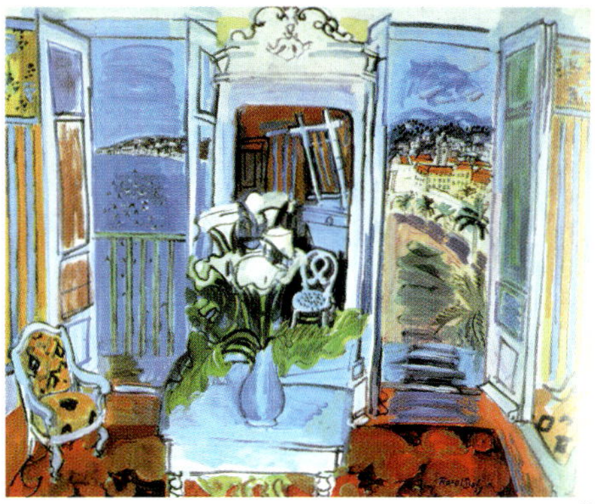

FIG. 23

Dufy, in fact, was obsessed with design in all its applications (fig. 23). His engagement with ceramics was just one of his many interests. He also collaborated with the couturier Paul Poiret, who had abolished the corset in 1907 and whose brilliant colors clothed the "new women" of the early twentieth century.[24] He designed textiles for the French firm Bianchini-Férier for 20 years (more than 3,000 of his designs are in the firm's inventory)[25] and he composed tapestries for several manufacturers, designed and illustrated books, made public murals, and created theatrical settings and fêtes. Although Dufy is not well remembered in America, in Europe he has been called one of the two or three artists who created the modern visual sensibility: "The vision was strong enough to affect, in a broadly disseminated, popularized manner, the colour, design, texture and imagery – the 'look' everywhere – of a very wide range of commercially manufactured products: book wrappers and record sleeves, perfume and *haute couture* advertisements, posters and stage décor, textiles for furniture and for clothes, decorated china and glass."[26] One activity influenced another: it is supposed that his experimentation with block printing for books and textiles encouraged a painting style which in printing could be called off-register, and there is some speculation that the arabesques he used in illustration and textiles originated in his memory of the linear decoration of the traditional earthenware pottery of his home region.[27]

FIG. 23 RAOUL DUFY
INTÉRIEUR À LA FENÊTRE OUVERTE 1928
oil on canvas; 65.5 x 81 cm

Among the early modernists' ceramics in the Kruithuis collection, works by **Fernand Léger** (1881-1955 – fig. 25) are the most adventurous dimensional abstractions. Léger's first training was in architecture and in addition to his painting he produced experimental films, made a mosaic facade for a church, did many stained-glass windows and was interested in typography. He made his first ceramics in 1949 at Biot, France, in the studio of one of his former students. His *Danseuse - composition en noir et jaune* (fig. 26) is a free-form allusion to

24. Bryan Robertson, "An introduction to Dufy," in Raoul Dufy 1877-1953, London: Hayward Gallery, 1983, p. 74.
25. Robertson, p. 50.
26. Robertson, p. 16.
27. René Simon Lévy, "The fabrics of Raoul Dufy: Genesis and context," in Raoul Dufy 1877-1953, p. 98.

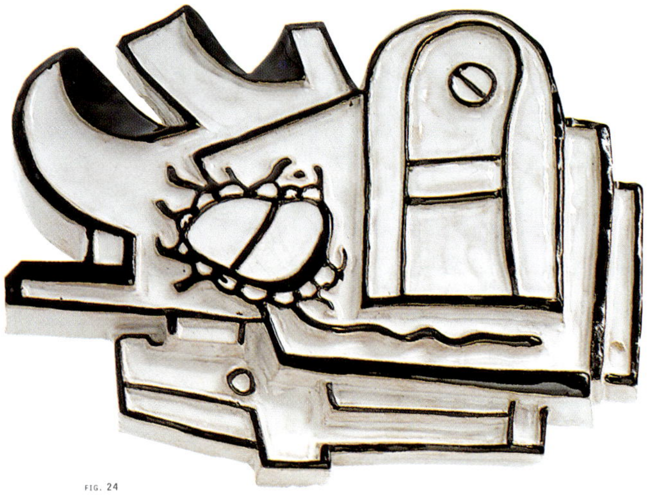

FIG. 24

movement. An irregular background of dark green sets off a white-sided protrusion with a yellow-and-black top that looks like a modernist cake decoration. Taken as an abstraction, it is a playful delight, with unpredictable ins and outs, the gloss of the lush yellow glaze confusing our perception of the exact positions of all these parts rendered in planes. The gloss also pulls light into the surface of the relief, which increases the impression of almost buttery tactility that the unusual surface presents. The title suggests, however, that the piece involves some degree of representation, and sends us on a treasure hunt. Perhaps the inverted black V toward the bottom identifies the space between the dancer's legs?

In *Bateau blanc* (fig. 24), a slightly larger and even more dimensional piece, Léger created a work that changes its character from every viewpoint and becomes a game of identification. Is that a capital letter A? Is that a circle with a diagonal line through it, like the current international symbol for No-this or No-that? Does that circle with the corona around it represent an eye, or a sun, or a lace-edged pillow, or a ciliated protozoan? The sculpture is constructed of low rectilinear blocks, one edge seemingly braced or buttressed, the opposite side flying out and up, giving a feeling of scurrying motion. The overall configuration can even, from a certain angle, look like a cartoonish head of a woman with an open mouth and an outlandish hat.

La pomme jaune (fig. 29) is highly colored. This is a still life of fruit painted in red, yellow and green on a white background of idiosyncratic shape. The disparity between the painting and the form creates a loose feeling, as if reality were slipping slightly – and that's a sensation that seems quite contemporary. The disharmony of color and form is a capability that ceramics has always offered but that traditional sculpture formerly did not. Before the 20th century, sculpture was

FIG. 24 FERNAND LÉGER
BATEAU BLANC 1951
relief; 27.5 x 34 cm
COLLECTION MUSEUM HET KRUITHUIS

FIG. 25 FERNAND LÉGER

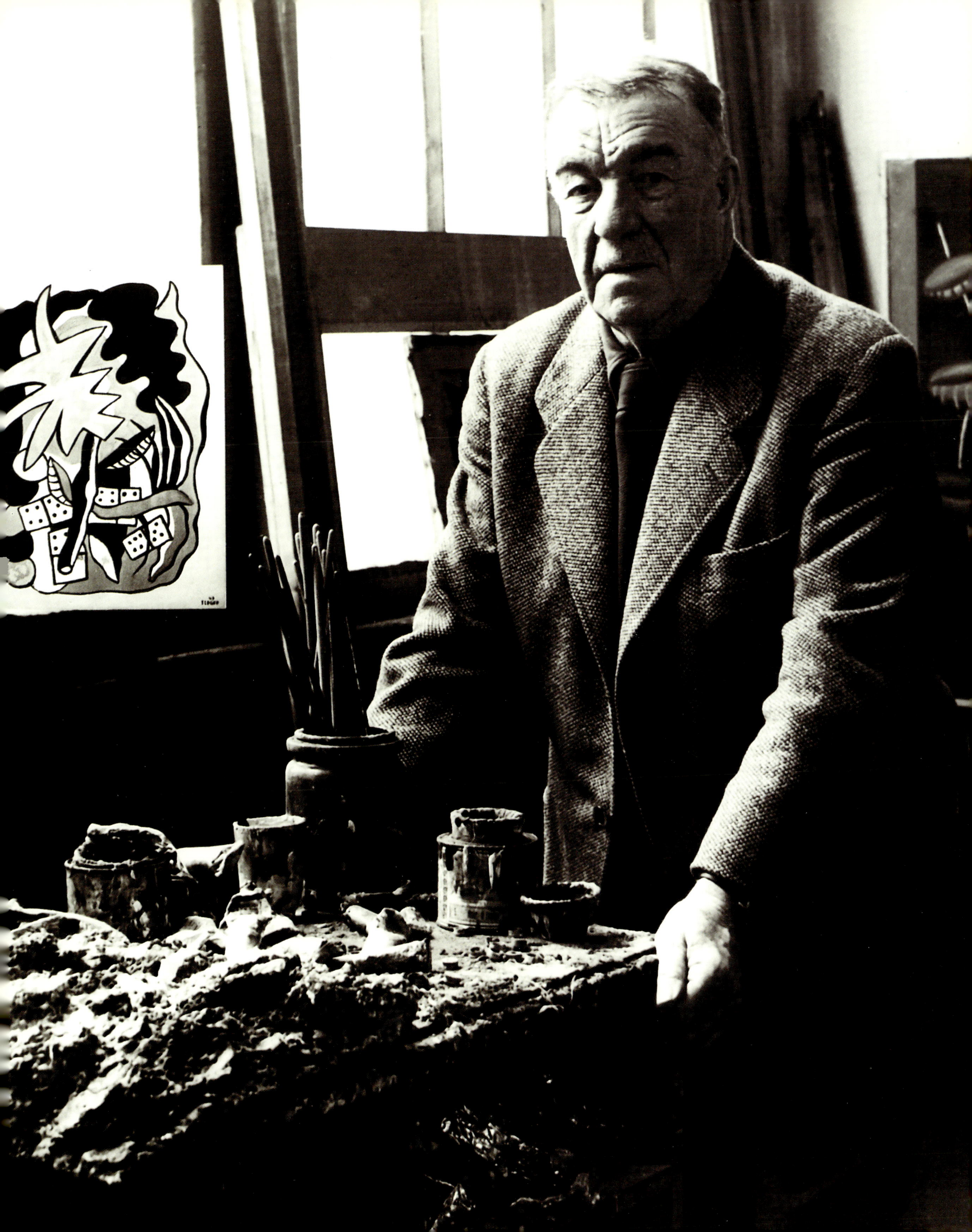

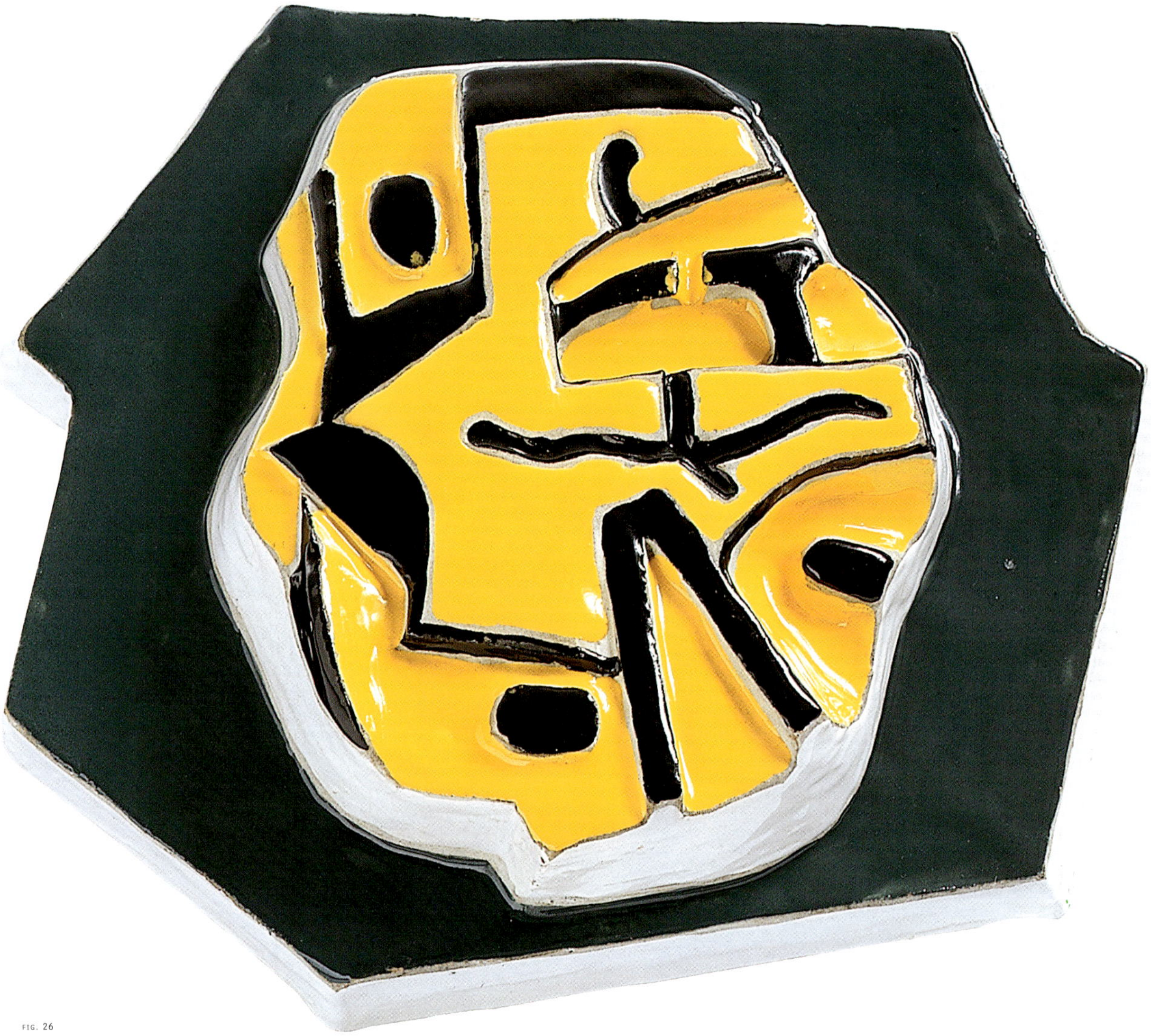

fig. 26

fig. 26 Fernand Léger
Danseuse - composition en noir et jaune 1951
relief; 21.5 x 25.5 cm
collection Museum Het Kruithuis

sometimes painted, but it was not abstract, so the applied color always supported representation. In ceramics the separation of making from painting encourages an independent consideration of each. Clay itself, the British art historian Herbert Read observes, is the most abstract of materials[28] (well, at least among the traditional materials; electronics has taken us into materials so abstract they have no substance). Ceramic objects may take nearly any form; a vase need not literally represent anything except itself (although, of course, it sometimes does allude to known forms) and its decoration has always included the option of being neither picture nor pattern but free abstraction. Painting came to this idea late!

Léger freely responded to ceramics' possibilities. One contemporaneous reviewer was appreciative, saying, "Here the tectonic chunkiness of Léger's style is bodied forth in a medium fully [in] keeping with it..."[29] The outlined geometric shapes that Léger used to suggest industry and modernity and even the human body in his paintings become palpable in these reliefs (fig. 27). But another reviewer, the young Hilton Kramer, responded in his typically acid terms:

"The digression into ceramics which has lately occupied the elder generation of painters in Paris has tended to isolate certain decorative and frivolous aspects of their talents at the expense of their expressive powers. The ceramic form itself is doubtless involved here, yet it ought to be recognized too that this digression has caught some of these artists in moments of relaxation, if not actual decline. Of Léger this is particularly true. The broad bands of color, the cartoon-like conceptions of figures, and the general lack of subtlety and expressive force in his recent painting have prepared us for the projection of these characteristics into his ceramic pieces. Most of these works are hung like bas-reliefs on the wall, and they afford the sensation of

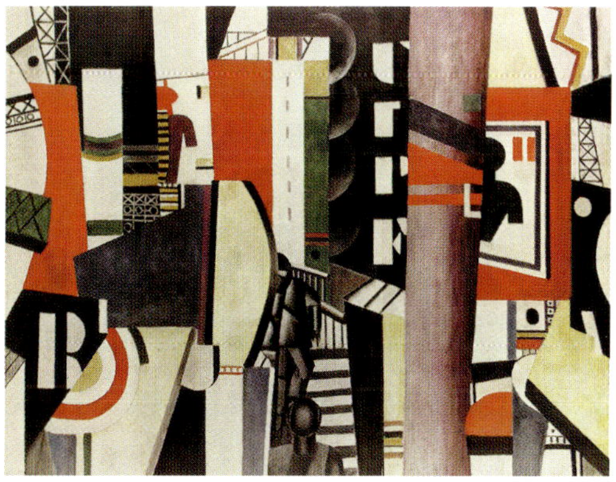

FIG. 27

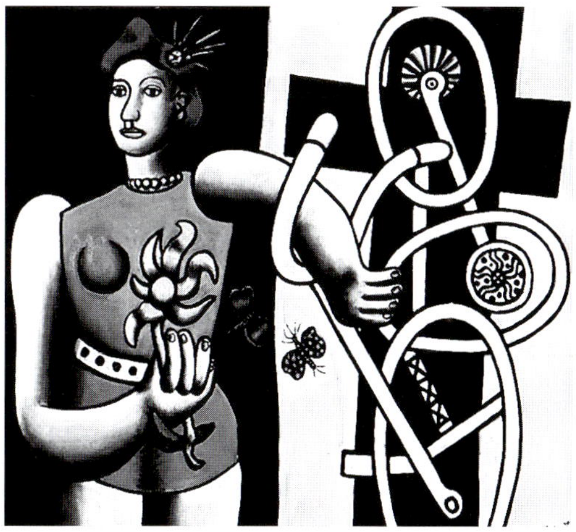

FIG. 28

FIG. 27 FERNAND LÉGER
THE CITY 1919-20
OIL ON CANVAS; 36 x 46 cm
COLLECTION PHILADELPHIA MUSEUM OF ART

FIG. 28 FERNAND LÉGER
LA GRANDE JULIE 1945
oil on canvas; 111.8 x 127.3 cm
COLLECTION THE MUSEUM OF MODERN ART, NEW YORK

28. Herbert Read, The Meaning of Art. London: Faber and Faber Ltd., 1931, p. 41.
29. M.R., ArtNews 59, November 1960, p. 17.

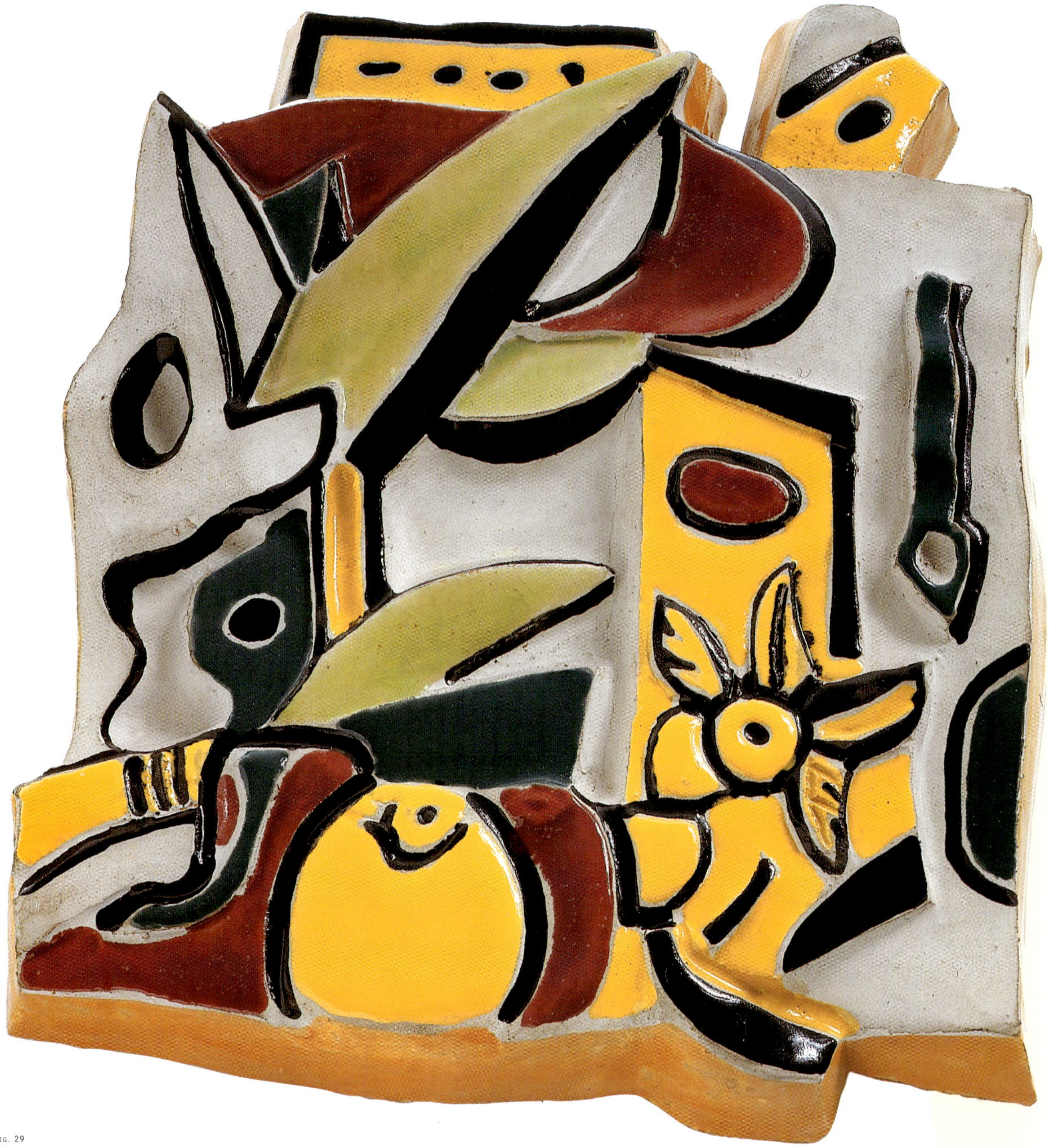

FIG. 29

FIG. 29 FERNAND LÉGER
LA POMME JAUNE 1951
relief; 28.5 x 25.5 cm
COLLECTION MUSEUM HET KRUITHUIS

seeing the forms of the artist's paintings emerging into three actual dimensions. The natural smooth ceramic surface also tends to disarm one's criticism of Léger's painted surfaces, for here the recent tendencies to slickness have a technical justification. By and large, it can be said that certain of Léger's mannerisms reach their logical goals in these works. This may be a dubious fate for a painter so far advanced in reputation as Léger, and as one passes from piece to piece in the current exhibition, one wonders inevitably how long such a reputation will withstand the onslaught of his recent works."[30]

Here is an example of the critic not considering the work on its own terms or for the strengths of its realization of spatial and optical effects, but only defining it as an activity both lesser than and subsequent to painting. If Léger had an "obsession with volume, defined by light, shade and contour"[31] why wouldn't this light-capturing relief present fascinating new options to him? And the "modernity" and coolness of the ceramic surface seem ideally suited to his long-time themes. In fact, some freestanding ceramic forms Léger made look forward, with their simple, brightly colored shapes, to the American Pop Art of a few years later, such as the sculptures of Claes Oldenburg.

Certainly it is true that Léger's reliefs are most interesting when the imagery is broken, incomplete or abstracted, and least interesting where it is straightforwardly depictive, particularly in the case of something as inherently appealing as a flower or a girl's face. Another observer enumerated the positive:

"First, Léger has been able to make ceramics in a manner completely consistent with all his previous output and without resurrecting or redesigning a museum of plates and pots that would never be used as such. Second, in making these works intended for walls, he has begun to fulfill his hope for "the collaboration of the three major art forms – architecture, painting, sculpture." Third, these reliefs are done in a manner simple, direct, yet original; wholly unexpected but natural; a manner that seems to have been waiting for Léger, but that only he could have invented... His use of bright color has always called for an extensive use of white, and his whites have

30. H.K., Arts Digest, vol. 29, Jan. 1, 1955, p. 22.
31. Nicholas Serota, Foreword, Fernand Léger: The Later Years, London: Whitechapel Art Gallery, 1987, p. 7.

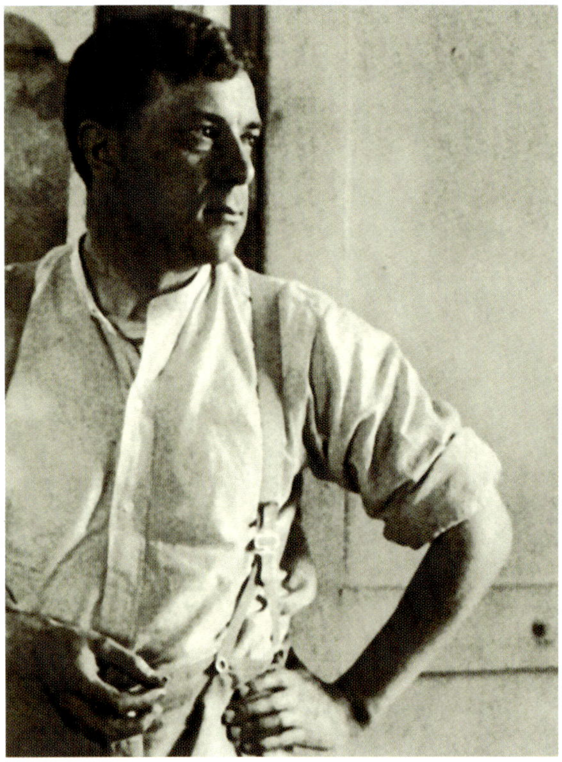

FIG. 30

FIG. 30 GEORGES BRAQUE

had a tendency to age. Fastened in ceramic, these whites and the colors that play against them are certain to resist the effects of time and unchangingly proclaim his joy in the physical world and his unquenchable optimism."[32]

Ceramics offered him particular and valuable artistic options.

Georges Braque (1882-1963 – fig. 30), Picasso's Cubist peer-competitor, also worked in clay (for a time with Artigas). The 1945 *Assiette à la mandoline* (fig. 32) has a centered image but one fragmented and masked in a quasi-Surrealist style. What presumably is the mandolin looks equally like an eye, and rests across a lettered handbill reminiscent of the collaged materials of Cubism. Other plates are simplified to the point of being emblems. *Profil* (fig. 31) consists of a white outline around a female near-silhouette on a coarse and stony gray plate. What's interesting about this piece is the opposition of the profile's flatness to the objectness of the thick and blunt plate with its prominently irregular surface.

In *L'oiseau blanc* (fig. 33), the bird, a design that Braque devised in 1949 and reproduced on a limited-edition plate in 1960, could almost be a cutout. Yet it suggests tumbling, fluttering movement with its shape that's almost an asterisk – all those wings evoke motion. Here again the simple shape plays against a very different background: Braque has used the same stony gray glaze but it is not evenly extended across the rim of the white plate. The result is a strangely contradictory one: the bird seems more ethereal, more a flight of insubstantial imagination or memory because of the hesitant,

32. Otis Gage, "Fernand Léger: ceramist," Craft Horizons 15, January 1955, p. 14.

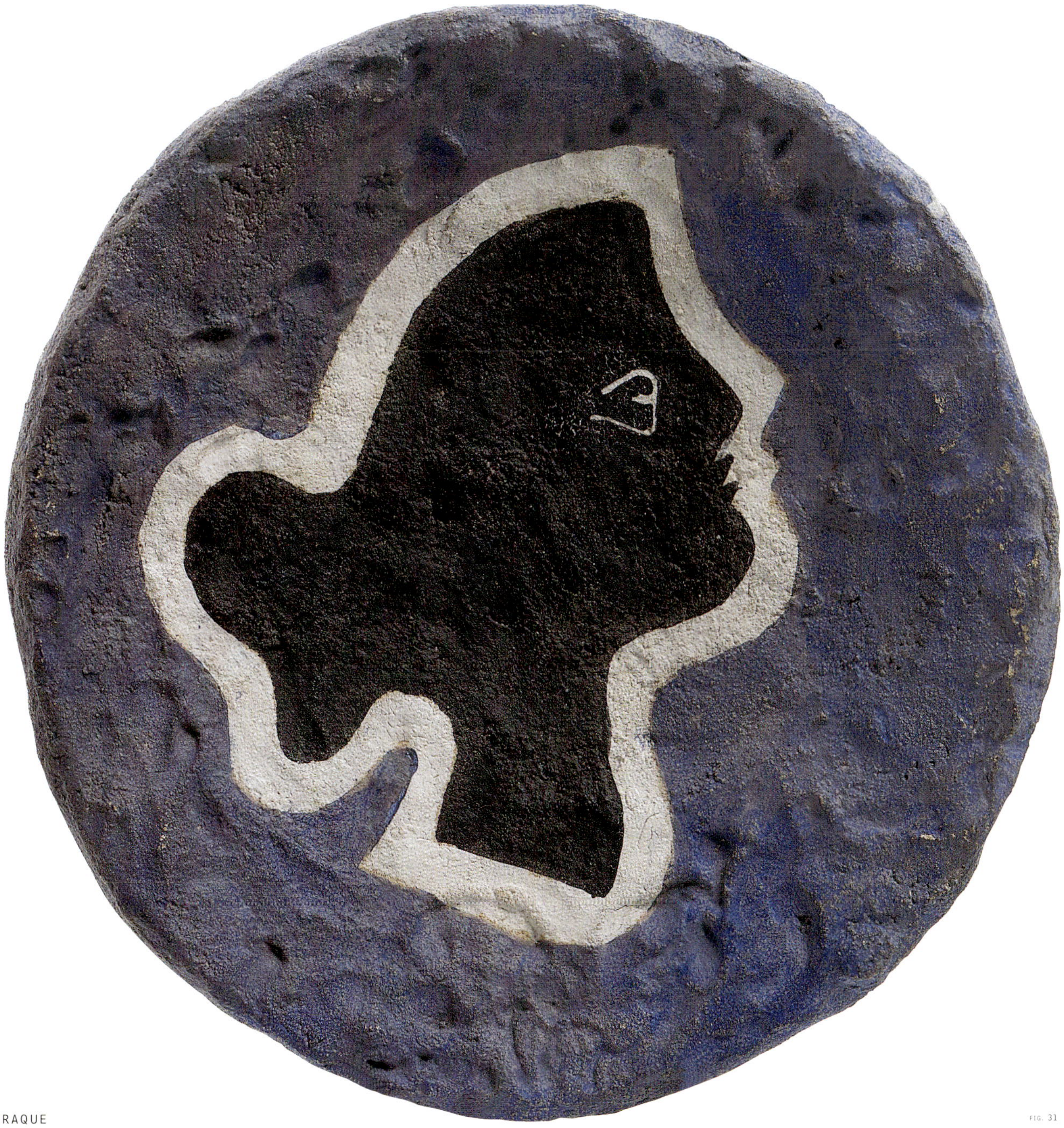

FIG. 31

FIG. 31 GEORGES BRAQUE
PROFIL (ED. 2/50) 1960
plate; ⌀ 27 cm
COLLECTION MUSEUM HET KRUITHUIS

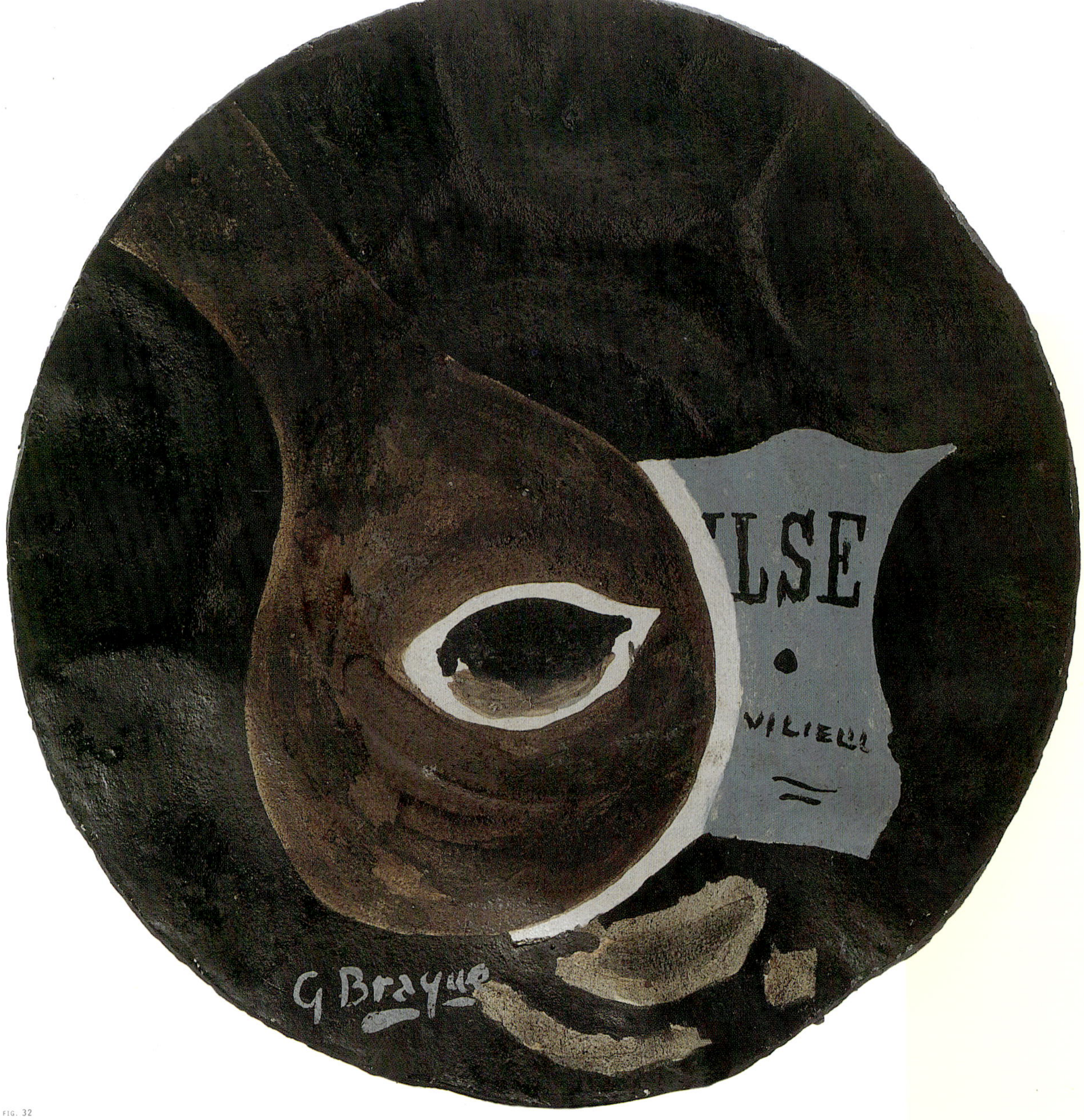

FIG. 32

FIG. 32 GEORGES BRAQUE
ASSIETTE À LA
MANDOLINE (ED. 3/30) 1945
plate; ø 26.5 cm
COLLECTION MUSEUM HET KRUITHUIS

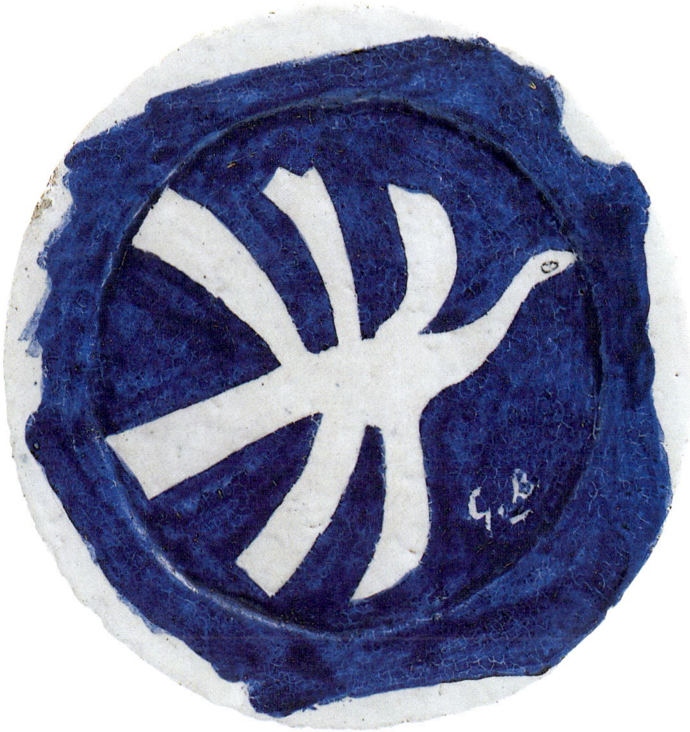

FIG. 33

fragmentary appearance of this background. At the same time, the plate as an object is very direct, so the glaze-and-image combination seems more artificial in comparison, because it is the outcome of an artist's subjective manipulations. This mixture of effects becomes more interesting the more you think about it, and the impact is not verbal or conceptual but overwhelmingly visual and physical (you can sense the contrast in your body).

After his Cubist days, Braque developed into something of a classicist. He excelled at still lifes and depicted objects in lithographs, tapestry cartoons, stained glass and ceramics, as well as in painting. He also made jewelry, drawing on his characteristic iconography (the designs, executed by Heger de Lowenfeld, were shown at the Musée des Arts Décoratifs, Paris, in the early '60s). This work was described as expanding the "magic import of his hermetic glyphs" with titles referring to alchemy or Greek mythology.[33] Braque seems to have been concerned above all with the definition of shapes. Henri Laurens once remarked that a painter becomes curious about how his painted forms look on the other side, and makes sculptures of them in order to find out.[34] This seems apropos of Braque, whose small number of bronze and plaster sculptures are two-sided, shallow forms and whose ceramic work concentrates on applied shapes.

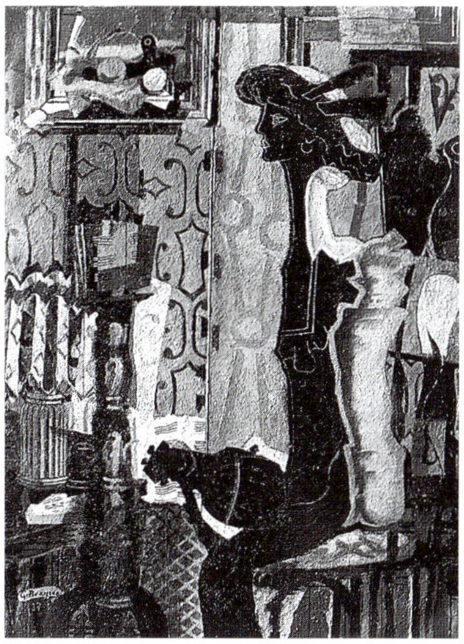

FIG. 34

FIG. 33 GEORGES BRAQUE
L'OISEAU BLANC (ED.) 1960
plate; ⌀ 23 cm
COLLECTION MUSEUM HET KRUITHUIS

FIG. 34 GEORGES BRAQUE
WOMAN WITH A MANDOLIN 1937
oil on canvas; 130.2 x 97.2 cm
COLLECTION THE MUSEUM OF MODERN ART, NEW YORK

33. D. Renzio, "Letter from Paris: Modern Artists Turn to Jewellery," Apollo, May 1963, p. 420.
34. Quoted in Henry R. Hope, Georges Braque, New York: Museum of Modern Art, 1949, p. 132.

Among the ceramic works of **Marc Chagall** (1887-1985 – fig. 35) is a plate painted in 1962 (fig. 36), which could be called a rather late work except that "late" becomes meaningless with an artist who continued working into his '90s. It shows a murky, atmospheric scene and has a ragged texture comparable to impasto in painting. Chagall depicted two figures, one of which is a human-size rooster. A story is implied but not spelled out, as in most of his paintings. Chagall once said, "For me a picture is a surface covered with representations of things (objects, animals, human beings) in a certain order in which logic and illustration have no importance. The visual effect of the composition is paramount."[35] This indefinite scene provokes a mixture of humor and melancholy.

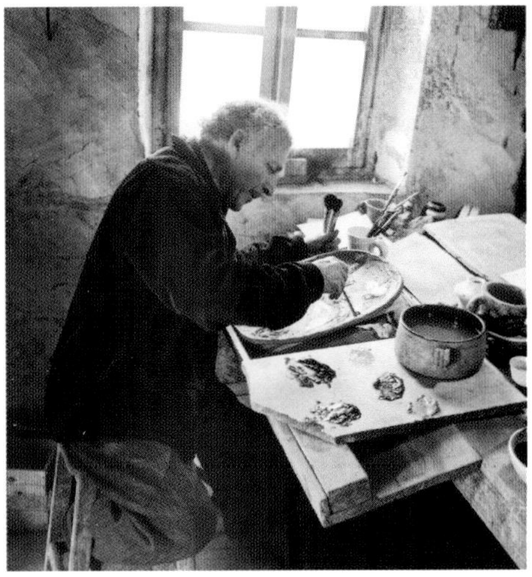

FIG. 35

FIG. 35 MARC CHAGALL WORKING IN THE STUDIO IN VALLAURIS

Chagall is generally regarded as a precursor to Surrealism because he first became known for his dream-inspired paintings that hark back to his childhood in the Jewish Pale of Russia. His family was Hasidic; Hasids were known for their mystical state of mind. The attitude has been described so:

"According to their belief, the souls of great sinners were transmigrated into the bodies of animals as punishment for their faults, and they wandered for centuries between paradise and hell. Since childhood, the Hasid was surrounded by a mysterious world of the Cabbala and fantastic, ancient legends. This was without any doubt the source of the lyrical fairytales of Chagall, of his people and animals flying between sky and earth, imponderable, enchanted, carried on the wings of love. Jewish literature is plunged in this mystical atmosphere where unreality has as much importance as reality."[36]

While there is no action within the confines of Chagall's small plate, the unreal size relationship of the figures gives the quality of a dream or memory, and the roughness of the depiction conforms to the imprecision of memory. The rich darkness of the image is a reminder that, in addition to his

35. Charles Sorlier, ed., Chagall by Chagall (trans. J. Shepley), New York: Abrams, 1979, p. 53, quoted by Norbert Lynton, "Chagall `over the Roofs of the World'," in Susan Compton, Chagall, New York: Harry N. Abrams, 1985, p. 21.
36. V. Marcadé, Le renouveau de l'art pictural russe 1863-1914, Lausanne: L'Age d'Homme, 1971, p. 228, quoted in Compton, p. 31.

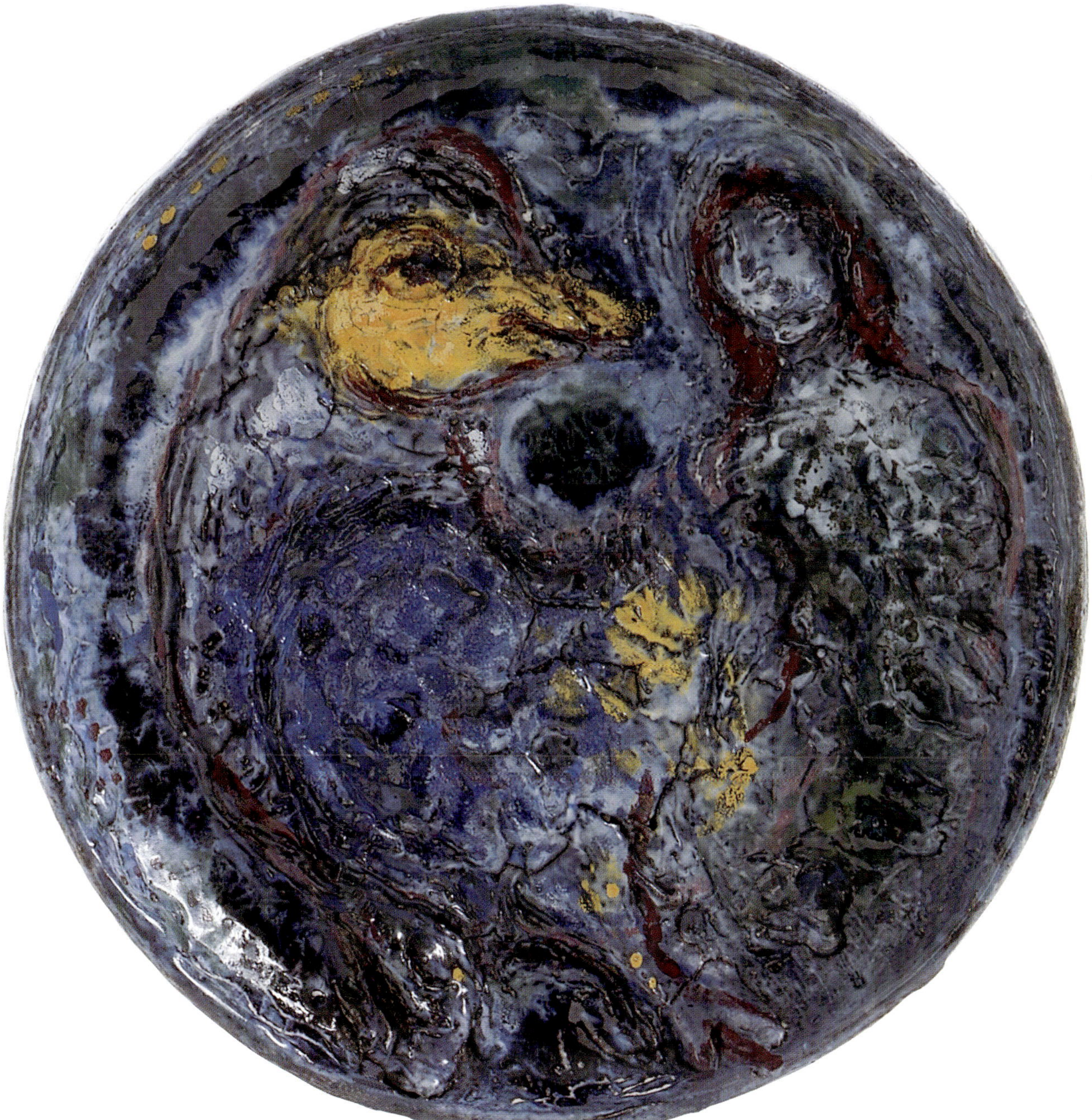

FIG. 36

FIG. 36 MARC CHAGALL
FEMME AU COQ 1962
plate; ο 24.5 cm
COLLECTION MUSEUM HET KRUITHUIS

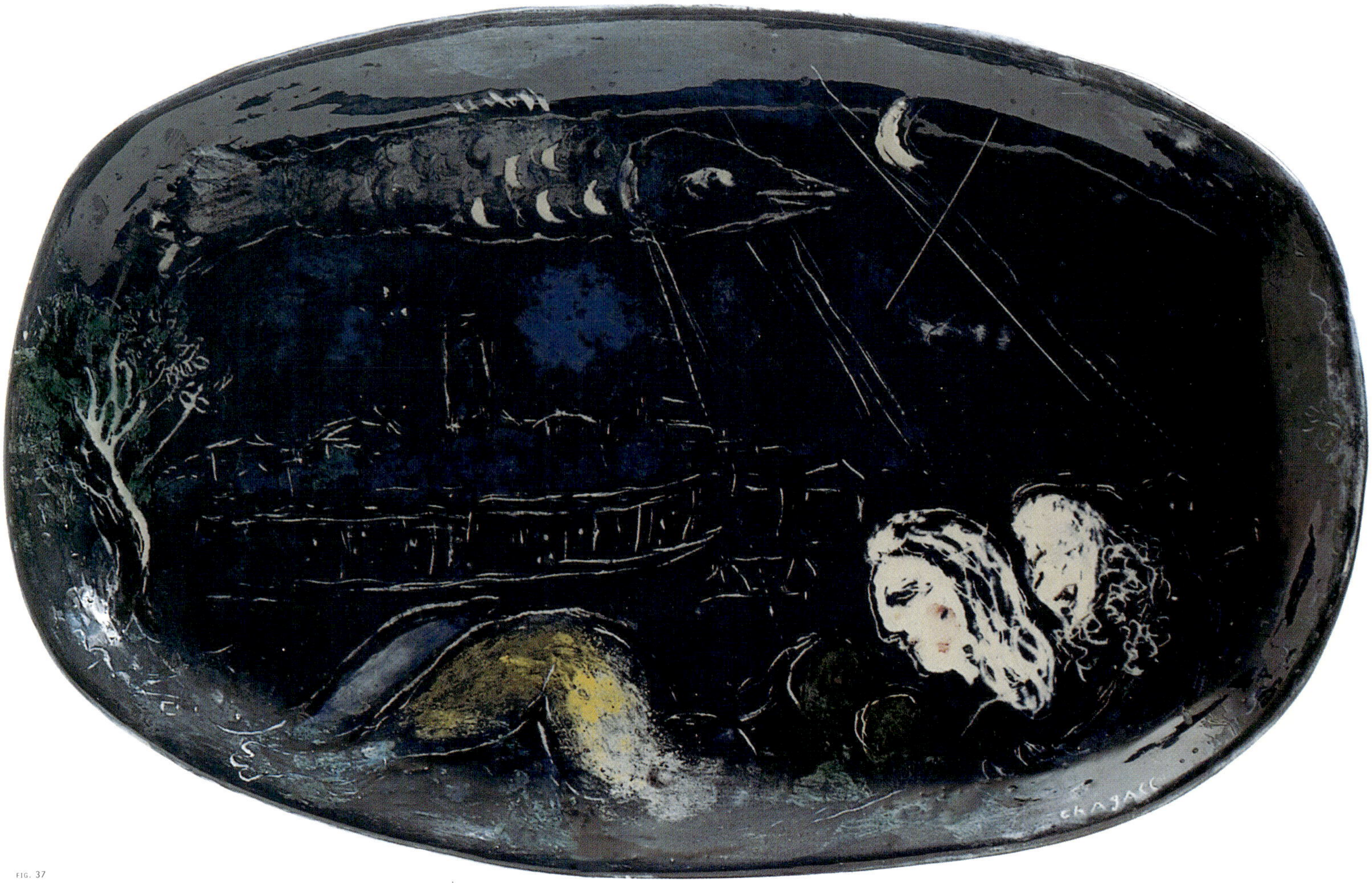

FIG. 37

FIG. 37 MARC CHAGALL
POISSON ET AMOUREUX DE VENCE 1955
plate; 30.3 x 48.5 cm
COLLECTION MUSEUM HET KRUITHUIS

recurrent themes of lovers and the circus as well as peasant life, Chagall has often addressed themes of suffering and death.[37]

This plate, entitled *Femme au coq*, seems to share the references of his many paintings which mix animals and people. *I and the village* (fig. 38), for instance, is dominated by a large animal face (perhaps a lamb?). The 1929 painting *The rooster* has a woman riding on the back of a horse-size rooster and embracing its neck. The rooster is historically associated with the sun and fire, with elementary spiritual power, and with the masculine principle.[38] A woman appears holding a rooster to her chest in another Chagall painting, *The soul of the city* (1945). This painting is filled with dichotomies and tensions, including a floating image of the artist's wife, who had recently died, depicted as a bride. She contrasts with this more symbolically sensuous woman with bird.

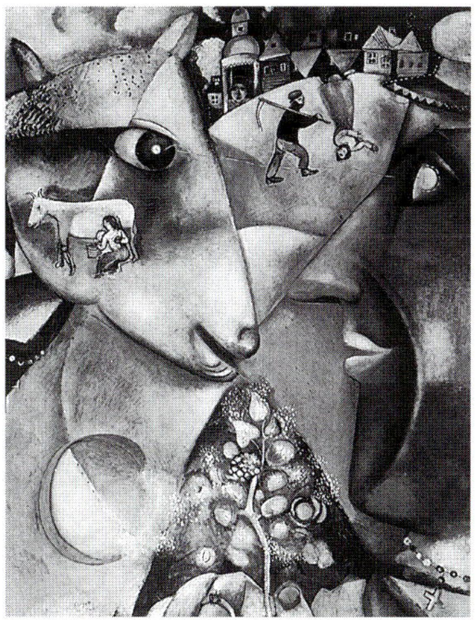

FIG. 38

A larger Chagall plate, *Poisson et amoureux de Vence* (fig. 37), also involves the combination and people and creatures, as in his paintings. Here it's a fish flying through the moonlit sky over a pair of lovers. In his paintings Chagall expressed the euphoria of love in many ways, often with the lovers flying or blended into flowers or shrubs; magic is the essential sensation.

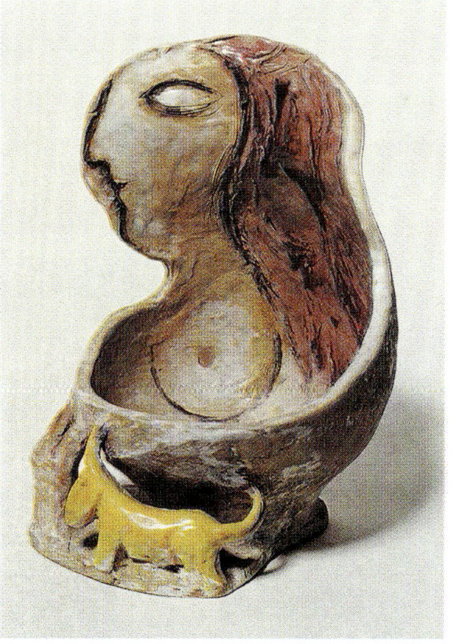

FIG. 39

Chagall made ceramic works in Vallauris, on the French Riviera, with the aid of Georges and Suzanne Ramié, who also assisted Picasso. He spoke at one point of the uncertainty that is part of subjecting ceramics to the flame of firing: "Often the fire lets the products of my pains come out of the oven in a recognizable form, but many times also in a grotesque and ridiculous shape. The old elements remind me all too often of the fact that my possibilities are limited."[39] Chagall also made unusual and interesting vase-sculptures in which the container is painted with a scene, from which figures emerge into actually three-dimensional space by means of the alteration of handles or the partial cutting away of the vessel wall (fig. 39).

FIG. 38 MARC CHAGALL
I AND THE VILLAGE 1911
oil on canvas; 192.1 x 151.4 cm
COLLECTION THE MUSEUM OF MODERN ART, NEW YORK

FIG. 39 MARC CHAGALL
VASE SCULPTÉ 1952
vase; 45 cm

37. Dr. Roland Doschka, "Art Can Not Be Made With Theory," in Terra Sculptura, Terra Pictura, p. 32.
38. Compton, p. 210.
39. Doschka in Terra Sculptura, Terra Pictura, p. 32.

Maurice De Vlaminck (1876-1958) was one of the pioneer Fauvists, the French painters in the early years of this century whose use of vivid colors earned them the epithet of "wild beasts." Dufy was also a Fauvist, but De Vlaminck was apparently one of the few in the movement who actually fit that description in character. An example of what has been described as his "swashbuckling egotism," comes from De Vlaminck's autobiography: "What is Fauvism? It's me. It's the manner I had in those days, the way I revolted and set myself free all at once, the way I broke away from the School, from bondage: my blues, my reds, my yellows, my pure, unmixed colors."[40] He also said, "I wanted to burn down the École des Beaux-Arts with my cobalts and vermilions. I wanted to express my feelings without troubling what painting was like before me... When I've got color tubes in my hand, I don't give a damn about other people's pictures. Life and me, me and life – that's all that matters."[41]

De Vlaminck first painted in a proto-Expressionist style. His color was ignited when he saw a retrospective of van Gogh's work in 1901 and met Matisse almost immediately thereafter. Fauvism began to wither about 1907, with the rise of influence of Cézanne after a memorial show of his work, and the subsequent beginnings of Cubism. De Vlaminck, however, persisted in the Fauvist style and fell into reproducing himself. That doesn't diminish his early importance, however.

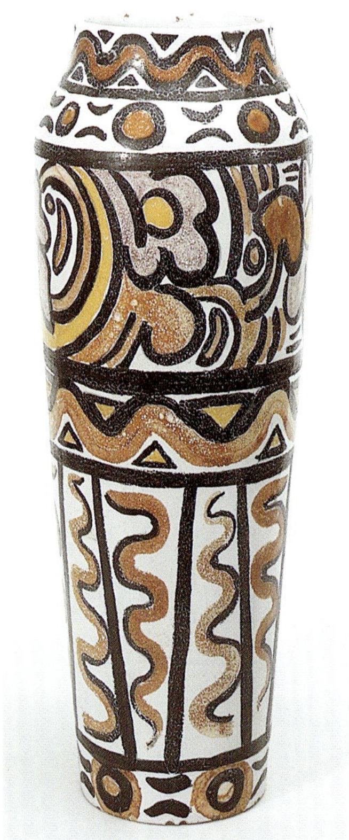

FIG. 40

FIG. 40 MAURICE DE VLAMINCK
TUBE VASE 1907-09
vase; 54 cm
COLLECTION MUSÉE D'ART MODERNE VILLE DE PARIS

De Vlaminck's ceramics can look like exercises in pattern-making and show little or no relation to the painting for which he is famed. But his first ceramic works, made at the studio of André Metthey around 1907-09, provide an intermediate step (fig. 40). For instance, a tube vase almost two feet tall is decorated in bands of waving lines, dots and flowers that look like they are undulating. The colors are clear and brilliantly contrasting. It seems half way between the heightened-color, naturalistic settings of his Fauve works and the patterns we see in his ceramic works such as fig 42 and 43. But these works offer an

40. Jean Leymarie, Fauves and Fauvism, New York: Rizzoli International Publications, 1987, pp. 29-30.
41. Leymarie, p. 36.

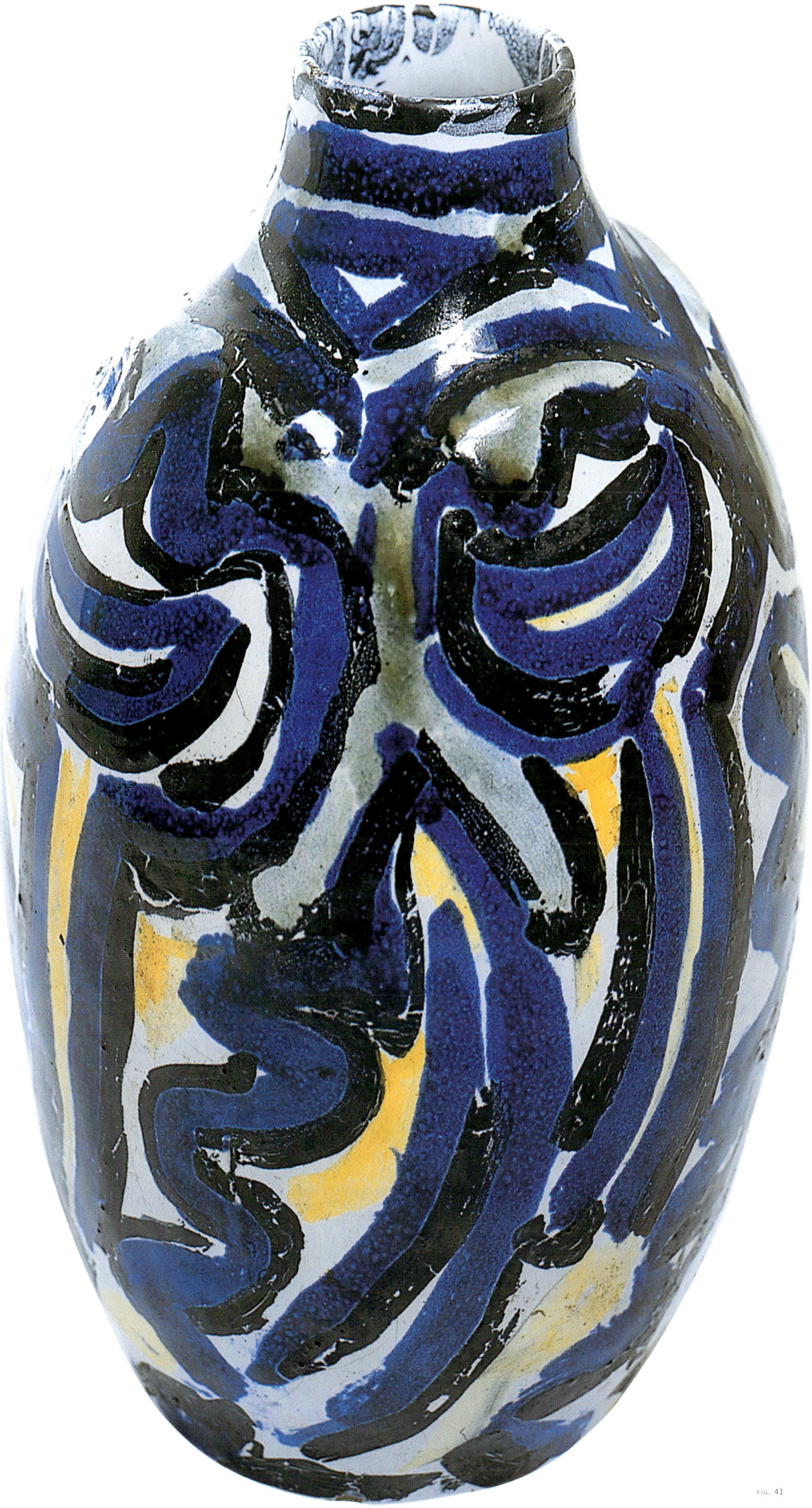

FIG. 41 MAURICE DE VLAMINCK
VASE BLEU
vase; 26.7 x 15.5 cm
COLLECTION MUSEUM HET KRUITHUIS

FIG. 41

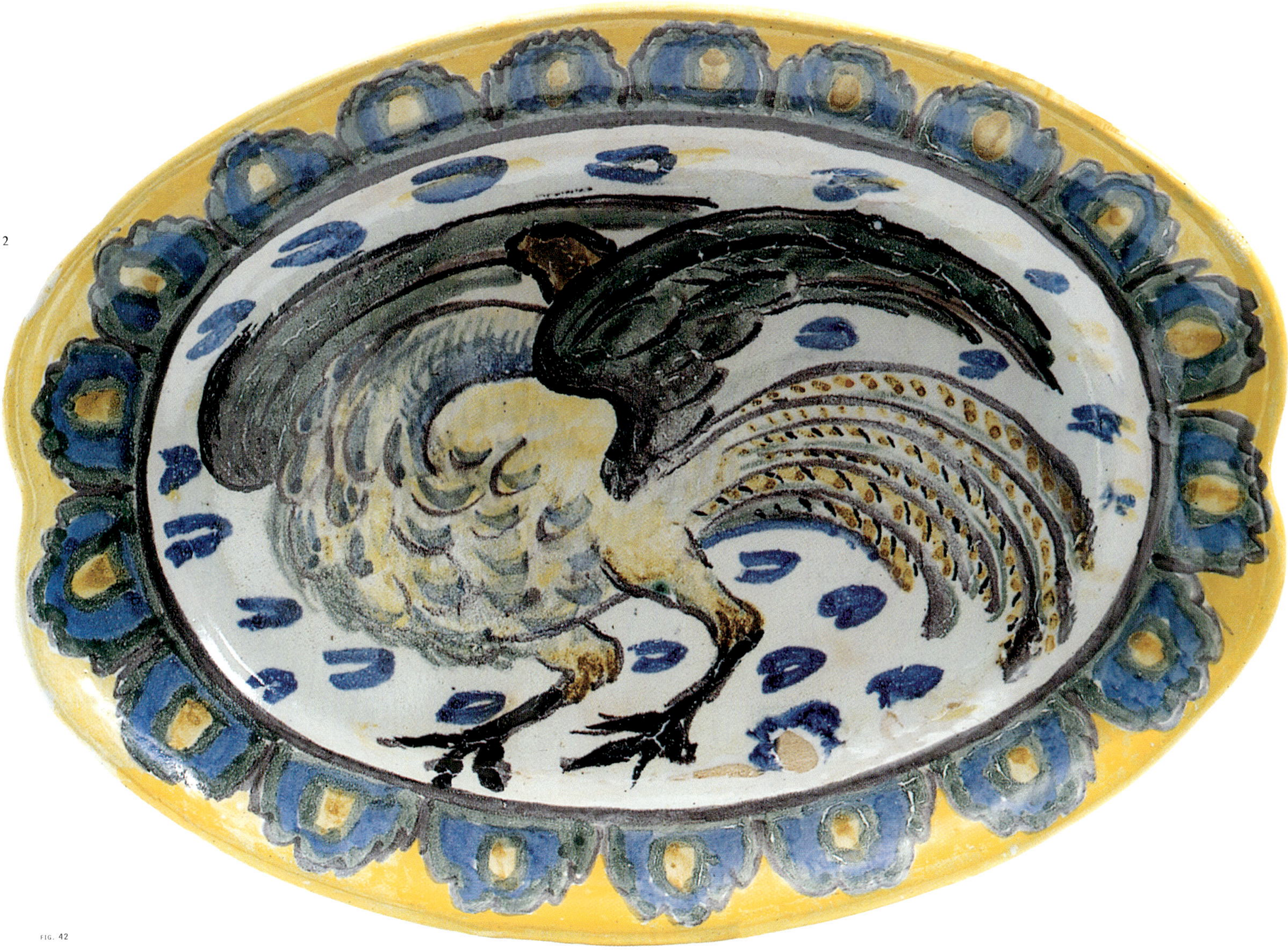

FIG. 42

FIG. 42 MAURICE DE VLAMINCK
UNTITLED
plate; 25 x 38 cm
COLLECTION MUSEUM HET KRUITHUIS

interesting and instructive contrast to the treatment of plates we have seen so far. In one work, the plate is merely a tondo for his painting of a fluttering bird spreading its wings. The closest thing to an acknowledgment of the plate form is a double-band decoration on the rim. The bands frame the image like the frame around any canvas does, yet the overall effect is reminiscent of Middle Eastern pottery decoration.

De Vlaminck also directly responded to a round, flat ceramic blank, using the kind of sinuous organic line that has been combined happily with the curves of ceramic forms since the beginning of time, it seems. This work still seems very much a painting, because the decoration has a fluid brushiness that almost looks like watercolor (fig. 44). The rosette he has painted is thinner in the center, resisting what must be an instinctive human impulse to make round things radiate from a dense center to a dissolving periphery, and also resisting a ceramic tendency for glazes to pool in the slightly indented centers of plates. Instead, in a painterly fashion he incorporates light into his "canvas" through the central openness of the design.

FIG. 43 MAURICE DE VLAMINCK
COMPOSITION 1907-09
plate; ø 35 cm
COLLECTION MUSEUM HET KRUITHUIS

FIG. 44 MAURICE DE VLAMINCK
UNTITLED
plate; ø 35 cm
COLLECTION MUSEUM HET KRUITHUIS

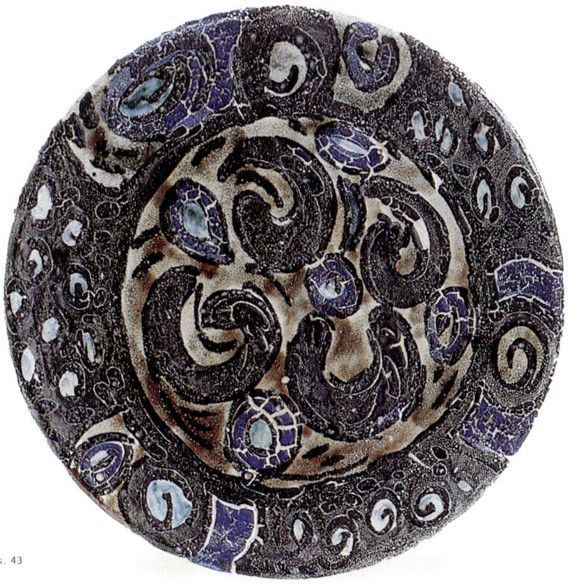

FIG. 43

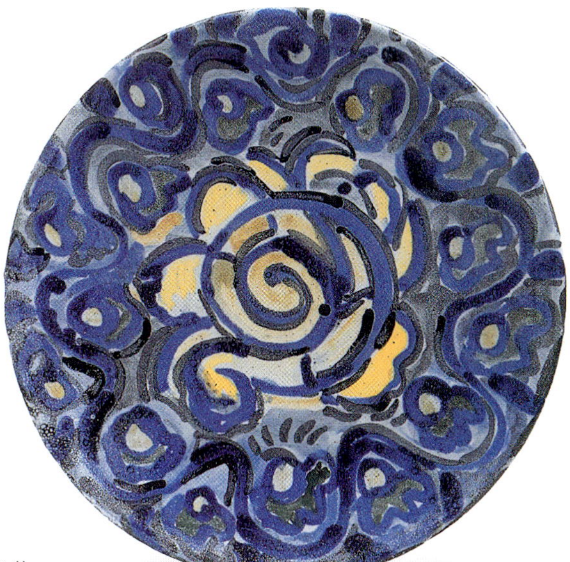

FIG. 44

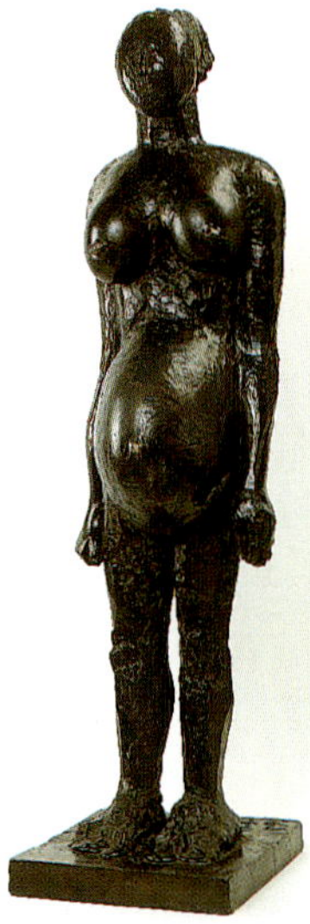

FIG. 45

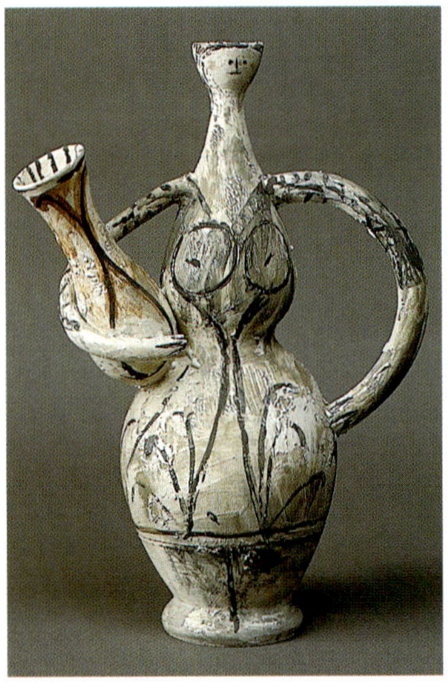

FIG. 46

"Picasso (fig. 47) began to experiment with ceramics in Vallauris in 1947-48. In 1946, on vacation, he had seen a pottery show and stopped by the Vallauris studio of Suzanne Ramié, known as "Madoura". He modeled by hand a faun's head and two bulls, and left them to be fired. A year later he returned and saw the fired works. His infatuation with ceramics is said to date from that moment.[42] The Madoura studio immediately became a center of attention as people stopped by to see "in what curious fashion this illustrious Cubist painter could be dealing with the rotundities of the balls of potter's clay."[43] Picasso later said, "In the ceramic work the artist can show his creativity and the power of his imagination, like in a painting but with on top of this the spontaneous characteristics of what is tangible, material, hand-made."[44]

An early outcome was a vase that looked like an owl, which was produced as a limited edition according to his design. A simplified human face is scratched sgraffito-style into a black patch on the owl's breast.[45] Within the first year or two Picasso had produced a variety of works – pitchers carved and painted with images of flowers and dark-skinned women, plates with line drawings of his characteristic nudes, rudimentary modeled figurines that looked pinched and others that look like modifications of svelte bottles, plates and jugs with bullfight scenes, casseroles remodeled into masks, strips cut from slabs pressed together to shape doves, painted tiles, various bird or woman-shaped vases. He produced so much ceramic work – an estimated 2,000 pieces his first year at Vallauris[46] – that books have been devoted to the subject.

Woman-shaped vessels seem to have been a particular specialty, which is not surprising, but the variety is impressive. A few small pieces are straightforwardly modeled in terracotta, others are collapsed or deformed vases or bottles, and still others are hardly manipulated at all but capitalize on the natural associations of pot and figure already discussed. These associations go toward the female more than the male, given

FIG. 45 PABLO PICASSO
LA FEMME ENCEINTE 1950
sculpture bronze
COLLECTION MUSÉE PICASSO, PARIS

FIG. 46 PABLO PICASSO
FEMME À L'AMPHORE 1947-1948
vase; 42.5 x 32.5 cm
COLLECTION MUSÉE PICASSO, PARIS

FIG. 47 PABLO PICASSO WORKING IN THE STUDIO IN VALLAURIS

42. Georges Ramié, Ceramics of Picasso, Barcelona: Ediciones Polígrafa, 1985, p. 8.
43. Ramié, p. 15.
44. Mathey, Terra Sculptura, p. 35.
45. See Cobra and Contrasts, Detroit: Detroit Institute of Arts, 1974, pp. 86-87.
46. Tamara Préaud and Serge Gautheir, Ceramics of the 20th Century (translation from the French by Office du Livre), New York: Rizzoli International, 1982, p. 90

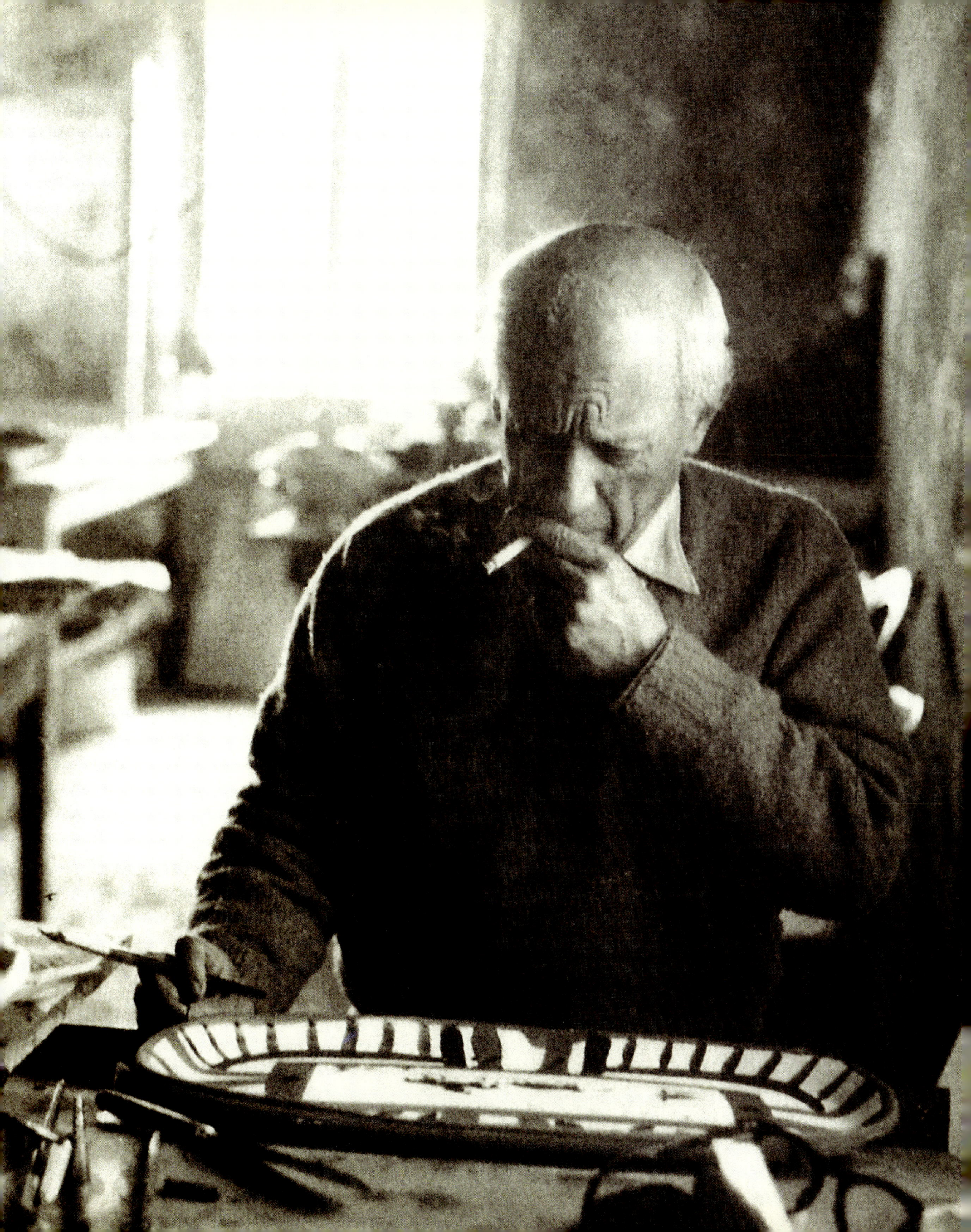

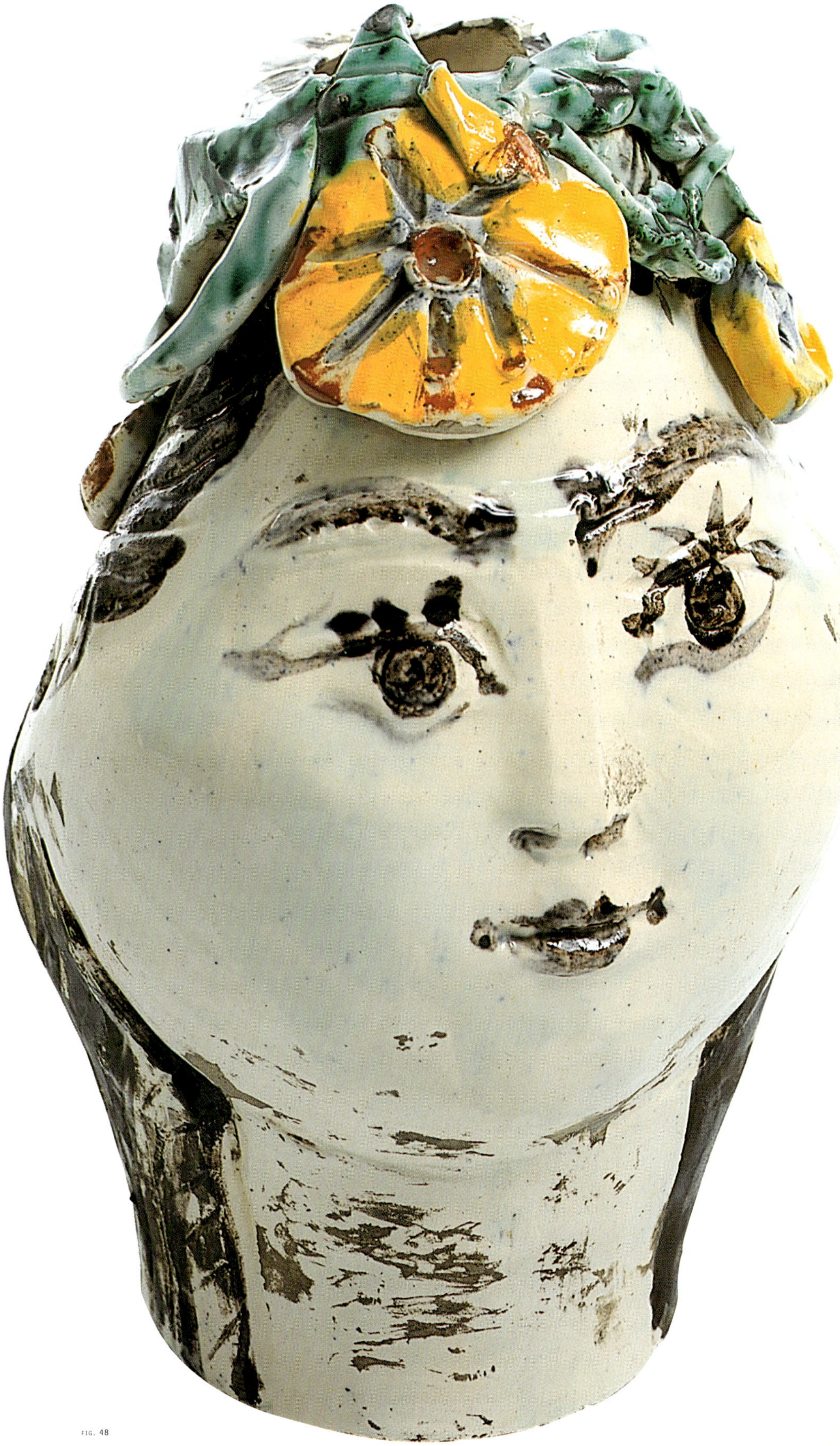

FIG. 48

FIG. 48 PABLO PICASSO
VASE FEMME 1954
vase; 25 x 18 x 14 cm
COLLECTION MUSEUM HET KRUITHUIS
[ACQUIRED WITH SUPPORT OF
VERENIGING REMBRANDT, AMSTERDAM]

the roundness of wheel-thrown pottery volumes. Sometimes he hardly did more than draw breasts and a face on a waisted vessel. His humor is often apparent in works such as the 1947 Vase in the form of a female figure (fig. 46) in which a modest, cup-like rim serves as the tiny head of a voluptuous, full-hipped woman. One handle of this vase swells from the narrow shoulder and rests insouciantly on the hip, while the other handle has been altered to hold a smaller pot, as if she is walking back from the well. Picasso also drew on the woman-as-vessel association in bronze sculptures such as his 1950 Pregnant woman, in which he embedded large ceramic jars in the plaster cast, positioned like breasts and belly (fig. 45).

FIG. 49 PABLO PICASSO
SCÈNE DE TAURO-MACHIE (ED. 27/150) 1954
bowl; ø 16 cm
COLLECTION MUSEUM HET KRUITHUIS

FIG. 50 PABLO PICASSO
UNTITLED (ED. 18/100) 1956
plate; ø 42 cm
COLLECTION MUSEUM HET KRUITHUIS

One example of Picasso's ceramic production is an untitled and undated small bowl (fig. 49). Conceptually though not physically the bowl parallels his little pitcher discussed – earlier in its playful merging of a standard ceramic form with something from the real world that shares its configuration – although in this case it is something of a vastly different size. Picasso created a bullfighting scene, a theme familiar from his paintings, on the inside of the bowl. It is made to be seen from a single viewpoint, which is contrary to the three-dimensionality of bowls, yet it takes on a peculiar life because of the way the curved walls of the bowl allow an evocation of an amphitheater's circular form. This looks like an aerial view, as if the Goodyear blimp hovered over the corrida.

Picasso also made innumerable plates, of course, to which he adapted motifs familiar from his paintings. The crude vigor of a horned faun (fig. 50) is carried through in his approach to the object on which this image appears: he stabbed the still-soft clay with a round stick, peppering the

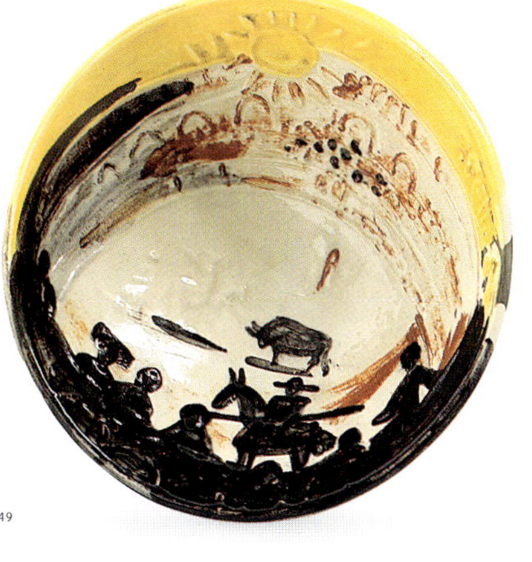

FIG. 49

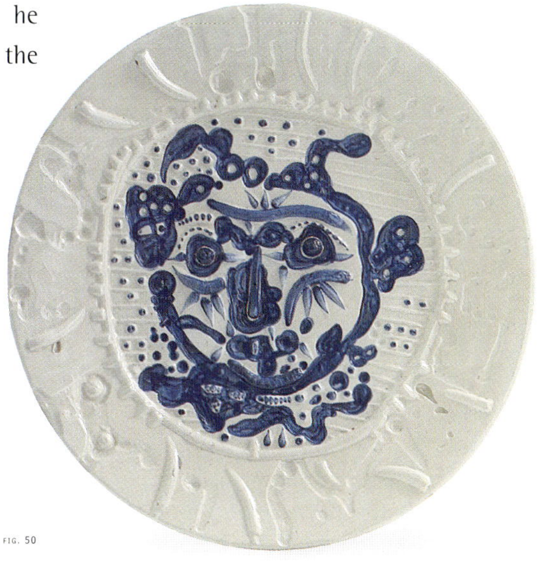

FIG. 50

plate with shallow indentations that look like spangles around the head – or maybe they're flies. He also gouged the rim in a linear pattern and piled up dots of clay between these notches. What's more, the actual painting of the face has an unmistakable dimensionality. This piece looks as quick and intuitive as many of Picasso's works in other mediums. Part of his genius, it would seem, is his attention to the qualities of materials and his ability to bring out the strengths of each substance he uses.

The Argentine-born Italian artist **Lucio Fontana** (1899-1968 – fig. 51) worked in clay extensively, perhaps more than any of the other Modernists discussed here. He is a generation younger than most of them, but he began working in clay before Miró and Picasso did. Fontana is best known for the body of work he called "Concetto Spaziale" (Spatial Concept), which began in 1948 when he punched holes in a canvas, utterly changing the terms under which it could be regarded (in 1958 he began to slash canvases as well – fig. 53)

FIG. 51 LUCIO FONTANA

One can hardly imagine how radical this action was at the time.[47] The painter's canvas had been a surface to be acted *upon*, not *through*. A perforated canvas is no longer a plane on which to fabricate an illusion, or even a ground for nonrepresentational arrangements of pigment. It is changed into a record of a gesture and a demonstration of the occupation of real space. The canvas becomes an interface between the obvious space in front of it and the once-hidden space behind it. That was why he called the works "Concetto Spaziale."

Fontana proclaimed, not facetiously, "Today we have entered the Space Age."[48] He wanted to make an homage to science and to incorporate a fraction of "cosmic space" as a palpable reality.[49] He asserted that the era of rockets inevitably influenced the creative spirit of artists and required a new development in artistic means. "Stone and bronze have to give way to new techniques in art," he wrote.[50] He spoke of making holes in the canvas to make a new dimension:

"I say dimension because I cannot think what other word to use. I make a hole in the canvas in order to leave behind me the old pictorial formulae, the painting and the

47. Erika Billeter, "Lucio Fontana: Between Tradition and Avant-Garde," in Lucio Fontana 1899-1968: a Retrospective, New York: Guggenheim Museum, 1977, p. 18.
48. Lucio Fontana, "Why I Make Spatial Art," in Lucio Fontana: Paintings and Sculptures, Paris: Galerie Karsten Greve, 1989, p. 18.
49. Billeter, p. 16.
50. Fontana, p. 18.

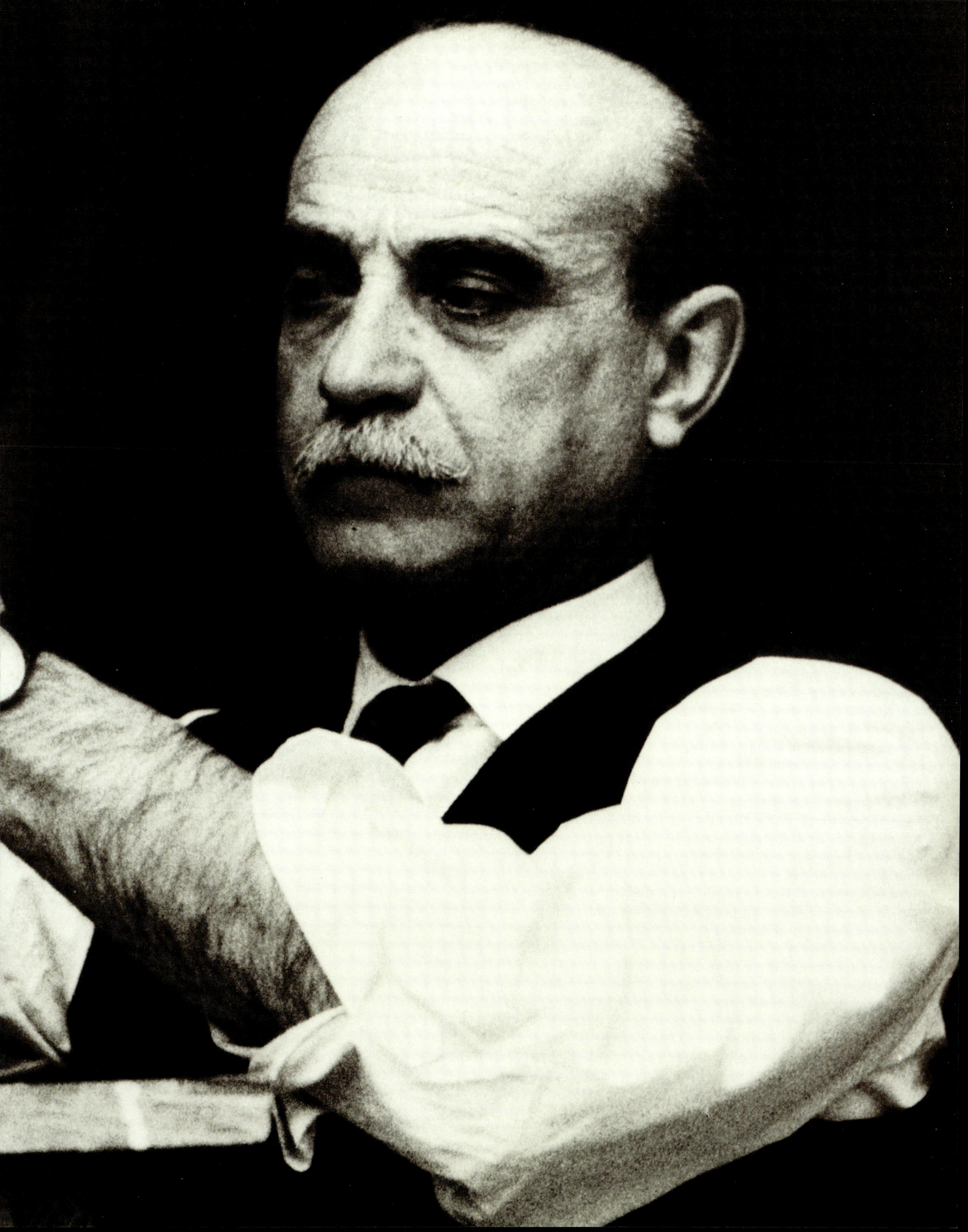

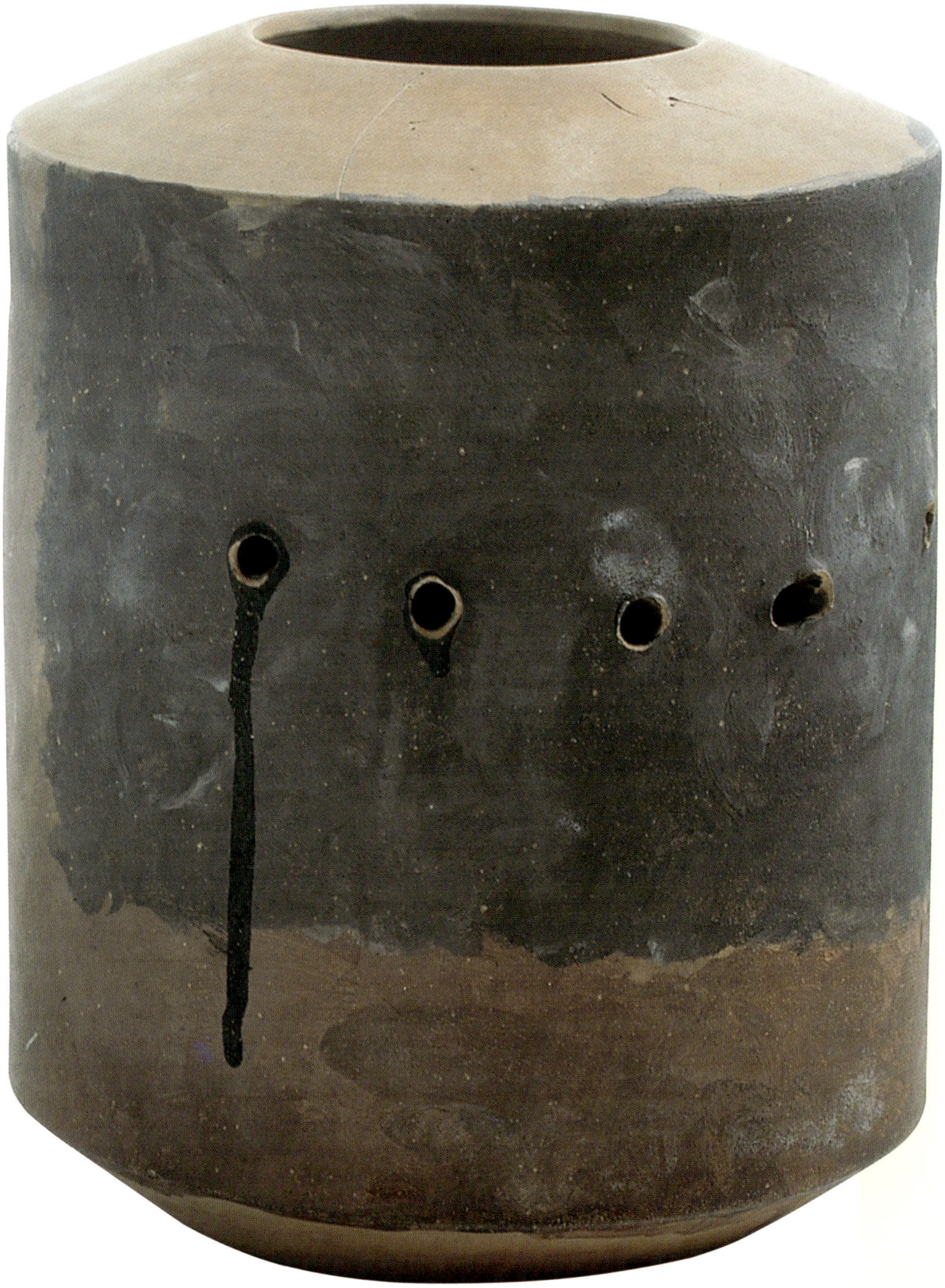

FIG. 52 LUCIO FONTANA
CONCETTO SPAZIALE 1958
vase; 18 x 14.5 cm
COLLECTION MUSEUM HET KRUITHUIS

FIG. 52

traditional view of art and I escape symbolically, but also materially, from the prison of the flat surface. As for Pollock... He was looking for a new dimension of space, but all he could produce was Post-Impressionism, because he threw paint *onto* the canvas, although he wanted to go *beyond* the canvas."[51]

The Kruithuis collection includes examples of Fontana's cylindrical vessels and plates that are slashed or punctured in accordance with his "Spatialist" practices (fig. 52 and 56) These, however, may look less shocking than the canvases. Clay is a soft material when the artist works with it and is receptive to this sort of manipulation. With clay, Fontana is operating in a different spatial arena as well. His cylinders already occupy three-dimensional space and make reference to an interior volume which already has a means of access, the vessel's mouth. By slashing or puncturing he makes the vessel wall seem more vulnerable, but he does not reveal an unexpected space. Oddly, it may be that he makes the vessel wall more like a canvas through his action: when he punctures, he calls attention to the wall in isolation from other aspects of the vessel, and presents it as a membrane that can be breached. The slashes are a slightly different case (although he claimed that holes and slashes "are the same thing"[52]). The slashes in the cylinder do not go completely through the wall to the interior space, so they are manipulations of the surface rather than structural changes. The interior surface is unblemished. This is possible with clay, a thicker membrane, whereas cloth could not be cut only on its front (fig. 54).

Fontana sometimes augmented the appearance of depth of a slashed canvas by applying a layer of black gauze to the back. He applied a black matte pigment to the face of these terra-cotta pieces. The incision goes through this top layer. The black pulls back slightly, like a dried cut in the peel of a fruit. The slash reveals the terra-cotta color below and thus make a visual connection to the bare clay exposed elsewhere on the vessel, as does the much finer free-hand scratch outlining the black field.

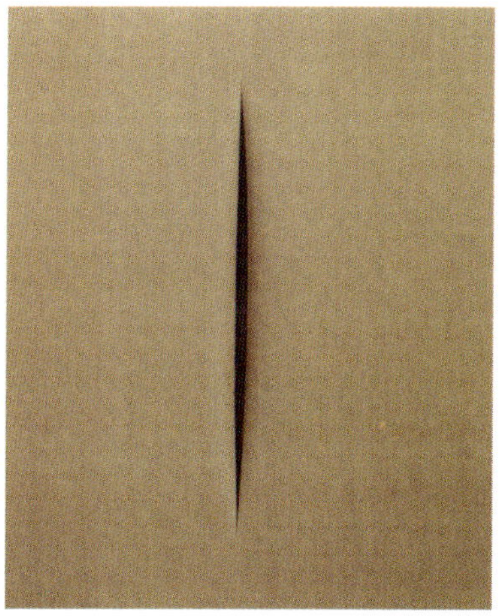
FIG. 53

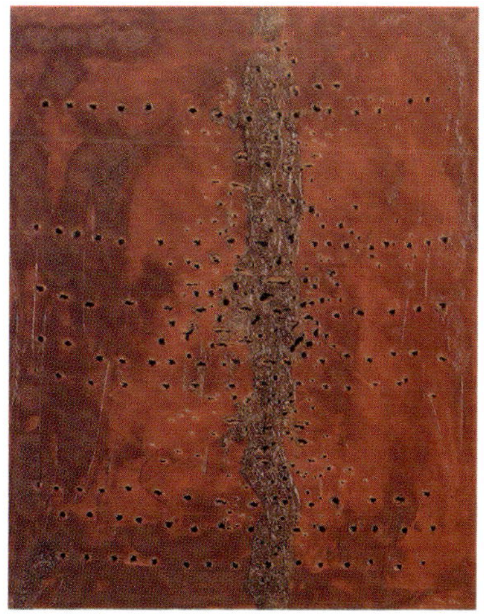
FIG. 54

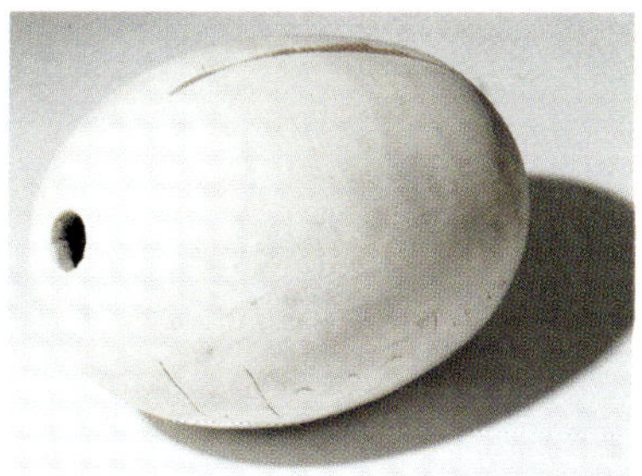
FIG. 55

FIG. 53 LUCIO FONTANA
CONCETTO SPAZIALE ATTESE (NOT DATED)
raw canvas; 73.6 x 60.4 cm

FIG. 54 LUCIO FONTANA
CONCETTO SPAZIALE 1960
oil on canvas; 100 x 81 cm

FIG. 55 LUCIO FONTANA
CONCETTO SPAZIALE CA. 1964
object; 16 x 24.5 cm

51. Tommaso Trini, "Last interview given by Fontana," in Lucio Fontana: Paintings and Sculptures, p. 27.
52. Ibid.

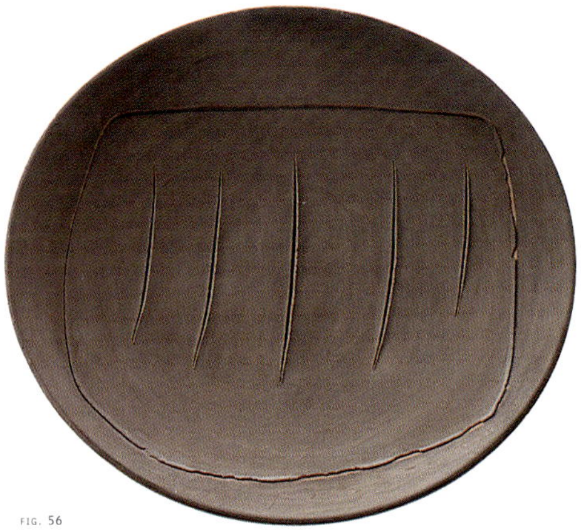

FIG. 56

In such works, Fontana creates an effect that seems almost Japanese. The utter simplicity of the forms and their dry, austere surfaces make a very strong contrast to virtually all of the works of the Classical Modernists discussed here, which are either more decorative or more illustrative. Fontana has made a stage so bare that his isolated, decisive gestures have an almost explosive impact. Imagine, for comparison, that such cuts and punctures appeared on one of De Vlaminck's plates. In that visually eventful, busy context, they would hardly be noticeable as minor incidents amid complex activity. Here they are isolated on the blackness, drawn out in an acute tension as taut as a bowstring, to give us a physical sensation of an action preserved in the receptive body of clay. On the slashed cylinder and plate, the arena of action is designated by the spidery, hand-drawn outline, which is as struggling or hesitant as the slashing is bold. On the perforated cylinder, the sense that the object has been wounded is reinforced by the weeping or bleeding of darker blackness from some of the holes.

Fontana was not alone in developing the "Spatialist" idea, but he is particularly identified with the Spatialist Manifestoes of 1948 and 1950 and the subsequent promulgation of the concept. It's interesting to wonder if he was affected by his pre-art-school work as a businessman dealing in granite and marble for the construction of buildings; these materials clad the surface of structures that have interior volumes: inside the beautiful face is the useful part. The same is true of ceramic vessels. As early as 1931 Fontana was making terra-cotta objects. In 1936 he worked as a ceramist at Tullio Mazzotti's ceramic works in Albisola, Italy. In 1937 he worked at the French porcelain manufactory at Sèvres, and his first solo show in Paris, that same year, was of ceramics.

Among Fontana's early works in clay are loose depictions of fruit and expressionistic figures as much as three feet tall. He also decorated classical vases with painting and relief. His earliest ceramic vessels given the "Concetto Spaziale" series title date from the second half of the 1950s and resemble the examples from the Kruithuis collection. His "Concetto Spaziale/Natura" series of 1959-60 consists of boulder-like masses of clay or bronze shown on the floor. Each large, rough-surfaced ball has a gash or puncture cutting into the interior. Each is essentially monochrome and earth-colored, but there is a considerable range of hues. All reveal the marks of their making, including finger marks.

FIG. 56 LUCIO FONTANA
UNTITLED CA. 1958
plate; ⌀ 49.5 cm
COLLECTION MUSEUM HET KRUITHUIS

Another "Concetto Spaziale" series, without subtitle, dating from the late '50s and early '60s, consists of egg-shape vessels with rounded bottoms that rest tentatively on their sides (fig. 55). These show a variety of colors and glaze effects, including a satiny copper color and stony charcoal grays. Each of the extremely simple forms has a small opening through which one may look into the interior. Sometimes, in the case of a white egg-shape vessel, the hole at one end recalls a blown egg. These vessels may also have slashes and punctures; they do not look violent but seem as graceful as the forms themselves. In the same period, Fontana made irregular-shape plaques on which the front surface was given a coat of color and also slashed. The spatial concept could be applied to any form or material, and he also worked in sheets of metal. Even though Fontana specifically adopted repetition as a means of giving order and significance to his marks, he was able to keep his work from being repetitive because of his fine sense of balance and proportion that makes these reductive works elegant and beautiful.

FIG. 57 LUCIO FONTANA
CRISTO CA. 1958
sculpture; 42 x 35.5 cm
COLLECTION MUSEUM HET KRUITHUIS

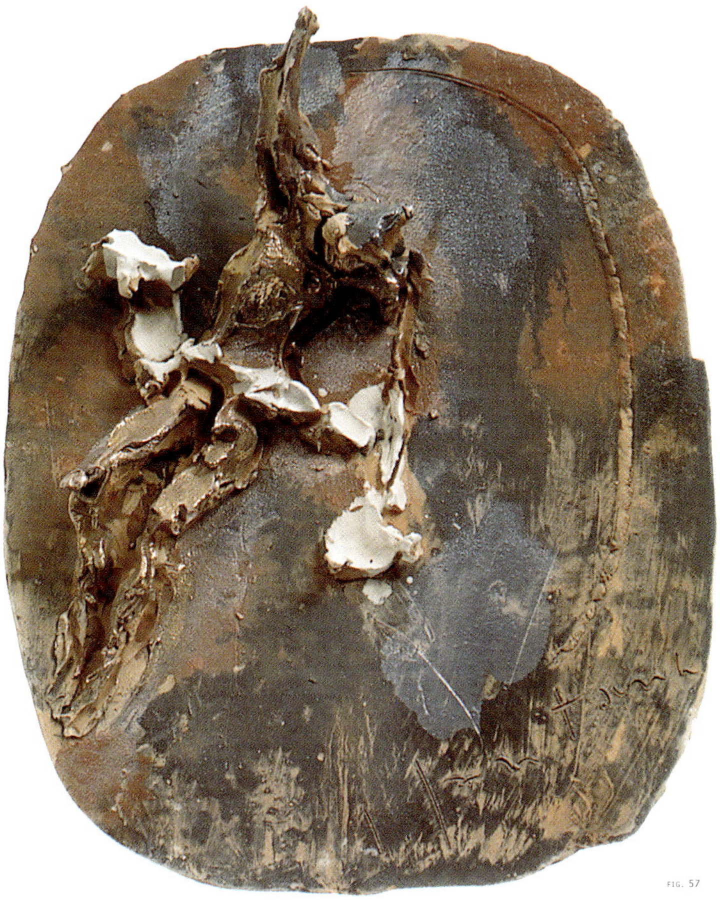

FIG. 57

COBRA

The COBRA artists (fig. 58) were a loosely affiliated group of Northern European painters, sculptors and poets who, between 1948 and 1951, shared viewpoints, activities and exhibitions, and put out publications. Several went on working in the characteristic style even after the group had dissolved.

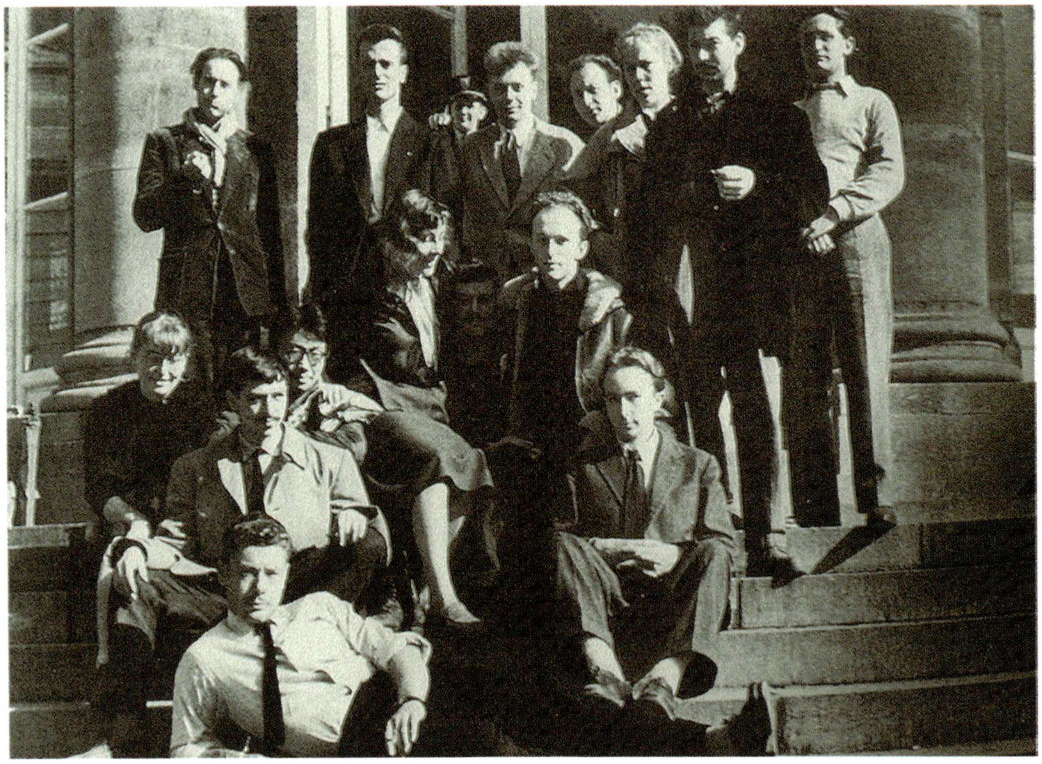

FIG. 58

FIG. 58 MEETING OF COBRA ARTISTS IN PALAIS DES BEAUX-ARTS 1951
BACK FROM LEFT TO RIGHT: CORNEILLE, ROBERT KAUFMANN, A STAFF MEMBER OF THE MUSEUM, JEAN RAINE, THEO WOLVECAMP, TONY AND KAREL APPEL, K.O. GÖTZ; MIDDLE: MICKEY ALECHINSKY, REINHOUD, PIERRE ALECHINSKY; FRONT: JANINE CORNEILLE, HANNOSET, SHINKICHI TAJIRI, LUC DE HEUSCH AND MICHEL OLUFF.

Most of them lived in Copenhagen, Brussels or Amsterdam, and from the first letters of those cities' names they took their group name. As a reaction to the horror of the war they had just survived, they rejected rational Western culture and "sought a spontaneous, expressionistic, anti-classic art which would return to primordial sources of creation."[54] They looked to the art of "primitive" peoples, Asian calligraphy, prehistoric art and the art of the Middle Ages. In contemporary Western culture they responded to folk art, naïve art, and the creative products of children and the mentally ill or mentally handicapped.[55]

54. Frederick J. Cummings, Foreword and Acknowledgements, Cobra and Contrasts, pp. 8-9.
55. Willemijn Stokvis, Cobra: An International Movement in Art after the Second World War, Barcelona: Ediciones Polígrafa, 1987, p. 7.

The COBRA movement is distinctive for its international fraternization and cooperation as well as its anti-specialization stance. "Painters wrote poetry, poets painted and drew, they established contacts with filmmakers, fashioned sculptures, took photographs, made works of art from rubbish, worked together on murals, canvas and paper."[56] Experimentation was a way of avoiding skill and academicism and working with a childlike directness. "When these artists were in the process of creation, they would often let themselves be guided by the properties peculiar to, and the accidental qualities of, the materials they were using. This method of approach was for some of them consolidated by the theories of the French philosopher and psychologist Gaston Bachelard (1884-1962), who believed that matter, in the form of the four elements, was the great source of human inspiration."[57] Among the materials with which they experimented together or individually was ceramics.

COBRA was close in time and in some ways close in spirit to *Informel* painting in France and Abstract Expressionism in the U.S., but it blended with such "action" painting a Surrealist fantasy as well as what we would now call "outsider artist" effects. COBRA paintings nearly always retain a trace of the figure, as often animal as human (not surprisingly, these artists respected the work of Miró). The emotional tone can be gathered from a 1948 statement: "a painting is not a construction of colors and lines, but an animal, a night, a cry, a person, or all of that together."[58] Most COBRA paintings involved bright, unmixed colors, applied in patches and connected with distinct lines. The creatures that populate the paintings, many of them hybrids, can be seen as expressing the artists' wish that man return to his origins among the plants and animals.[59] There were, of course, some differences within the movement: the Danish COBRA participants tended to be more Norse and gloomy and to make reference to myth; the Dutch were more likely to be inspired by children's drawings as well as modern art predecessors such as Picasso, Kandinsky and Klee in addition to Miró.[60]

56. Stokvis, p. 7.
57. Stokvis, p. 19.
58. In Cobra and Contrasts, p. 33, the words are attributed to Constant; in Karel Appel: Sculpture, Note 44, p. 172 (see FN 66, below), they are attributed to Karel Appel!
59. Stokvis, p. 20.
60. Stokvis, p. 20.

In the early autumn of 1948, shortly before COBRA officially came into being with the signing of a manifesto, the Dutch artists Karel Appel, Constant, Corneille and Anton Rooskens had an opportunity to try their hand at ceramics at a factory managed by one of Rooskens's old friends. Rooskens later recalled that "the workers at the factory used to call our department 'the circus.'"[61] Appel, Constant and Corneille (these latter two, along with the poet/artist Lucebert, use only a single name) showed ceramics and drawings at an exhibition in Amsterdam in October of that year, and revisited the factory to make more work in 1949. Lucebert was introduced to ceramics in 1950-52 by a friend who was a potter, and he drew and painted on dishes she made as well as handmaking a relief of an owl himself.[62] The Danish artist Asger Jorn had worked in clay as early as 1933, and in 1952 he worked at the studios of several potter friends in Denmark, where he both decorated existing dishes and had vessels made to his design.[63] Jorn was responsible for a sustained opportunity to make ceramics for himself and several other COBRA artists, beginning in 1953 when he visited Albisola, Italy, and then took up residence there the following year. He and his friends made works or decorated artisan-made pottery at the ceramic factory of Tullio Mazzotti.[64] Jorn's stay at Albisola is also important because he founded an organization of artists and writers that was an early stage of what became (in Paris) the Situationist International.

FIG. 59 KAREL APPEL

The COBRA artists embraced clay as a new sort of surface for painting whose earthiness gave an additional resonance to their primal figuration. Much COBRA ceramics in the Kruithuis collection is vessel-oriented and show a painterly approach. However, many of the COBRA artists also used ceramics as a sculptural material. A rather brutalist variety of "action" ceramics is a second strain of COBRA work.

As in painting, in ceramics COBRA imagery is often figurative, with a particular emphasis on animals. **Karel Appel** (b. 1921 – fig. 59) made plates that have very much the spirit of his painting, extending even to the thick, clunky almost cubic form of the ambiguous figures, and a feeling that they are too

61. Willemijn Stokvis, "Cobra and Ceramics" in Everything Valuable is Defenceless: ceramic work by COBRA members," 's-Hertogenbosch: Museum Het Kruithuis, 1993, p. 14.
62. Everything Valuable, p. 15.
63. Everything Valuable, pp. 16-17.
64. Stokvis, p. 21.

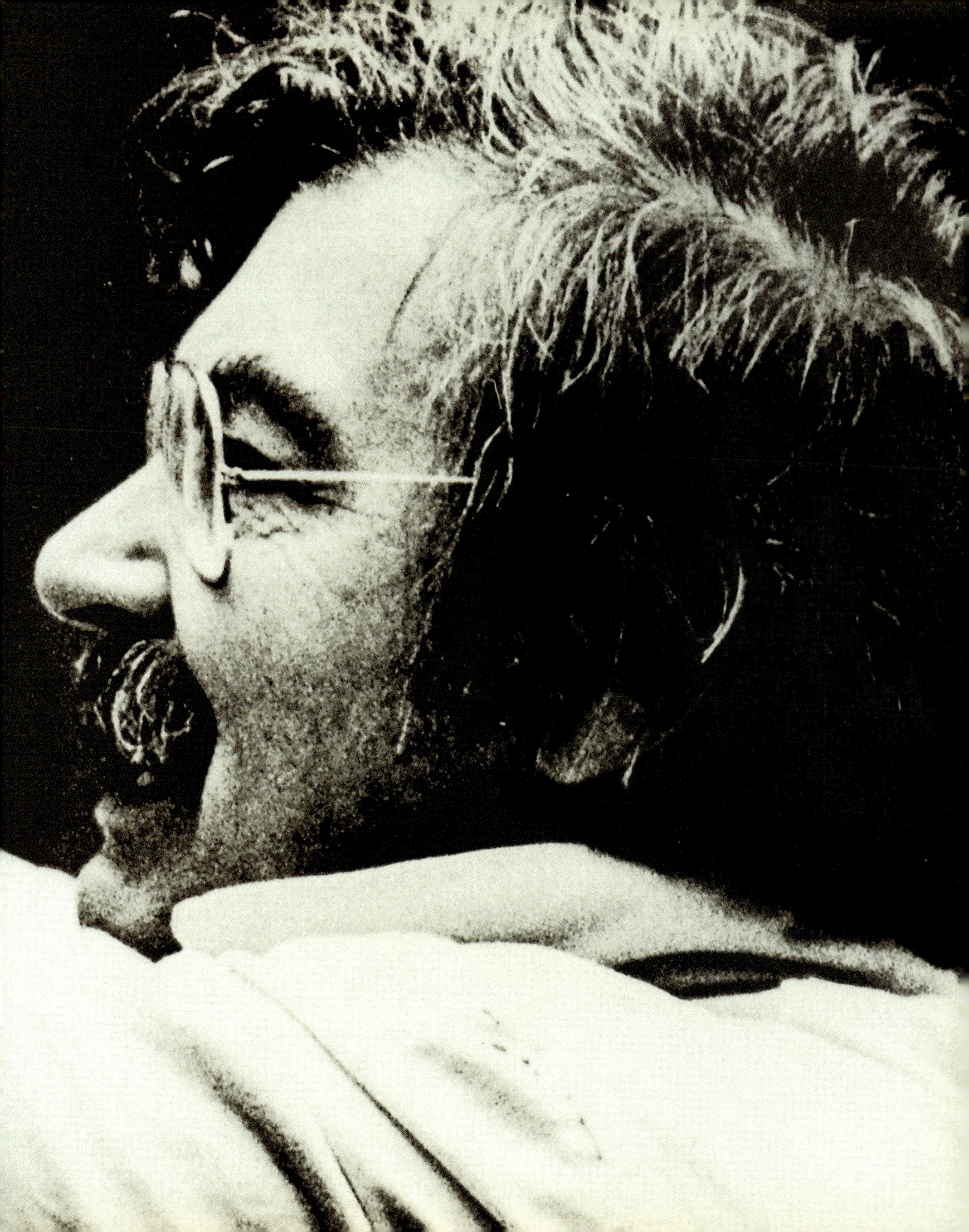

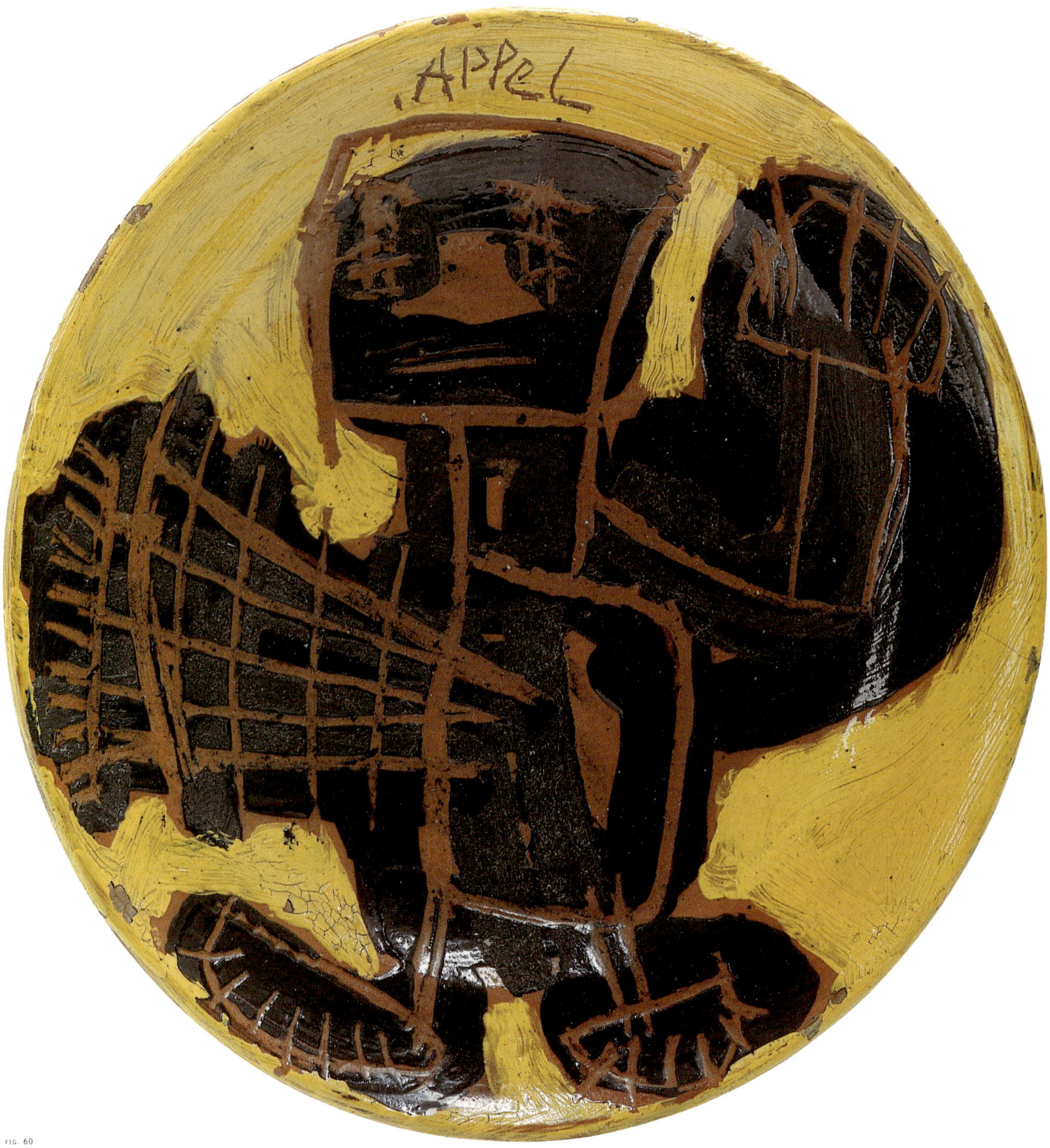

FIG. 60

FIG. 60 KAREL APPEL
UNTITLED 1948-49
plate; ø 35 cm
COLLECTION MUSEUM HET KRUITHUIS

big for the canvas (or clay) that encloses them but too slow to escape from it. We might look at the image on a plate he made in 1950 (fig. 60) and think this odd form represents a bird with a strangely human – and sad – quality to its "face," a bird that can't stretch out its wings in this cramped space. But it has very un-bird-like feet. Maybe it's not a bird, or only one in its imagination. Appel has painted large, blocky wing-like appendages, but upon these dark areas the orange lines at one side look like an upraised fist, while at the other side is a splayed grid that might represent a shield. So those blocky areas might not be wings at all, but simply indications of the massing of the limbs of a figure in motion. And if so, the figure may be Everywarrior. The warm, dark, layered colors give this work an intensity that holds our interest until we arrive at some interpretation of identity.

An Appel plate from 1953, (fig. 61), is both like and unlike the first. Again there is a single, central, ambiguous but vigorous-looking figure; again the plate is treated like a canvas and the figure seems confined. But if the image on the other plate might be called Brutalist, and might be reminiscent

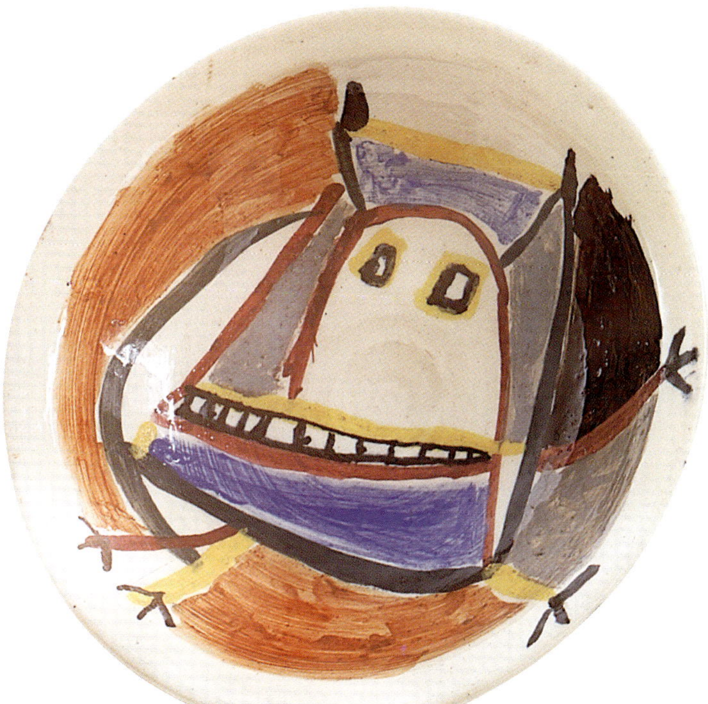

FIG. 61

FIG. 61 KAREL APPEL
UNTITLED 1953
plate; ⌀ 21 cm
COLLECTION MUSEUM HET KRUITHUIS

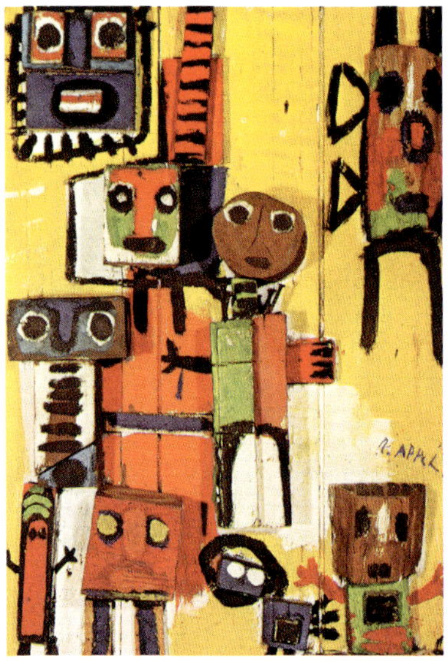

FIG. 62

of Dubuffet in its harshness (though not in its smooth surface and bright hues), this one seems straight from a kindergarten drawing. It is all head and mouth. Although the excess of teeth might seem fearsome, the creature is without density and unconstrained by gravity, so the feelings it conveys are exuberance and energy. It seems to have antennae and so might seem to be a cartoonish space creature, but this time it has very bird-like three-part feet. There are, however, four of them, in an arrangement something like arms and legs, so Appel is not making identification easy. This figure, like many of Appel's, seems "primitive" in a knowing way, and seems to have a sense of humor behind it.

Appel, along with Jorn, is the most famous of the COBRA artists. His early works are the most clearly influenced by children's art. They often consist of thick, owl-like birds with bright harlequin heads, or simplified representations of children with square heads that feature only large round eyes (fig. 62), plus rectangular torsos with stick arms and legs, always executed in vivid colors. But in the early '50s his work became vastly more expressionistic. After 1953, when the Parisian art promoter Michel Tapié took an interest in Appel, "his work became more emotional. He could now afford better materials

FIG. 62 KAREL APPEL
VRAGENDE KINDEREN 1949
wooden relief, painted in oils; 87 x 60 cm

FIG. 63 KAREL APPEL
KOP 1958
sculpture; 21.7 x 25.7 x 33.1 cm
COLLECTION KRÖLLER-MÜLLER MUSEUM, OTTERLO/NL

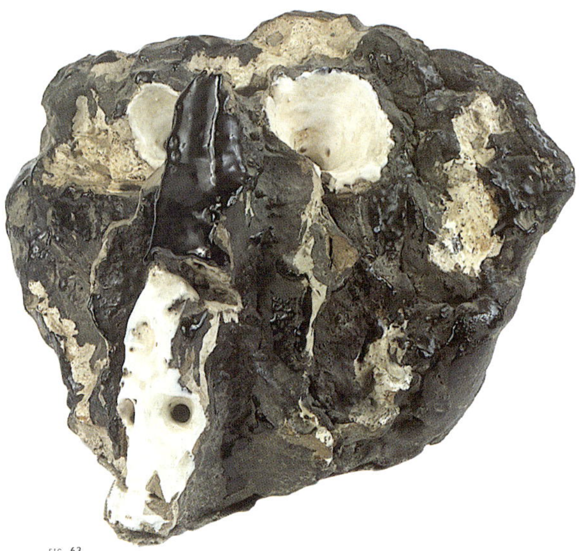

FIG. 63

and larger canvases. His world of childlike creatures was devoured by the paint, which started to move around the canvas with ever increasing force. Creatures could still be discerned, making their presence felt through the vague traces of eyes and mouths, though now possessing a more demonic nature."[65] Appel was the only COBRA artist included by Tapié in the 1952 show and manifesto *Un art autre*, which endorsed a violent, temperamental and matter-oriented art.[66]

In 1953 and '54 Appel made glazed terra-cotta heads (fig. 63) that are almost mask-like in having only small eyeholes and a rudimentary nose or a slit to indicate a mouth. The features appear in a surface so irregular that it resembles a rough sea. These intense and mesmerizing works concentrate on the most known and communicative aspect of the human body. But at the same time Appel also made untitled and unnameable chunks of clay, squeezed, twisted, riffled, torn and scarred, that in form alone (to say nothing of their fierce colors) resemble the increasingly ferocious surfaces of his paintings at the time. Appel regularly worked in sculpture in a wide variety of mediums. Some of his sculptures "seem like folk art, others like quick graffiti sketches made three-dimensional. Many use found materials and found objects; others are made of plaster, steel, and wood. Some are elaborate constructions, others seem deftly carved or modeled. Virtually all are painted."[67] His painterly instinct literally colors his work in all mediums.

An animal also decorates an untitled 1948 work (fig. 71) by the Dutch/Belgian artist **Corneille** (b. 1922 – fig. 67). It appears to be an anthropomorphic bird. This one, unlike Appel's, comes with appropriate feet and a beak. It is amusingly wide-eyed, and it is decorated with some ornamental medallion that looks interestingly like a seed with eyes. But the bird has little to suggest wings. Rather, arms seem to hold aloft a banner that shows sun, stars and other markings. The heavens above the bird's head invoke something rather more elevated than the normal territory of such a modest little avian. Perhaps it's for that reason that birds seem to have attracted the COBRA artists. But also, perhaps, because of the symbolism of birds in a time when war was only a few years in the past:

65. Stokvis, p. 22.
66. Donald Kuspit, Karel Appel: Sculpture, New York: Harry N. Abrams, 1994, Note 34, p. 171.
67. Kuspit, p. 33.

the connotations of flying away and of freedom were particularly meaningful.

Corneille's COBRA paintings were generally quieter than Appel's, with a graphic strength. They tend to concentrate less on expressionistic brushwork than Appel's, and to fill up nearly all the space of the canvas with compartments, some representing heads or bodies and some whose meanings are less clear, but always with a feeling of vitality. Beginning in the 1950s he painted labyrinthine cities (fig. 68) and what seem to be aerial views of the earth. Some of these are charmingly schematic depictions of a scene or place spread out flat for easy viewing. These compositions often show a round motif, such as a sun or a moon, or a square, which is to be taken as a place of rest.[68] With the renewed inspiration of folk and tribal art, Corneille's later paintings extend the COBRA themes with images alluding to the earth's fecundity.

The decorations on two 1954 plates by Corneille (fig. 64 and 65) represent fish rendered schematically. They consist of visually balanced elements rather than individual, portrait-like characteristics. Both are broad flat fish, like flounder. One has boxy protrusions from the four extreme points of the form; the top, bottom and rear protrusions might reasonably stand for fins, but not the one at the front, near what passes as an eye. At the rear is a much larger round shape, too big to be an eye, that brings to mind the sound hole on a mandolin or

FIG. 64 CORNEILLE
UNTITLED 1954
plate; ⌀ 27 cm
COLLECTION MUSEUM HET KRUITHUIS

FIG. 65 CORNEILLE
UNTITLED 1954
plate; ⌀ 27.5 cm
COLLECTION MUSEUM HET KRUITHUIS

FIG. 66 CORNEILLE
UNTITLED 1954
vase; 41 x 43 cm
COLLECTION MUSEUM HET KRUITHUIS

FIG. 67 CORNEILLE IN ALBISOLA

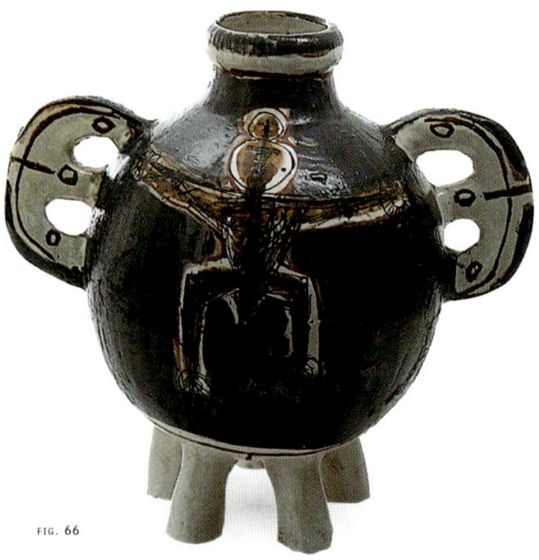

FIG. 66

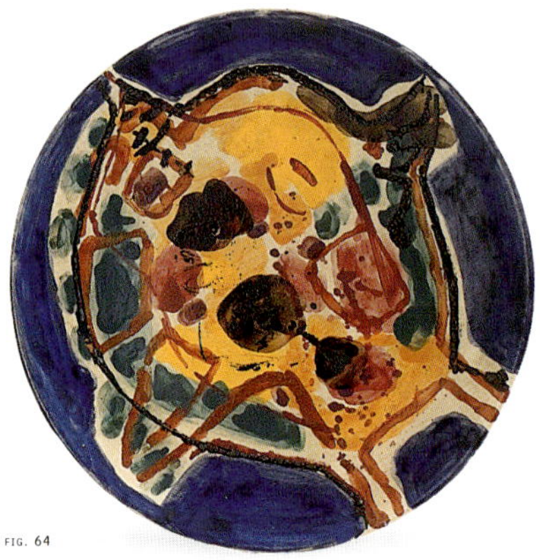

FIG. 64

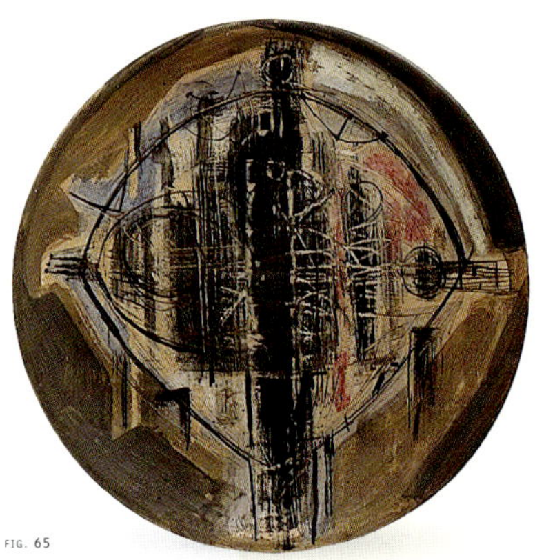

FIG. 65

68. Stokvis, p. 23.

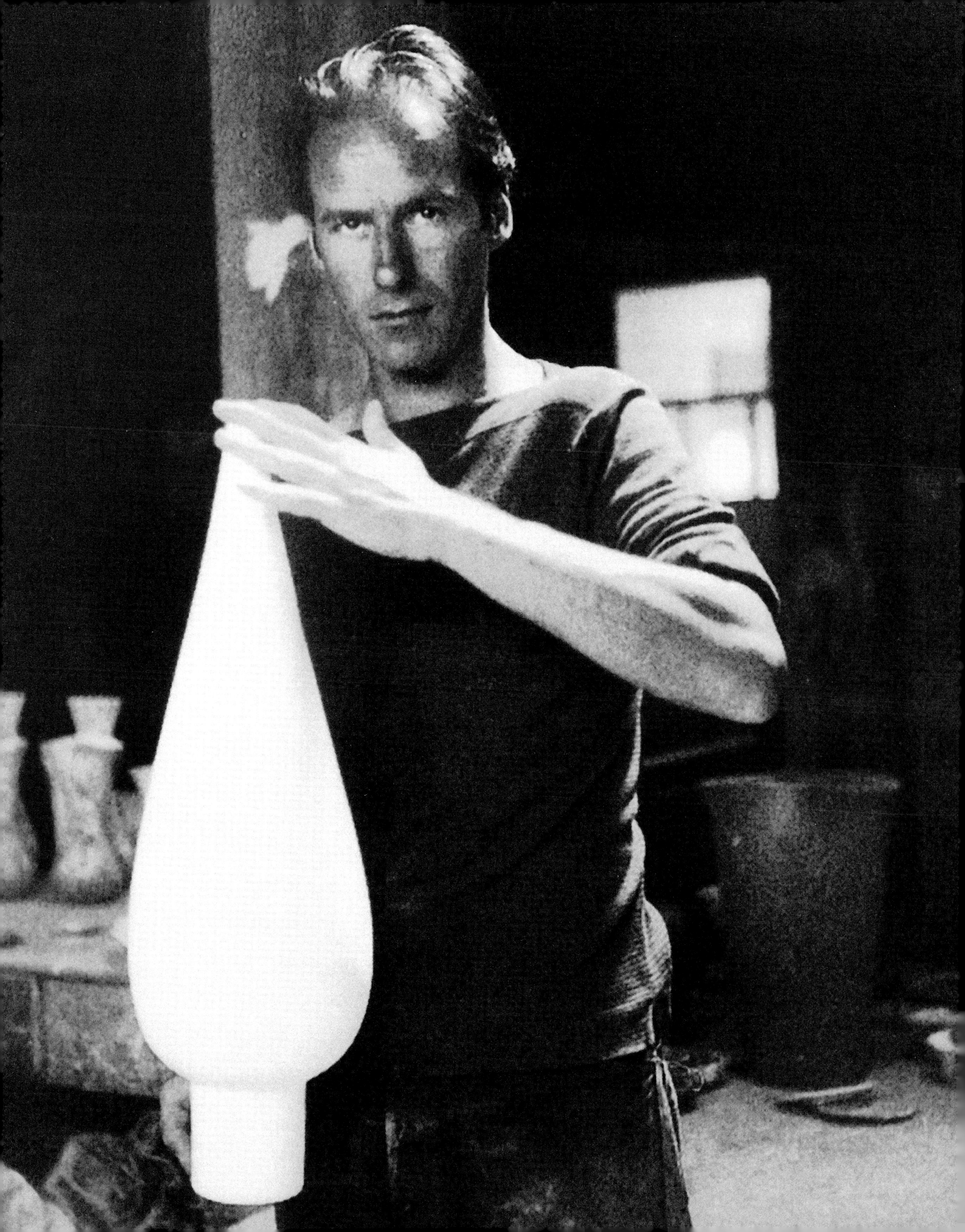

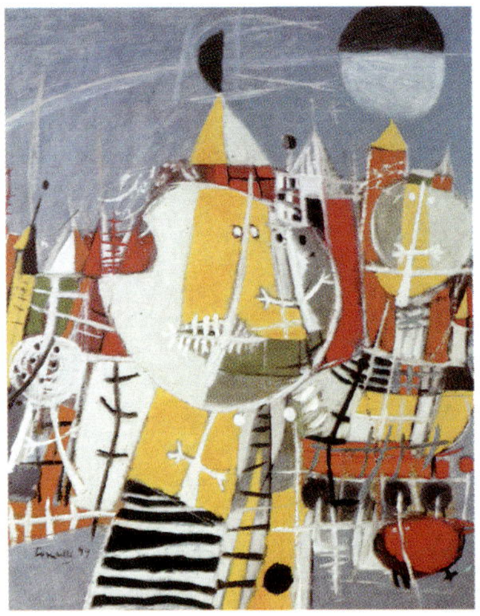

FIG. 68

similar stringed instrument. Corneille also stroked rough bands of black across the form. Some fish are striped, of course, but these stripes continue right across the edges. In addition, grooves scratched into the surface of the plate do not show representational considerations. It seems that Corneille both depicted and decorated. The same can be said of the second, and more colorful, piscine plate, where the shape is more reasonable: this fish has a pointed nose, fins at top and bottom, and a properly two-lobed tail. But Corneille is not striving for any precision here, either. His outline is partly in black, partly in a brown that does not coincide with the black. He could be suggesting a form in motion, one that has vanished by the time its appearance has registered in our minds. Or he could be extrapolating from the beauty of tropical fish, for the yellow, brown, red and aqua colors that mottle the outlined expanse are lyrical. Both plates could be used to serve fish or to eat it from; the consumption of the real fish would gradually reveal the imaginative one underneath. That would be in the finest tradition of functional ceramics: useful and yet engaging the mind and senses.

FIG. 68 CORNEILLE
LE RHYTME JOYEUX DE LA VILLE 1949
oil on canvas; 58.5 x 49 cm
COLLECTION STEDELIJK MUSEUM, AMSTERDAM/NL

FIG. 69 CORNEILLE
UNTITLED 1955
bowl; ø 24.5 cm
COLLECTION MUSEUM HET KRUITHUIS

FIG. 70 CORNEILLE
UNTITLED 1948
plate; ø 24.5 cm
COLLECTION MUSEUM HET KRUITHUIS

FIG. 71 CORNEILLE
UNTITLED 1948
plate; ø 24.5 cm
COLLECTION MUSEUM HET KRUITHUIS

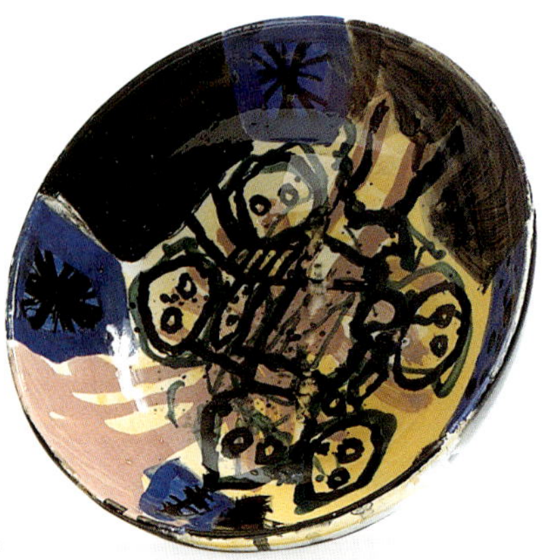

FIG. 69

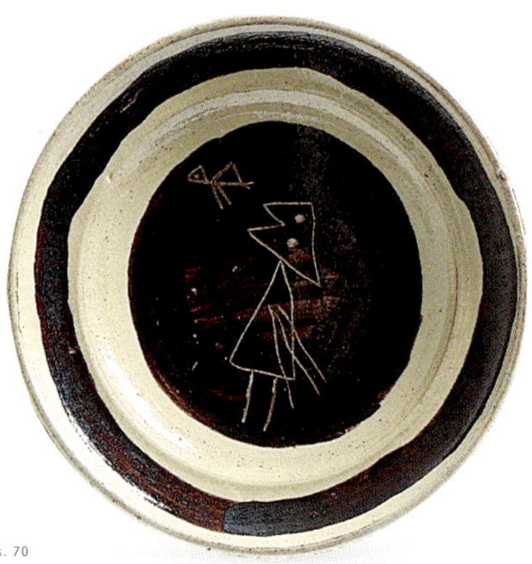

FIG. 70

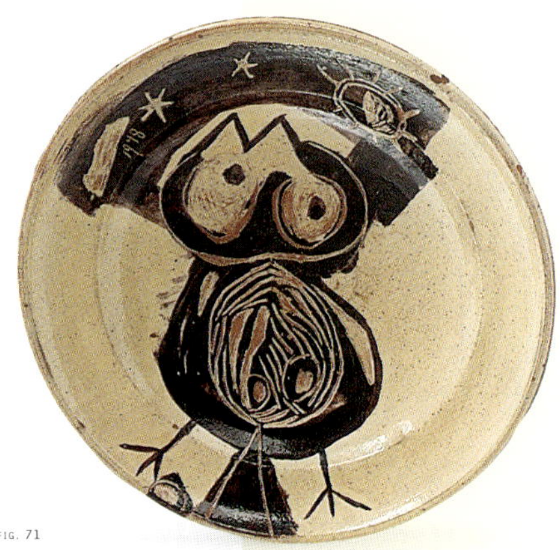

FIG. 71

FIG. 72 CORNEILLE
UNTITLED 1954
vase; 57 x 19.5 cm
COLLECTION MUSEUM HET KRUITHUIS

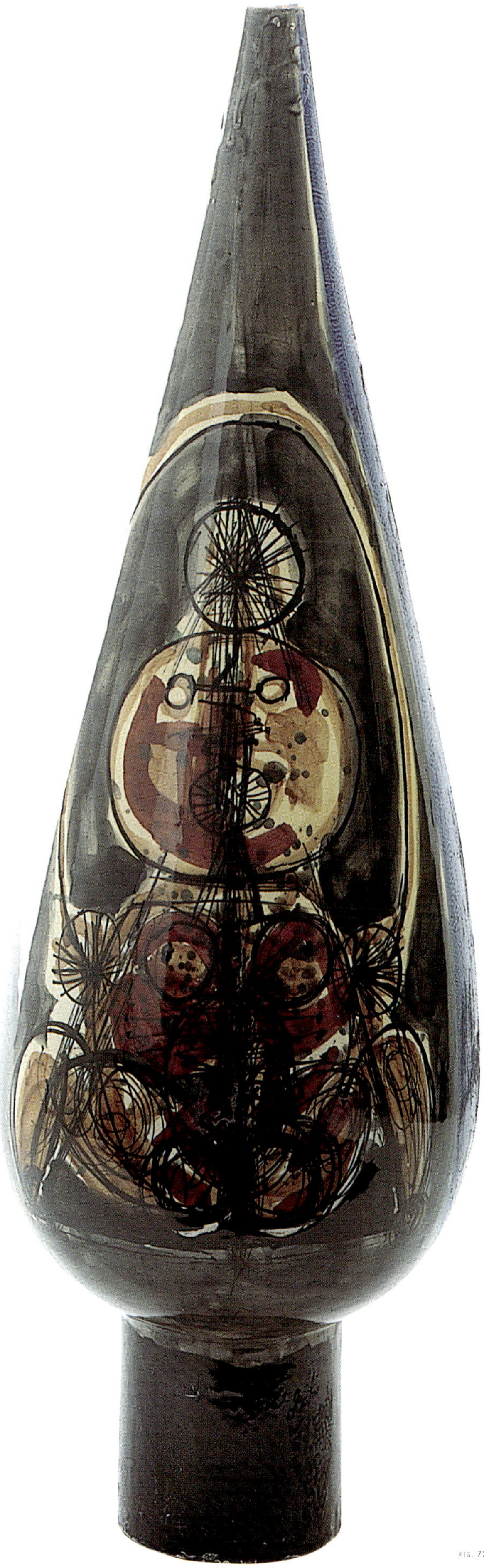

FIG. 72

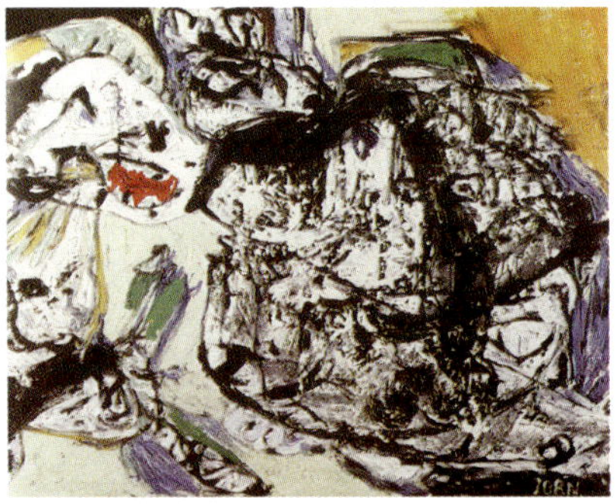

FIG. 73

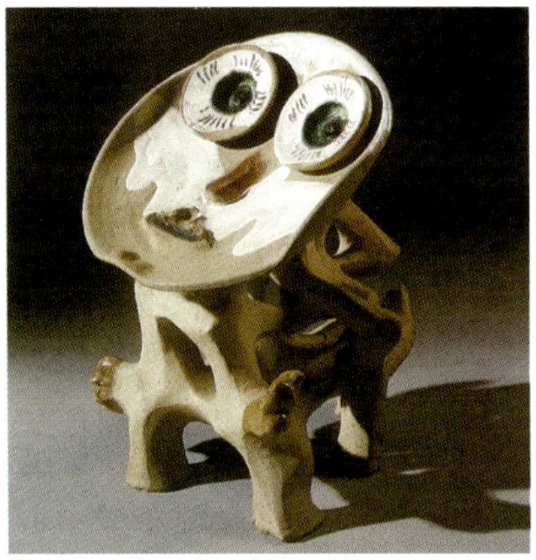

FIG. 74

Asger Jorn (1914-1973 – fig. 75) painted a plate in 1953 and unequivocally titled it *Vogel* (fig. 147). This fowl, however, seems most foul. Compared with Appel's light-weight bird and Corneille's bug-eyed one, Jorn's is a bird of prey with dark motives, clinging to a branch. The spiraling, complex line of his painting seems to compact inward with a wiry, propulsive energy. If Appel's birds look slow, this one seems on the contrary to have the potential of great speed. Its wings are held close to its sides, giving a sense of compression that is heightened by the darkness closing in around the bird and by the fact that it is rendered in lines only, not shading. It is transparent, as if its cold heart might be seen.

Only after the end of the "official" COBRA period did Jorn achieve his mature painting style: "paint was applied to the canvas with ever increasing vehemence, allowing the primordial forces of nature to burst forth in unrestrained rage. Mysterious, demonic creatures shelter among the motley shapes, while the splatters and blotches occasionally take on the humorous form of a somewhat confused ghost."[69] His surfaces are often so textured that the painting almost becomes an object (fig. 73).

Jorn made a huge variety of ceramic works. Some were playful, such as the 1953 *Man in the moon* (fig. 74), a foot-high dog-like sculpture with a carved, lattice body that includes four legs but also two stubby arms. A plate serves as a face and smaller attached disks make two large eyes. Some were monumental: he constructed a mural 27 meters long for a Danish high school (1959) that includes a dazzling array of colors and textures in a typically COBRA maelstrom of abstracted figuration. The mural consists of tile segments, in sizes amenable to firing in a kiln, that include quite irregular contours. This constructive "grid" through which the imagery is seen ranges from looking like mosaic tesserae to looking like a huge jigsaw puzzle.

More specifically human figures and visages also make frequent appearances in COBRA ceramics, just as they do in

FIG. 73 ASGER JORN
L'ACCROCHAGE 1958
oil on canvas; 97 x 130 cm
COLLECTION STEDELIJK VAN ABBEMUSEUM, EINDHOVEN/NL

FIG. 74 ASGER JORN
MAN IN THE MOON 1953
object; 33 x 25 cm
COLLECTION SILKEBORG KUNSTMUSEUM, SILKEBORG/DK

FIG. 75 ASGER JORN AND ELISEO SALINA
IN THE STUDIO IN SAN GIORGIO, ALBISOLA 1970

69. Stokvis, p. 21.

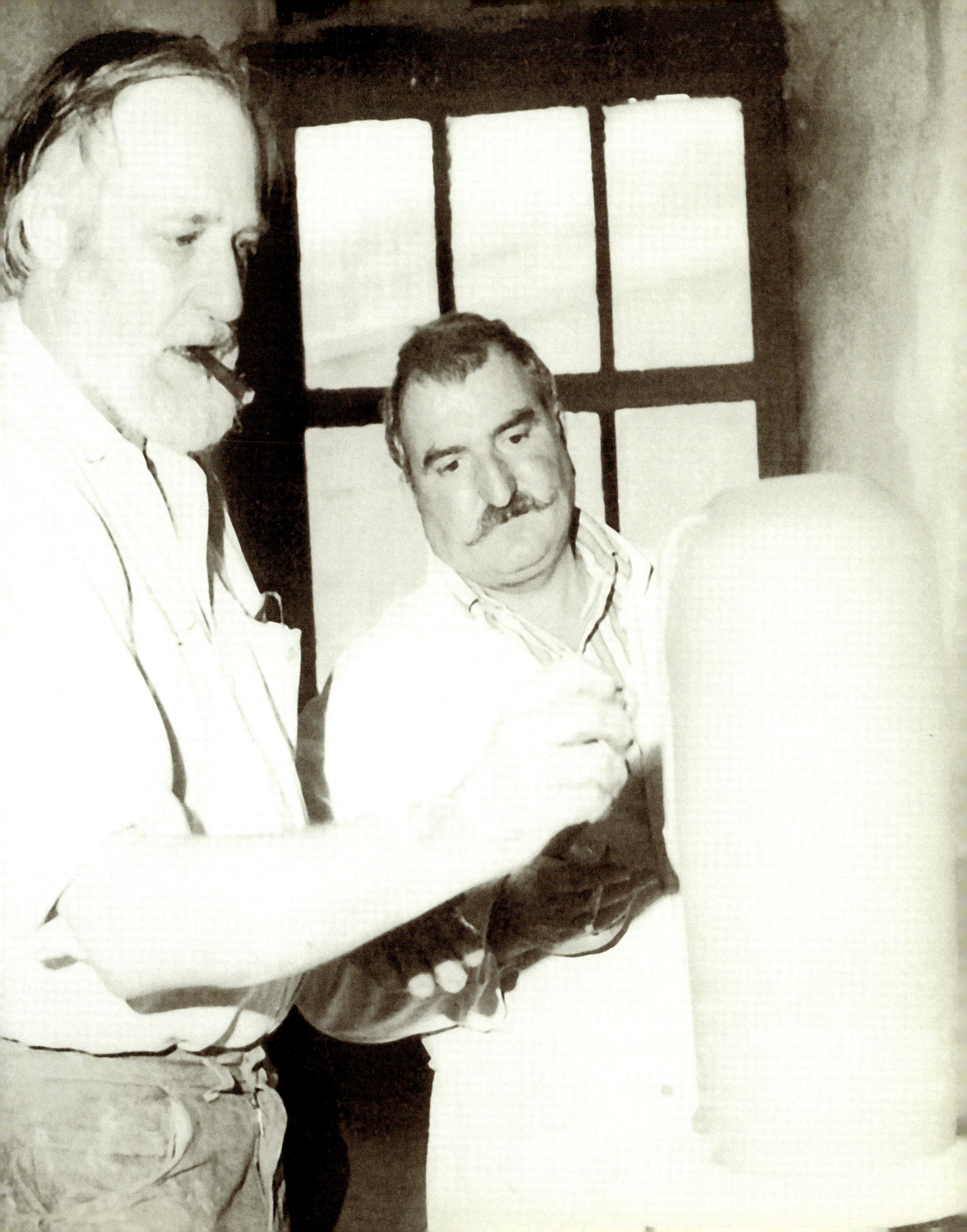

COBRA paintings. A 1953 oval dish by Jorn (fig. 78) is embellished with a quick and cartoony face that consists only of two eyes, one a circle and line and the other a spiral, and a set of gnashed teeth: no nose, no ears, no contouring of bones or flesh, just these isolated features within the width of the dish. The head is distorted because it occupies the width. To have presented it vertically on the oval would be closer to real-life proportions. In the same year, Jorn depicted a vastly different head on a smaller, rounder and flatter ceramic plate (fig. 77). This one does not devour the entire space, but is depicted within the confines of the plate, as on a tondo. It could almost be described as a realistic depiction, depending upon whether one sees this rather masculine-looking but long-haired head, with its fleshy face in which a big mouth contrasts with tiny eyes, as being exaggerated. If it is a caricature, the relative sizes of mouth and eyes are undoubtedly symbolic of differences between appetite and understanding. But sympathy, fondness and amusement seem to underlie this image; if the face is not exactly an ideal, it nonetheless seems to show the artist's empathy toward human weaknesses and flaws.

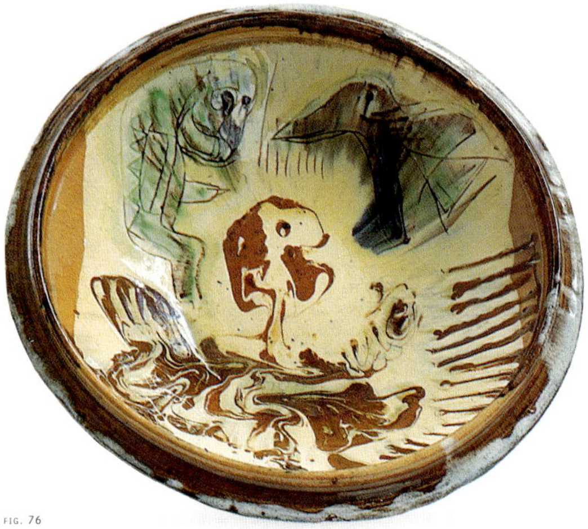

FIG. 76

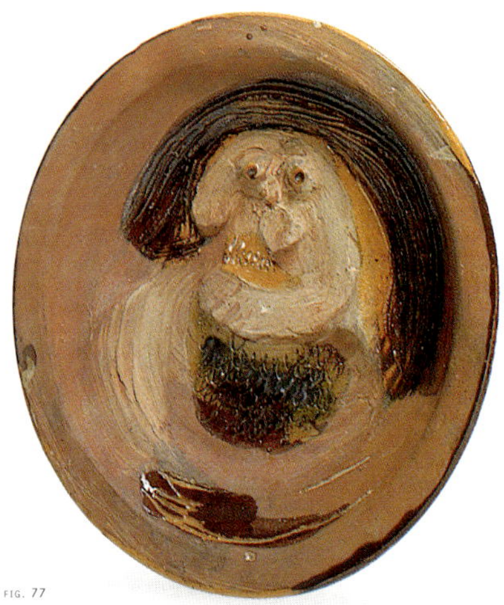

FIG. 77

FIG. 76 ASGER JORN
UNTITLED 1953
plate; ⌀ 30.5 cm
COLLECTION MUSEUM HET KRUITHUIS

FIG. 77 ASGER JORN
UNTITLED 1953
plate; ⌀ 18 cm
COLLECTION MUSEUM HET KRUITHUIS

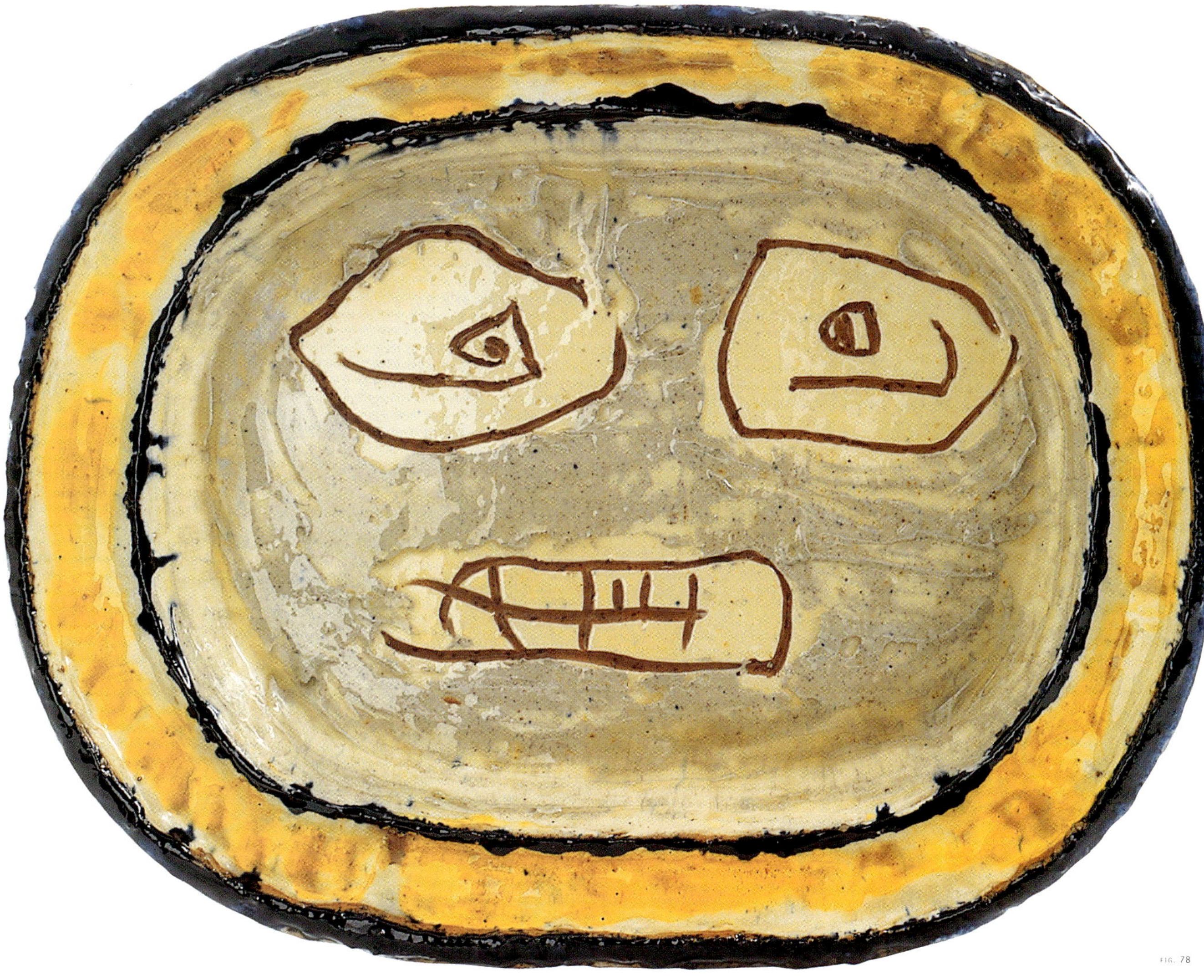

FIG. 78

FIG. 78 ASGER JORN
UNTITLED 1953
plate; 30 x 39 cm
COLLECTION MUSEUM HET KRUITHUIS

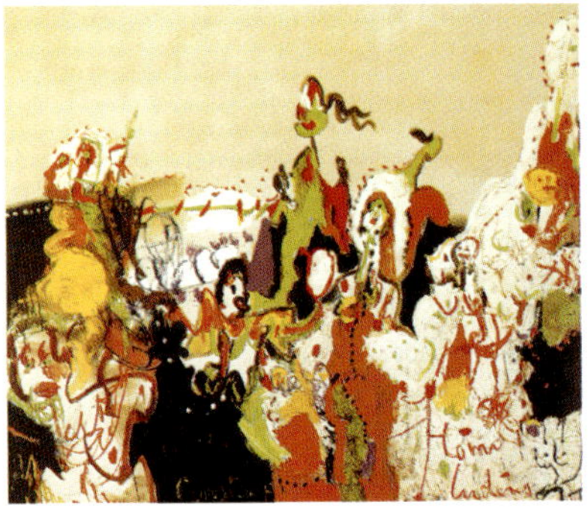

FIG. 79

One ceramic work by **Constant** (b. 1920 – fig. 81), a large plate, is scribbled with two non-human creatures – one is four-legged and the other looks like a crab – and random wandering lines, as if a child had attacked the plate with color crayons (fig. 82). Some of the background looks like flowers and leaves, but most looks like irrepressible scribbling. Although this drawing probably has a preferred orientation, with the animal on the bottom and the crab above it, there's no particular logic to that arrangement, and it's possible to look at the plate from every side without disorientation. That makes it more like a useful plate, which is designed to be seen flat on a table rather than "this end up" on a wall.

FIG. 79 CONSTANT
HOMO LUDENS 1964
oil on canvas; 160 x 185 cm
COLLECTION STEDELIJK MUSEUM, AMSTERDAM/NL

FIG. 80 CONSTANT
UNTITLED 1948
bowl; ø 9 cm
COLLECTION MUSEUM HET KRUITHUIS

Among the most charming of COBRA ceramics is Constant's small bowl, $3^{1/2}$ inches tall, which conveys a moving simplicity and innocence (fig. 80). The exterior is decorated with figures whose heads are cropped by the rim, yielding a shape reminiscent of a tulip. One thin, stem-like body actually looks like a flower (with appendages). A walleyed head is attached to a bulging pear-shaped body with two legs. There's some sort of bird with a tail, and what appears to be a cat (it has whiskers), and a child – eyes forward, legs splayed, but no arms. All these simple forms are separated by patches of swabbed-yellow tangible sunshine. Inside the bowl is a crackled white glaze that's almost spiritual in its worn asceticism, evoking vows of poverty. This implication is supported by the endless, timeless circularity of the living beings represented on the bowl's exterior.

The sweet naïveté of this work is a surprise, because Constant was the theorist and polemicizer among the Dutch members of COBRA. He himself has explained contradictions in his work as being the result of dialectical alternation that characterizes the whole of life in all its aspects – the explanation of a convinced Marxist.[70] Constant's early use of the imagery of children's drawings in his late-'40s paintings sometimes took a darker cast than his fellow artists' did – the idiosyncratic animals often seem threatening. It has been asserted that, "With his crude shapes and consciously clumsy lines, [Constant] appears to try harder than the others of the group to put into practice the anti-aestheticism" COBRA propounded.[71] In the '50s,

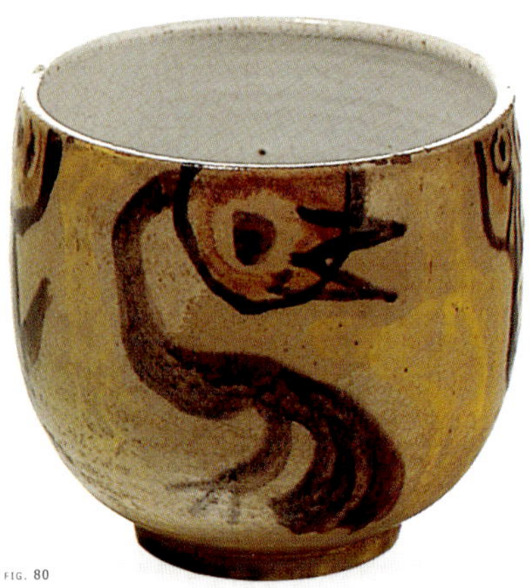

FIG. 80

70. Stokvis, p. 23.
71. Stokvis, p. 23.

he made an unquestionably darker series of paintings on war, gloomy in color and in subject matter. He seemed to revert back to the COBRA positivism in the early '60s, with a work such as *Homo Ludens* (1964) (fig. 79), with greens, oranges and yellows indicating busy-looking figures on a background horizontally divided into black earth and tan sky. *Homo Ludens*, a book detailing the concept of man as player, published in 1939 by the Dutch historian Johan Huizinga, influenced Dutch artists of the COBRA generation, who "saw themselves as homo ludens, ludic men, gamesmen; in contrast to their homo faber compatriots, they believed in childhood, play, violence, tinkering, and fooling around."[72] Constant later produced models and paintings based on an ideal of a city, and paintings of such constructive spaces enduring dystopian occurrences such as interrogations and massacres.

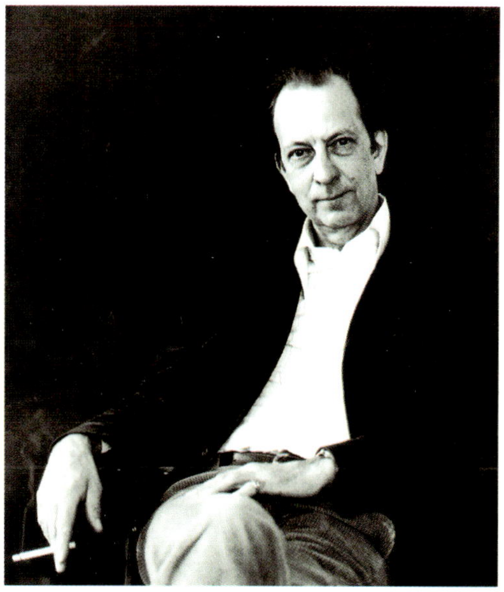

FIG. 81

FIG. 81 CONSTANT

FIG. 82 CONSTANT
UNTITLED 1948
plate; ⌀ 44.5 cm
COLLECTION MUSEUM HET KRUITHUIS

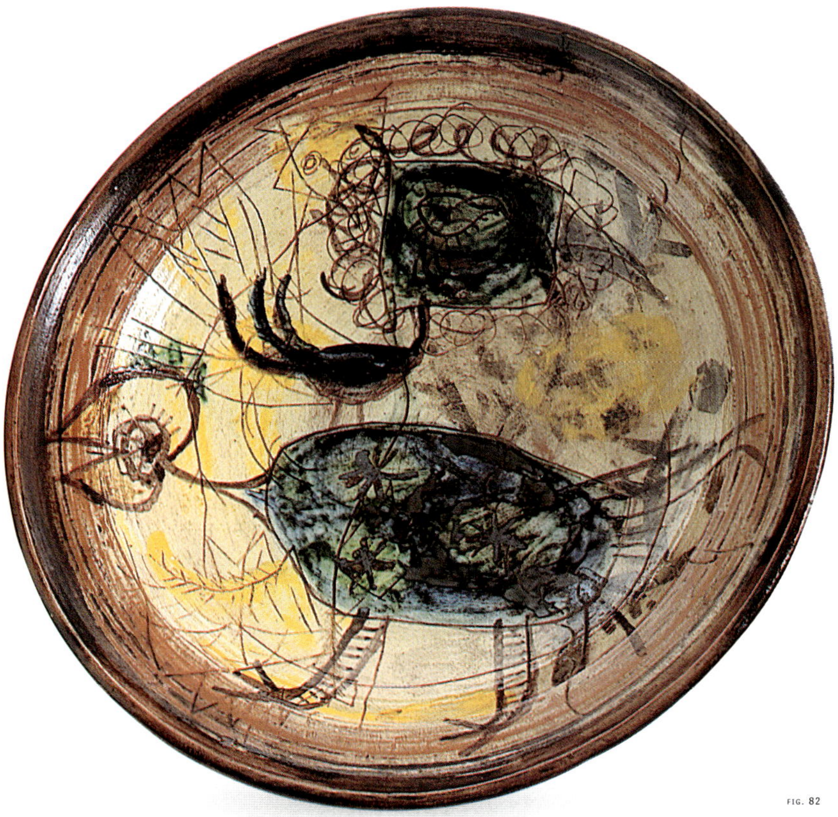

FIG. 82

Lucebert (1924-1994 – fig. 83), like Jorn, uses extremely tight framing on a head, so that the edge of a dish crops off its outside contours (fig. 141). Lucebert's 1951 example is flatter, smoother and glossier than Jorn's, which gives it an aura of perfection and an imperious air. The face is both Cubist and harlequinesque. Its division into bands of black and white (with areas of blue-gray) gives the clownish effect, but the rearrangement of features is more reminiscent of Picasso's grotesques: the eyes are seen from the front; the lips are in profile facing left; the nose might be seen as a profile silhouette facing right but reads most strongly simply as the two nostrils (which should not both be visible in a profile anyway, but is a Cubist convention). The hair waves upward in a pompadour beginning between the eyes. There are no brows, no forehead. In literal terms this is a monstrous face, but in emotional terms it is powerfully concentrated because of the focus on sensual and sensory aspects.

FIG. 83 LUCEBERT IN HIS STUDIO IN SPAIN

Lucebert came into COBRA as a poet but became equally known as a painter and draftsman. The movement stimulated his experimental poetry as part of a group called the *Vijftigers* (Fifties school) that sought a freedom in language comparable to COBRA's spontaneity in painting. Lucebert's own paintings presented animals and figures with mythological identities, at first rather playfully. But they soon seemed shadowed and allusive of entrapment. His paintings might be compared with Constant's in their darkness and intensity. In the '60s they changed entirely, with caricatural depictions of people and political themes and titles (e.g., *The prisoner*, fig. 84).

Corneille, whose *Plate with bird and banner* has already been discussed, also made vessels that incorporate a full human figure. His thick, sturdy vase of 1954 takes a stabilizing gravity from its five blunt legs and two handles (fig. 66). On one side he rendered a male, arms extended, with a circle on top of his head (or is it the face of a child?) and with circles for his hands and feet. Circles are rich symbolic forms, particularly associated with Buddhism but also often used to imply universality. Here the roundness is nicely consistent with the very full-bellied ceramic form. The decorated handles are equally round. The other side of the vessel has a female figure in the same splayed pose, with the same circle hands and feet,

72. Michel Ragon, Karel Appel: The Early Years 1937-1957, Paris: Editions Galilée, 1988, pp. 193, 202, quoted in Kuspit, Note 3, p. 170.

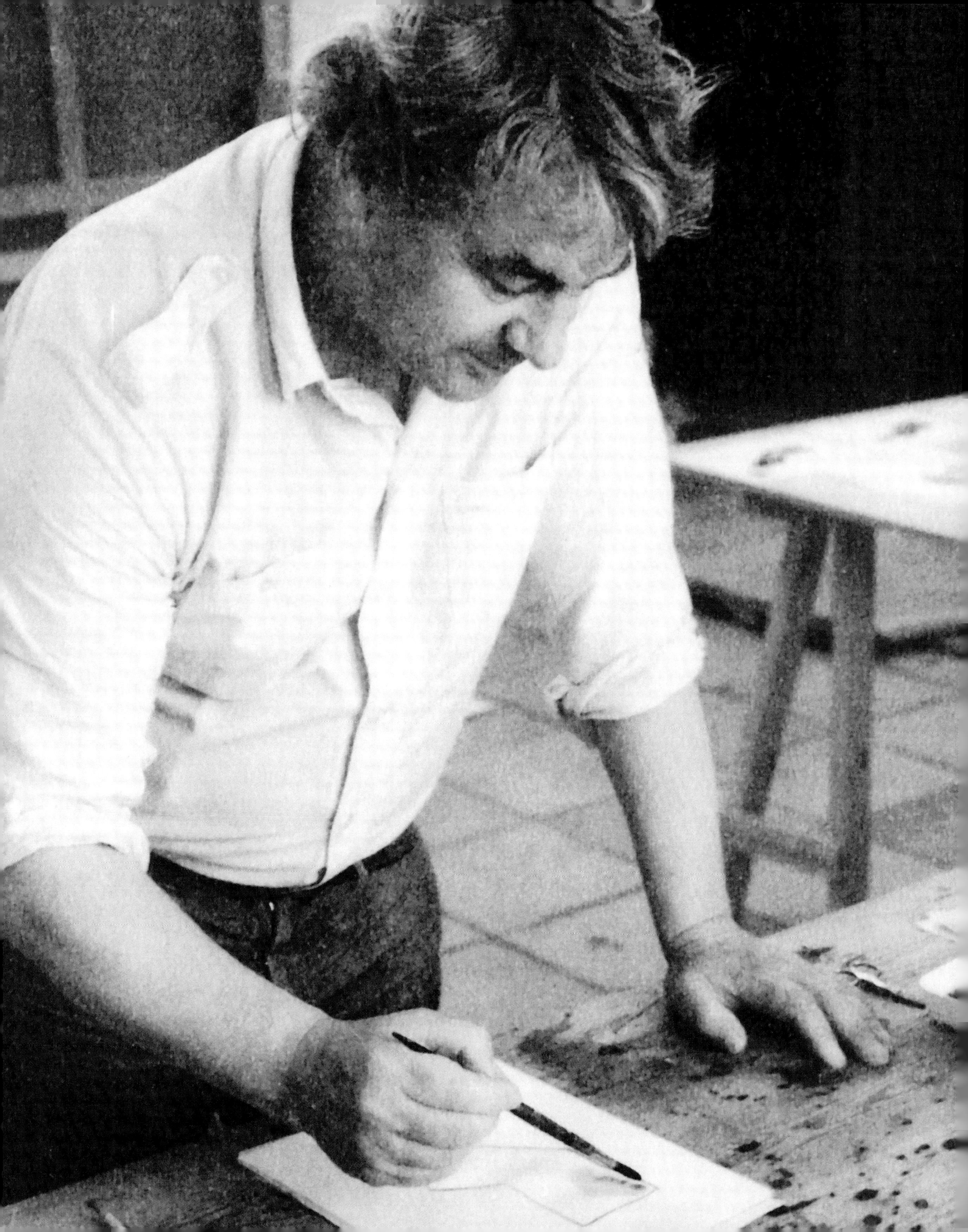

and the same child-face upon her head, and notable pubic roundness as well. These figures, depicted with layers of color and line that include black, white, brown and red (all skin colors, one might note), occupy a reserved space on the bluish, ripply surface.

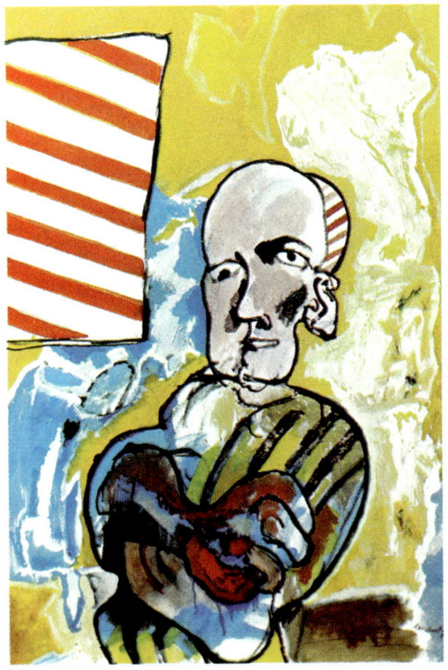
FIG. 84

One who is very old sings:

There is no more in little
Nor is there less
It is uncertain yet what there was
What becomes, becomes passive
Only when it is, is it in earnest
Remembering brings it no comfort
And there is always haste

Everything valuable is defenceless
Enriched by its openness to touch
And everything's equal

Like the very heart of time
Like the very heart of time

Lucebert

FIG. 84 LUCEBERT
THE PRISONER 1964
oil on canvas; 130 x 90 cm
COLLECTION STEDELIJK MUSEUM, AMSTERDAM/NL

In another vessel from the same year (fig. 72), Corneille repeats the wheel-like elements at the head, hands and feet of his figures, but presents them on a tall, narrow form that might be a finial or a conventionalized cypress tree. The shape is unusual. Corneille applies his colors almost transparently over a pale-colored clay, so that light seems to radiate up from beneath the glaze despite its peculiar shade of green, which is as ominous as an oncoming storm in a Romantic sublime painting. The red-brown-black drawing is similar to that on the round vase, and the circles, whether they are Buddhist wheels of life, symbols of the sun, or gears and spokes from some unknown machine, can again be seen as relating to the form, although this form is very different, not bulbously spherical but tauter and smoother. Still, the wheel echoes the cylindrical foot, the gently rounded belly of the vase, and the tight construction of the mouth. On one side, the vessel's form repeats in a blue drop shape. The blue has crawled and doesn't have the fineness and glossy seductiveness of the rest of the surface. It therefore seems more physical, less like a picture. On the other side is a figure composed of round parts. Its legs are splayed, it has a full, rounded abdomen and round breasts, and it is topped with a crown and aura, yet it's hard to tell whether it is meant to be pregnant female or a representation of prosperity in the Asian style.

COBRA artists put figures within scenes as well as in isolation. One of the simplest and most poignant of scenes is also a work by Corneille. It is a plate showing a rudimentary figure in a dark environment looking up at a passing bird (fig. 70). Both bird and person are depicted by means of incised lines, (sgraffito technique), with an unfinessed touch that is more reminiscent of Jorn's head/dish than any of Corneille's other works. This directness continues in the imperfect painted line of black that circles the rim of the plate and pulls our eyes back into the darkness of the central area. The plate has been given a shiny glaze which, one could argue, is inconsistent with the visual character. Yet its transparency discloses the clay's grainy texture, which, along with the thickness of the plate, suits the innocent and unrefined manner of depiction.

Lucebert, whose Cubist-head plate was discussed above, has also rendered a scene on a small plate that is titled *Children in the sun* (fig. 85). The drawing is stick-figure style, as if it were not just of children but by one as well. A person is depicted with shovel arms, wedge legs, and what one might call a sun head, except that there's a gigantic and radiant sun at another edge of the plate. This commanding sun is not hot. The colors on the plate are restricted to brown, blue, black and ivory, without the yellow or orange conventionally symbolic of heat or glare. On the plate are various beasts, most too abstracted – reduced to a head with eyes, or to two triangles

FIG. 85 LUCEBERT
KINDEREN IN DE ZON 1950
plate; ø 17 cm
COLLECTION MUSEUM HET KRUITHUIS

FIG. 86 LUCEBERT
UNTITLED 1950
plate; ø 18.5 cm
COLLECTION MUSEUM HET KRUITHUIS

FIG. 87 LUCEBERT
UNTITLED 1950
plate; ø 18.5 cm
COLLECTION MUSEUM HET KRUITHUIS

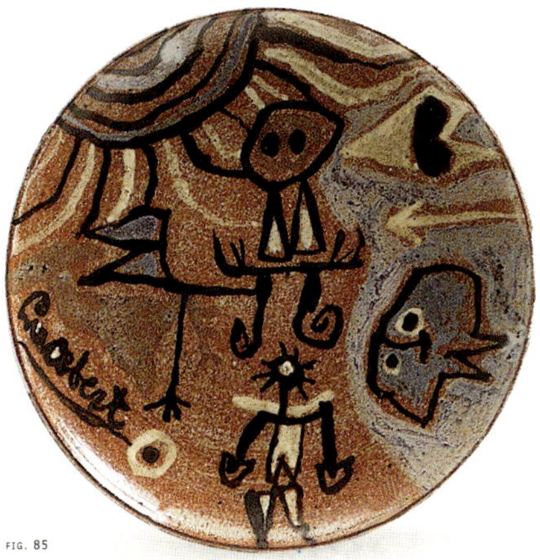

FIG. 85

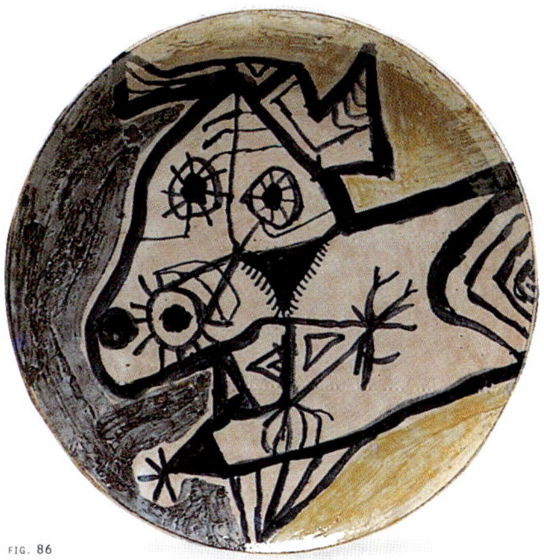

FIG. 86

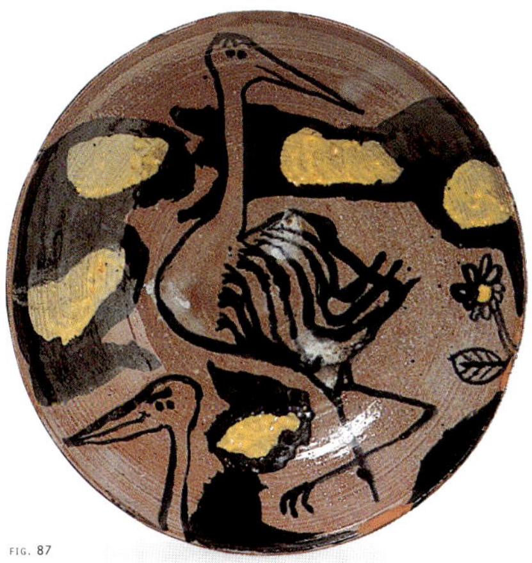

FIG. 87

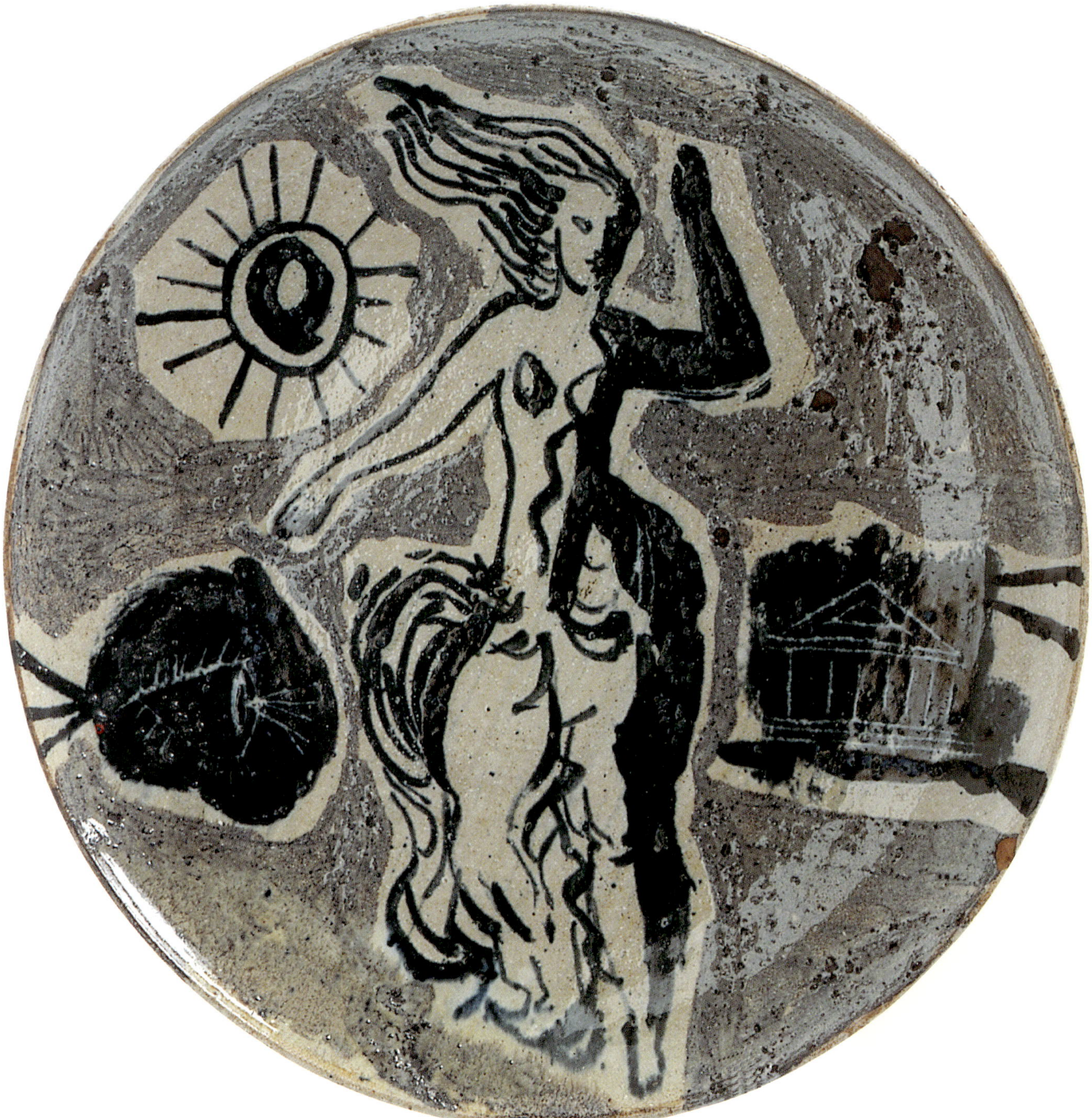

FIG. 88

FIG. 88 LUCEBERT
UNTITLED CA. 1951
plate; ø 19.5 cm
COLLECTION MUSEUM HET KRUITHUIS

atop one leg – to identify. The plate has an overall air of whimsy, and a sense of alert and active beings interacting. The title in this case tells us one obvious thing (that there is a sun) and something that is not obvious (that these varied morsels are children, presumably human ones!).

Lucebert worked in many stylistic formats. Another of his ceramic works uses imagery that speaks of Classicism (fig. 88) appearing on four reserved areas in a mottled light-brown field. Because they are separate there is no way to be sure that they're meant to be seen together or what the spatial relationship between them might be. At the center a partly nude woman with streaming hair and one arm raised as if testifying recalls Greek statuary. To her left, scratched into a patch of black, is, indeed, a Greek temple. A sun and a vase occupy the other two reserved spots, to the figure's right. The plate is sober, serious, and yet its apparent connection to the Mediterranean and the Golden Age gives it a lushness.

Other COBRA plates seem to be purely abstractions. They may be quite opposite in their treatments of the surface. Jorn, in a 1953 plate (fig. 76), has played with the glazes, dribbling them or perhaps applying them neatly but planning their placement to take advantage of the fact that they would melt and run during the firing process. The result is a Surrealist vision, with two strange semi-transparent creatures hovering in the air, one bird-like but the other looking rather like a fetus. Below and between them is an amorphous blob that seems to raise up its head in the middle, but is primarily just a mass of beautiful marbling.

Totally contrasting to Jorn's fluidity, and to the way that the rim of his plate seems to rise up to contain this liquid vision, is the lapidary composition on a plate by **Anton Rooskens** (1906-1976 – fig.91). Rooskens, who was older than most of the COBRA artists and had a painting career before he joined them, collected primitive art. His own expression, however, was more controlled. His early paintings have been equated with magical signs[73]; from a contemporary perspective they look somewhat science-fictiony, with simple shapes – ovals or eye-shapes or boat-shapes – floating in indefinite spaces (fig. 89). These shapes are filled with incident, whereas the backgrounds are still and uneventful. They may be light against a

73. Stokvis, p. 24.

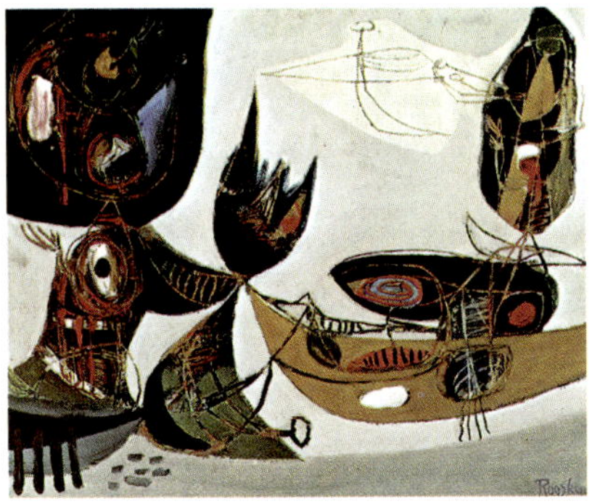
FIG. 89

dark background (in which case they seem to radiate), or the reverse. Only in the late '60s did Rooskens' paintings adopt figurative imagery and the bright colors usually associated with COBRA, and in such works the complex figure is often isolated against a nonspecific and uninflected background, as earlier.

In his plate (fig. 90), Rooskens fashioned a large central group of rectilinear elements and two smaller groups at the sides, each defined with precision. Nearly all elements are triangular, which makes them seem like constructed emblems rather than random abstractions. The most striking exception to the general character is a spiral at center, a segmented and graduated curl that suggests a snail shell or some microscopic organism. The triangles are raised surfaces upon the plate, and while they all look hand-drawn (as if squeezed from a pastry tube) and reflect different degrees of exactness, all involve a visible urge to order. The rim is treated much more lightly yet extends the geometric orderliness of the whole. The expressionistic gestures of so much COBRA work are absent here.

FIG. 89 ANTON ROOSKENS
COMPOSITION 1952
oil on canvas; 95 x 114.5 cm
COLLECTION STEDELIJK MUSEUM, SCHIEDAM/NL

FIG. 90 ANTON ROOSKENS
UNTITLED 1948
plate; ⌀ 34.5 cm
COLLECTION MUSEUM HET KRUITHUIS

FIG. 91 ANTON ROOSKENS

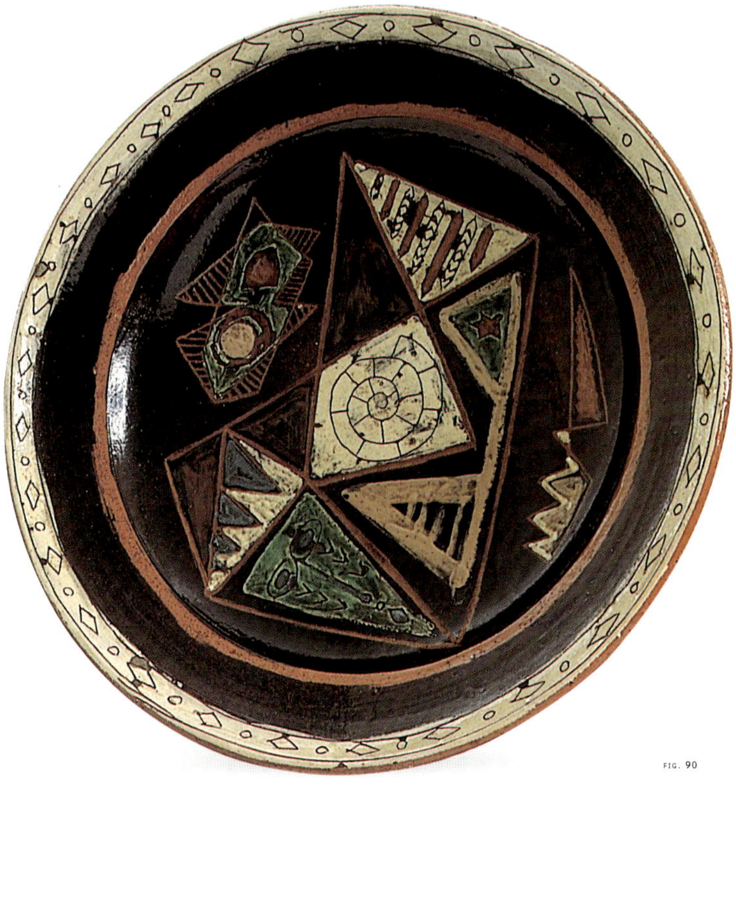
FIG. 90

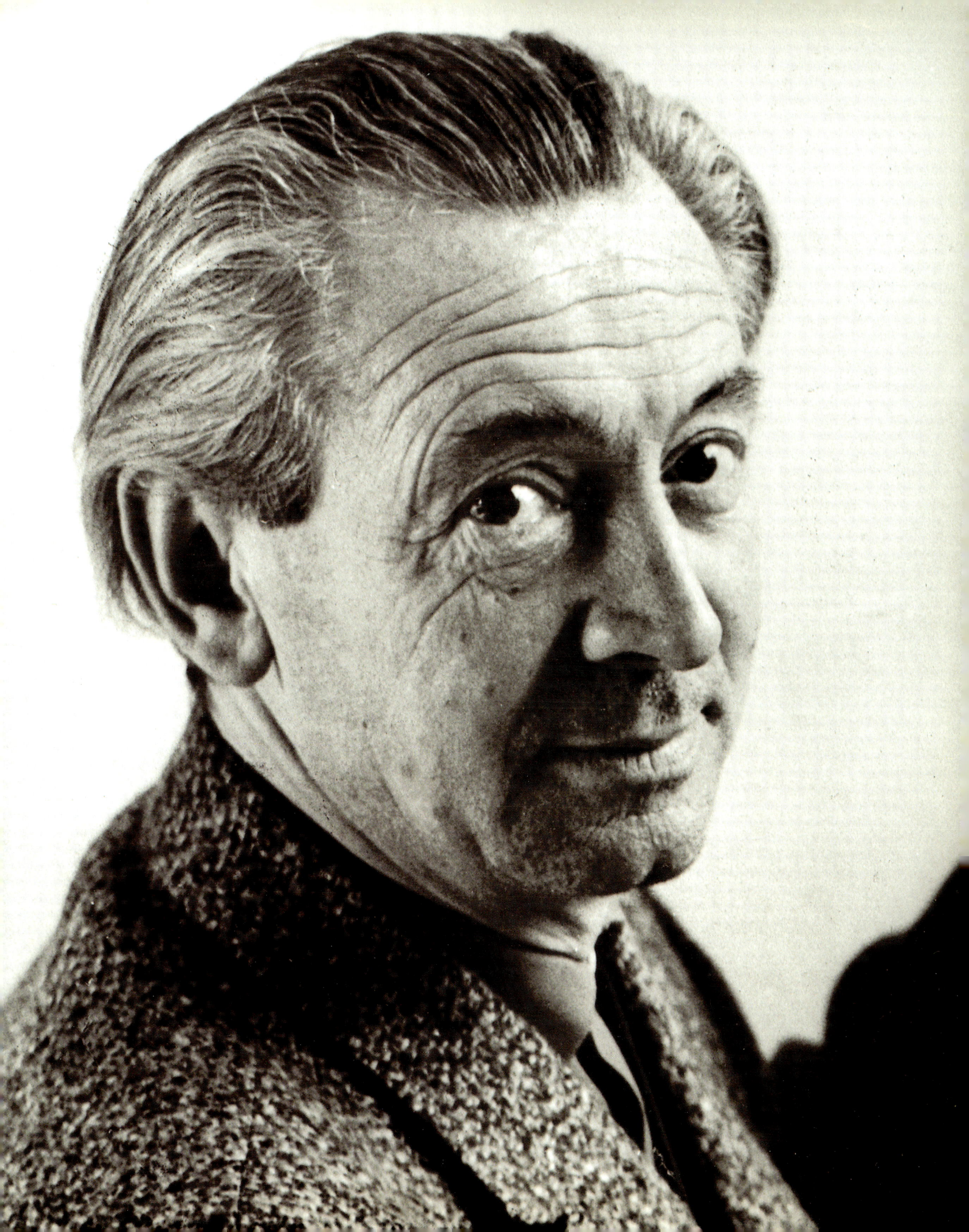

Contemporary Artists

Within the theme of "Artists' Pottery" that is the subject of this book, the broadest range of approaches to clay is seen in the work of the most recent "visitors to clay." That may reflect the increasing openness of the artworld itself. **Mimmo Paladino** (b. 1948 – fig. 93) has made a series of 34 little vases with ball stoppers called "Vasi Ermetici" (Hermetic Vases). Among them is one that has a bright yellow neck and shoulders and is black below (fig. 92). It's very glossy and smooth, which suits the perfection of the form. On one side of this vessel Paladino has drawn a vestigial flowering tree. There is a head at each side that is somehow skull-like, although no bones are depicted. All these emblems are outlined in shiny gold. The rest of the vessel is undecorated, so the part with images registers as the front.

FIG. 92 MIMMO PALADINO
UNTITLED
(SERIES VASI ERMETICI) 1993
vase; 26 x 19 cm
COLLECTION MUSEUM HET KRUITHUIS

FIG. 93 MIMMO PALADINO 1992

One has to decide how the artist means for these vases to be understood. They are not particularly being treated as sculptural, since they are symmetrical (and therefore predictable); in fact, all vessels in the series have precisely the same dimensions, so they are probably blanks, made with a mold, interchangeable, and not inventively or individually modeled as sculptural forms. Each also has a single, privileged viewpoint. Even though these factors put the emphasis on shape or outlines, they certainly have more presence than cutouts would. Maybe they're of interest to Paladino as images – as representations of vases which also happen to occupy space like vases (a conceptual ploy). Are they specific symbols of some ritual that is meaningful to him? Are they game pieces in a cultural puzzle, to be seen as part of some larger context?

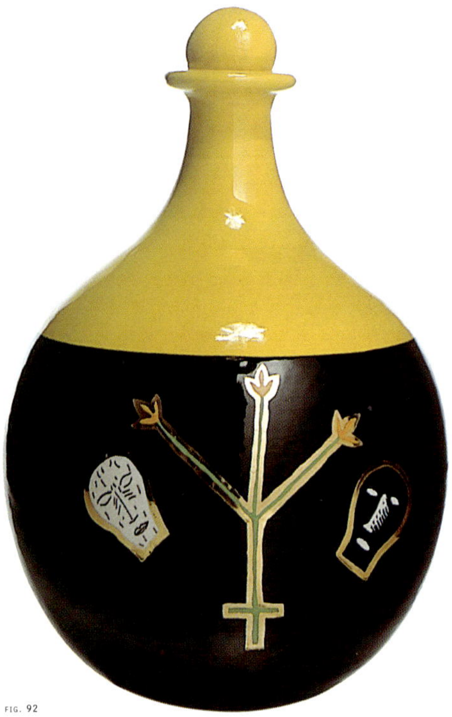

FIG. 92

Two other examples from the series are white (fig. 96). The symbolic and puzzle possibilities are foregrounded on one of these white bottles, on which a variety of little emblems and letters are drawn in a configuration that reproduces the overall shape of the bottle itself. In red, O is shown with a flower; in gold, D has a droplet; in yellow, L is accompanied by a lamb; another L, in gold, has a line of face and stem; a blue I comes with a rope; a black C is made into a face; the green V comes with a man squatting so that his thighs make a V. Perfectly placed, exactingly drawn, in a carefully worked out code; if

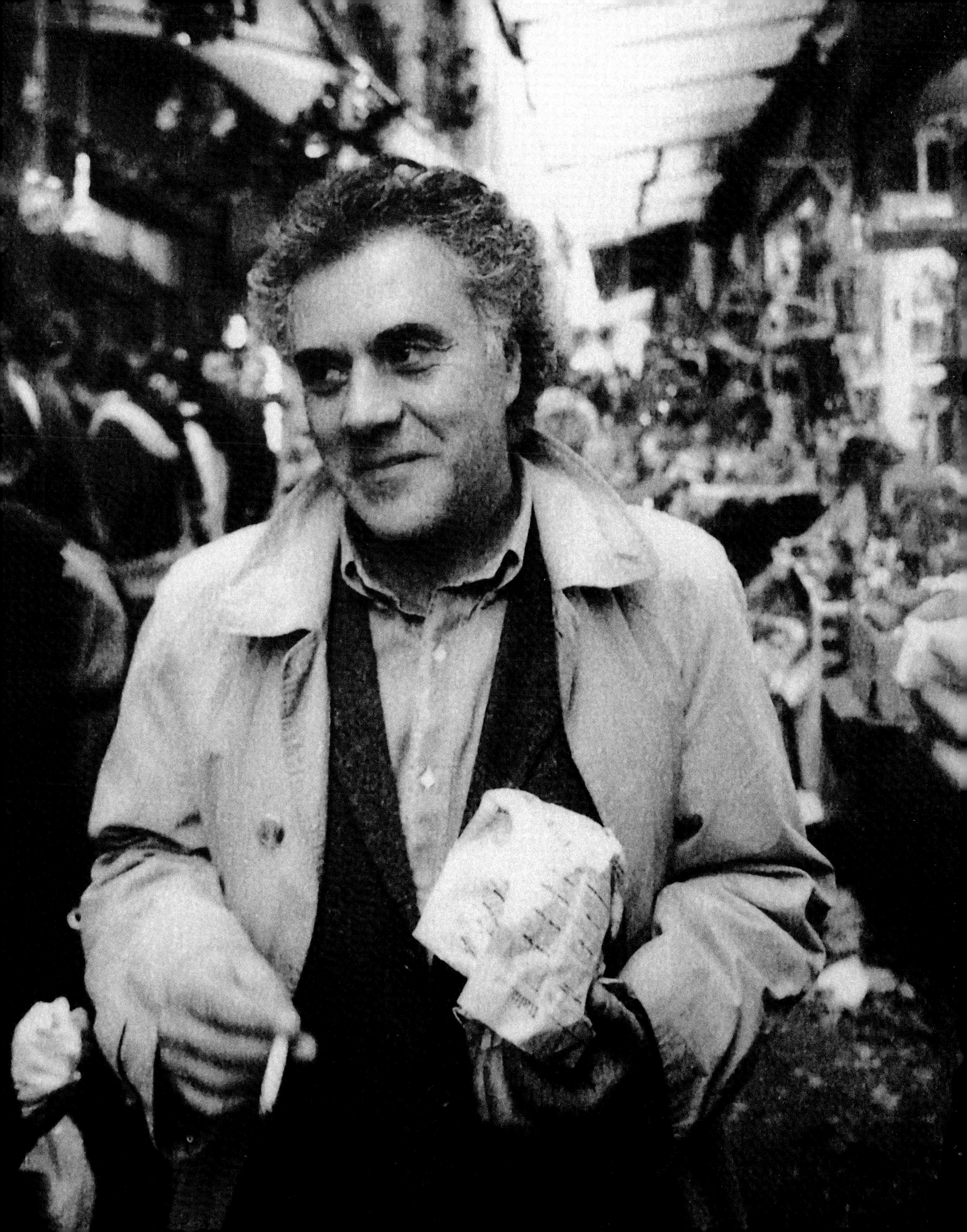

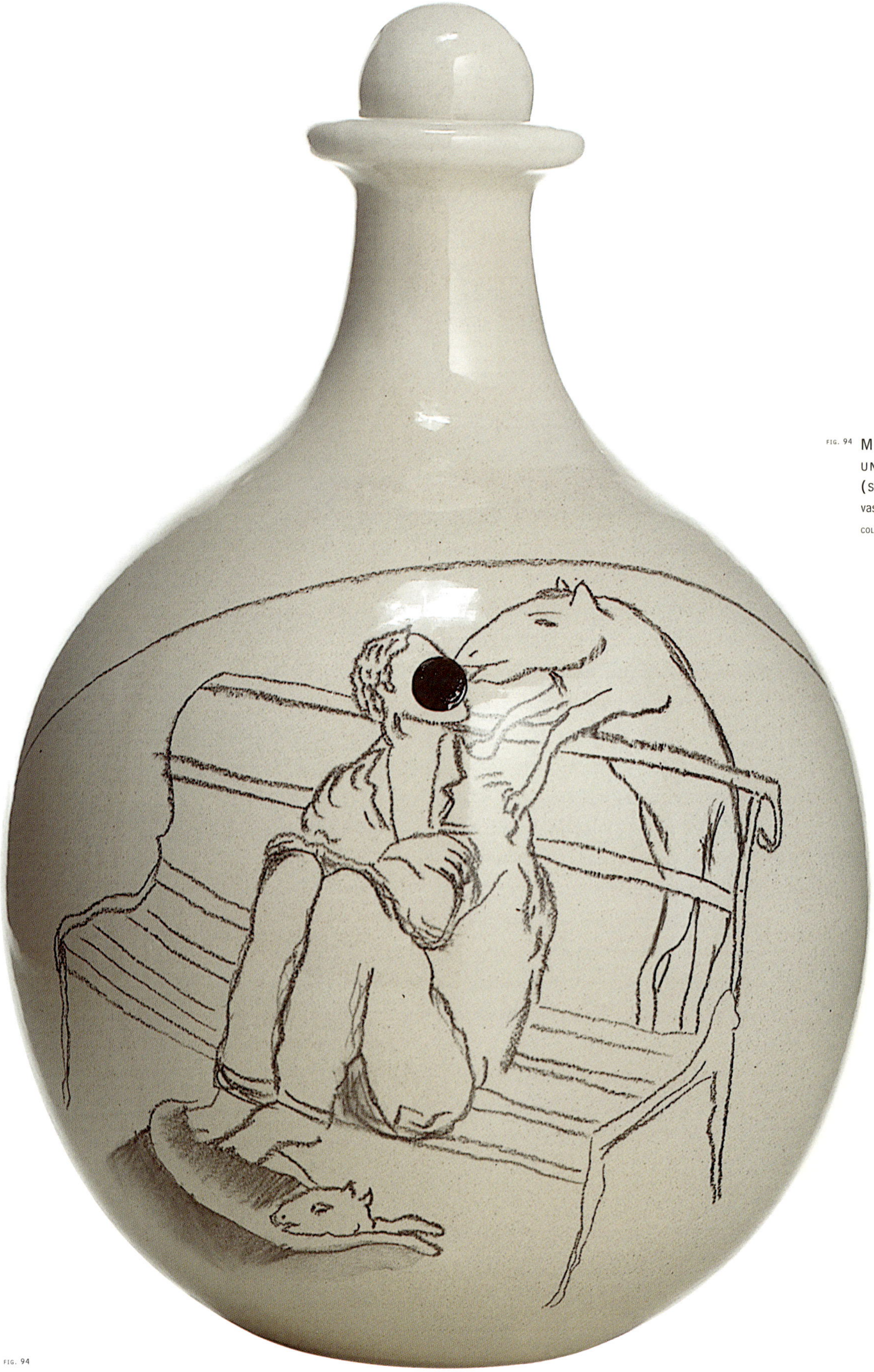

FIG. 94 MIMMO PALADINO
UNTITLED
(SERIES VASI ERMETICI) 1993
vase; 26 x 19 cm
COLLECTION MUSEUM HET KRUITHUIS

FIG. 94

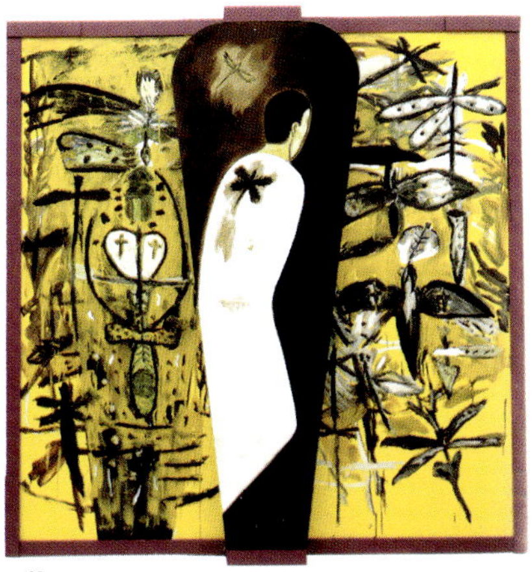

FIG. 95

only the casual viewer were privy to the meaning! Clear contrast and crisp execution yield works that are fully controlled and fully secretive, as the title of the series promises.

The other (fig. 94) is decorated with a man on a park bench with his feet on a dog and another dog leaning over the bench to lick his face, which is obscured by a gray circle, in a manner reminiscent of John Baldessari's alterations of movie and advertising images. This picture is drawn with a crayon. The smooth, white surface of the bottle is uninflected, like paper, and the line of the crayon shows the tooth of the clay, also like paper.

FIG. 95 MIMMO PALADINO
IL RESPIRO DELLA BELLEZZA IV, 1990-91
oil and enamel on canvas and wood;
205 x 205 x 30 cm

FIG. 96 MIMMO PALADINO
UNTITLED
(SERIES VASI ERMETICI) 1993
vase; 26 x 19 cm
COLLECTION MUSEUM HET KRUITHUIS

Paladino's painting practices offer some clues as to the implications of these bottles. It has been said that his work introduces us to "cardinal mysteries" and "rests upon the eternal coordinates of human creativity... it gathers fragments of memory and, with a cadence of classicism, scatters them in space... They are parts of a whole that concede nothing to narrative and symbol, for Paladino's art is primarily language: syntax over semantics, sign without referent."[74] His paintings sometimes refer to mythology or alchemy, and also to everyday life, but they do so with a determined taciturnity. He tells little. "He acknowledges the evocative power of the image: symbols will reveal themselves in any case because archetypes exist mainly in the human mind. In this way everything is left to the onlooker's sensibility."[75] Paladino only provides provocative "raw material" for meaning. Yet the elements must mean something to him, because they do not seem random.

It has been asserted that all Paladino's work has to do with death, both in regard to human biology and in a broader sense: "the overwhelming presence of absence metaphorically invokes the vacancy of meaning itself: the death of the unity of the sign. Meaning is 'buried' or 'shrouded' in mystery."[76] His conceptual agenda is related to his Italian pre0decessors, notably de Chirico ("By making the familiar strange, overturning spatial and temporal logic, de Chirico revealed the arbitrary basis of our linguistic systems."[77]), and also to several of his

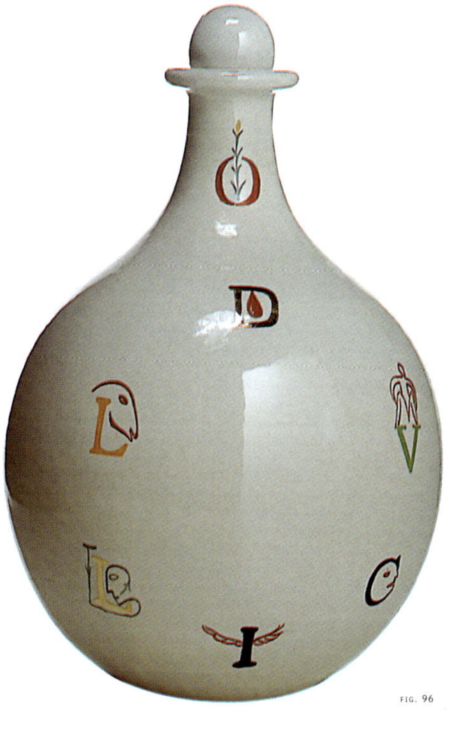

FIG. 96

74. AA.VV., "En Do Re," in Mimmo Paladino: En Do Re," Siracusa: Tema Celeste Edizioni, 1990, p. 13.
75. Demetrio Paparoni, "Tiresias of the Seven Rooms, or the True Story of the Disappearance of the Eighth Work of Mimmo Paladino's Cycle En Do Re," in Mimmo Paladino: En Do Re, p. 105.
76. Emily Braun, "The Spirit of the Dead Watching," in Paladino, Milano: Edizioni Charta, 1993, p. 19.
77. Braun, p. 22.

European peers, among them A.R. Penck. Paladino's work is, in the end, about "the survival of meaning in traces and fragments,"[78] probably at least in part because he lives in southern Italy, an area "overrun at various times by Egyptians, Phoenicians, Etruscans, Greeks, Romans, Early Christians, Normans all of whom have left extensive archaeological traces..."[79]

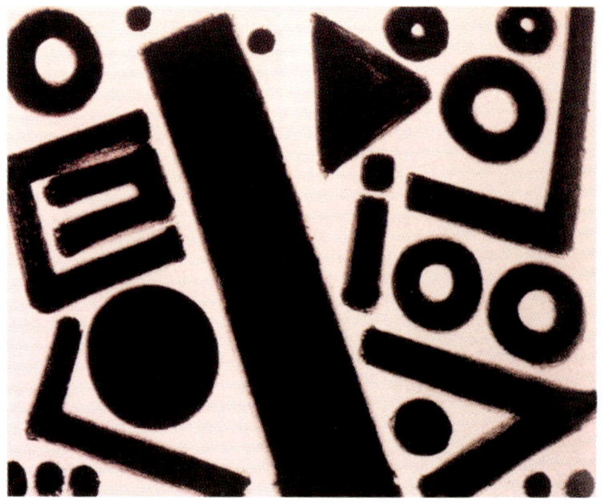

FIG. 97

The reticence of Paladino's pottery is thus in keeping with that of his work as a whole (fig. 95). Still, the series seems to be distinctive to pottery, since it does not repeat the symbolic forms and only a few of the codes that he uses in his paintings or in his many figurative sculptures in bronze and stone. He has addressed clay and made something new in it.

A.R. Penck (b. 1939 – fig. 99) has made a number of large ceramic jars, three feet tall or more. Penck is a name adopted by Ralf Winkler during the years when he was trying to keep a low profile in East Germany although his paintings were being shown in the West. He developed a vocabulary of graffiti-like stick figures that he did not intend to be seen as expressionist or primitive. "Rather, the paintings were meant to be understood as the objective evaluations of an artist-scientist, whose subject is the manipulation of information and understanding that routinely occurs within any modern society, and the various forms of aggressive behavior these manipulations encourage in people."[80] Penck was affected by the political climate in which he lived, by Wiener's *Cybernetics*, which was translated into German and published in paperback in 1963, by Picasso's graffiti-like figures of the late '40s, and by primitive art.

His work is a not-uncommon instance of public understanding of art diverging from the artist's intentions, for Penck's imagery reads as primitive, like cave drawing. On the surface of a large ceramic vase from 1993 (fig. 100) he has shaped elliptical medallions that he treats with yellow spirals and red-brown circles and then fills with a population of characteristic figures and emblems. Details differ, but each medallion has a central figure. There is an arrow pointing down at left, and one pointing up at right. A snake zigzags, there's also

FIG. 97 A.R. PENCK
STANDART WEST V 1982
painting; 130 x 162 cm

FIG. 98 A.R. PENCK
BODENVASE 1997
vase; 102 x 65 cm
COLLECTION MUSEUM HET KRUITHUIS

FIG. 99 A.R. PENCK

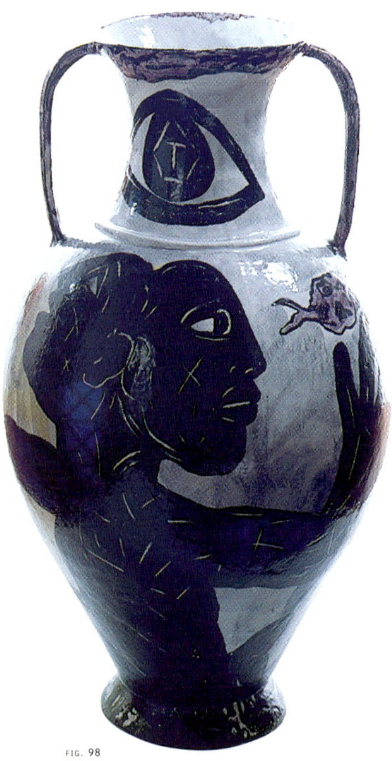

FIG. 98

78. Braun, p. 24.
79. Norman Rosenthal, "Mimmo and Memory," in Paladino, p. 38.
80. John Yau, A.R. Penck, New York: Harry N. Abrams, 1993, p. 15.

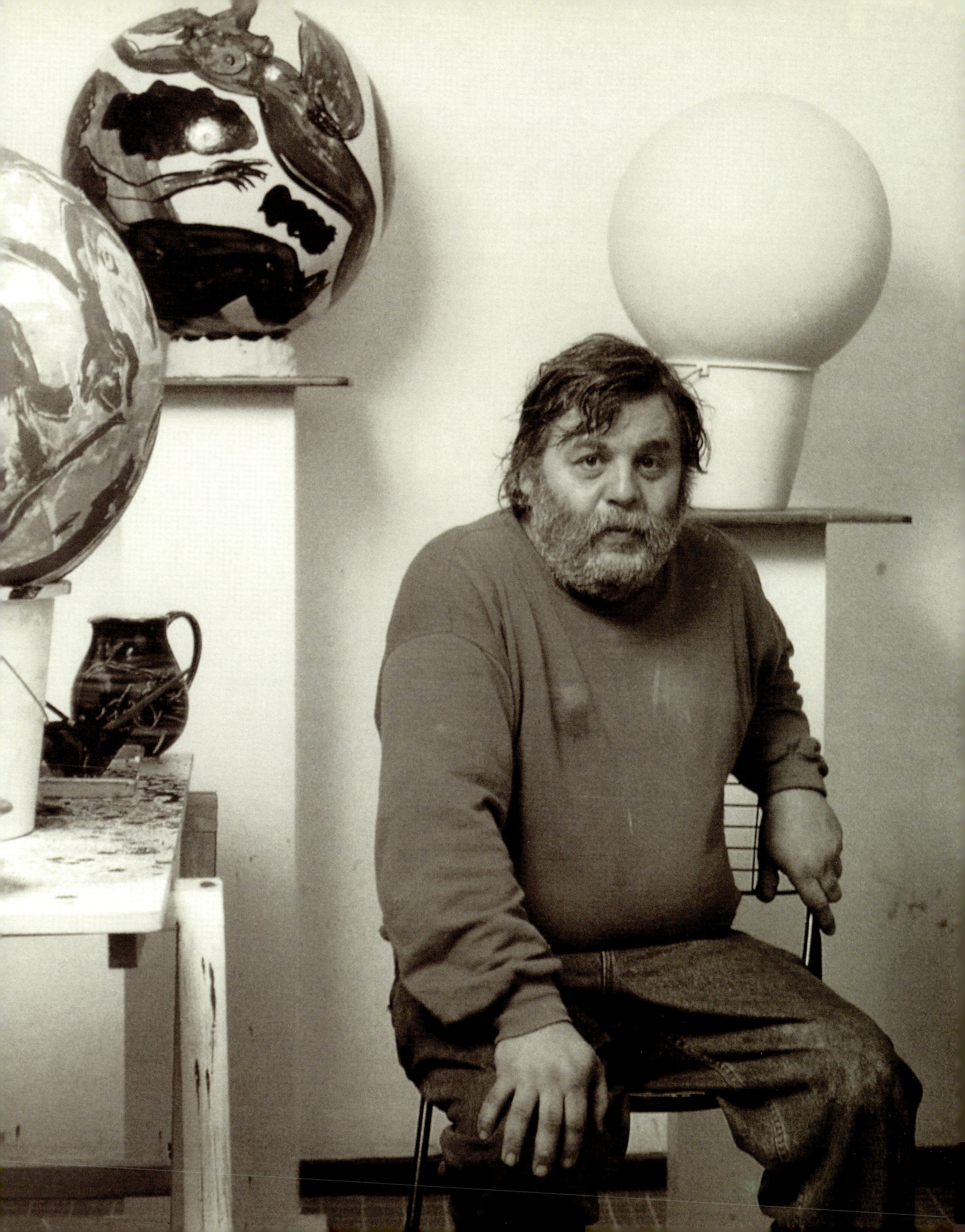

a bird, a house emblem and sometimes an eye in each. There's a lot of activity and movement among these figures (all of which appear to be male) plus a dog, a bird and many X shapes. The figures gesture, they lunge, they hold tools. On the black background of the pot itself Penck has drawn blue eye icons and figures, right side up or not.

"Penck's codification of his stick figure consists of presenting it frontally, arms raised and fingers splayed, a gesture that is repeated by the spread apart legs. The figure is somewhere between pictogram and design, capable of being an individualized type and/or part of a larger abstract pattern. The pose is still (with fear) and resolute (in control). As it faces the viewer, it is confrontational yet afraid, direct yet withdrawn, vulnerable yet standoffish."[81] After Penck emigrated to the West, the upraised arms, according to the artist, no longer indicated fear and resolution but discovery and puzzlement.[82] But here again, without the artist's verbal instruction, the pose might be understood differently, for in early Christian painting, praying figures were represented as standing with their hands raised from bent elbows, which was the practice of the time in churches which had no seating. This is not Penck's stated reference, but then, praying is just another Western behavior, ripe for analyzing or symbolizing.

This piece finds its strength in its proportions and in the vigor of the imagery drawn on the surface. It also elicits a kinesthetic response from viewers because we can't see it all from one viewpoint, but must move around it. Our movement bonds with that of the figures. The ceramic form Penck uses is a refined shape. It's also neutral, as he might wish a canvas to be. Although it's not a thick and primitive vase, Penck has opted for a bumpy, imperfect surface which gives a sense of hand and adds to the vitality, an effect also implied by his apparent haste in drawing. Then all this is "preserved in amber" under a thin, shiny layer of glaze, which distances the images from our eyes, as glass over a drawing does. This primitivism suggests performance rather than belief, which is also the case in Penck's sophisticated paintings and murals.

Even larger vases which Penck made in 1997 (fig. 98 and 101) reflect new developments in his painting. The mythic themes continue but the figures (animal and human) are

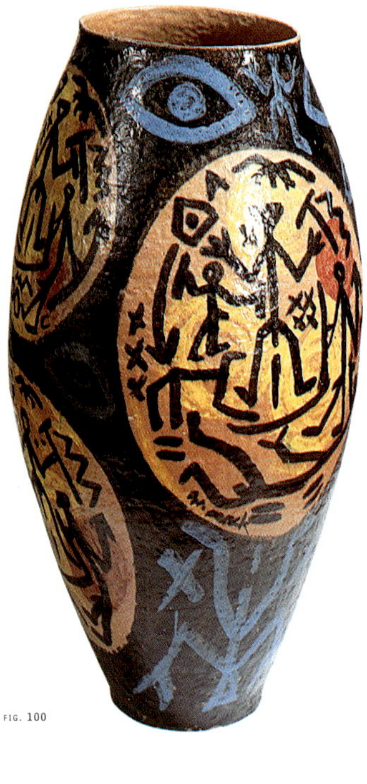

FIG. 100

FIG. 100 A.R. PENCK
BODENVASE 1993
vase; 99 x 52 cm
COLLECTION MUSEUM HET KRUITHUIS

81. Yau, pp. 46-47.
82. Yau, p. 61.

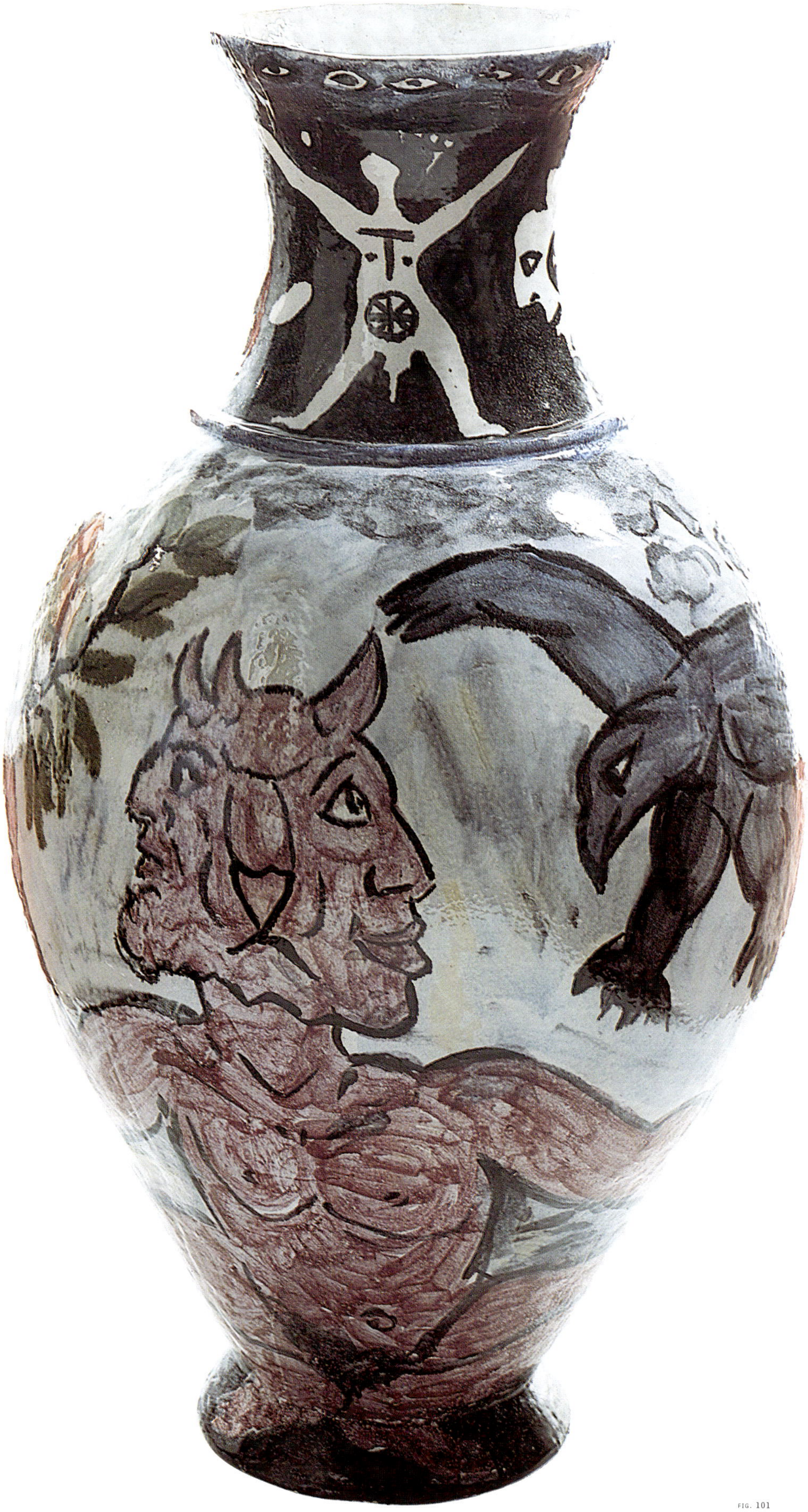

FIG. 101 A.R. PENCK
BODENVASE 1997
vase; 100 x 65 cm
COLLECTION MUSEUM HET KRUITHUIS

FIG. 101

now fleshed out, the surface of the vase is more continuously painted and has a chalky, somewhat fresco-like appearance. Eyes continue as a motif, and new symbols, such as a ball of heads and a wheel, add to the mix.

Alphons Freijmuth (b. 1940 – fig. 103) is a Dutch painter who became known in the 1970s for large, bold, intense paintings that were seen as extending the van Gogh-to-COBRA heritage of Dutch expressionism. The word Fauve was also applied to his work. Freijmuth paints contemporary interiors in which a densely patterned background seems to force a naked woman or a naked or suit-wearing man up against the picture plane. The backgrounds, rendered with force, bring to mind such contemporaneous German artists as Georg Baselitz, yet Freijmuth's underlying message is artifice and elegance rather than the anger or pain associated with Neo-Expressionist painting.

FIG. 102 ALPHONS FREIJMUTH
BIG HEAD 1990
bronze; 100 x 24 x 22 cm

FIG. 103 ALPHONS FREIJMUTH

He could be called savagely decorative. The backgrounds never violate the integrity of the isolated figure. Moreover, many of the paintings are reminiscent of Mondrian because of grids that appear in the paintings in the form of windows or floor tiles; also there is a kind of neatness or separation between the elements of the painting. A Dutch sense of order hovers around the edges of the violent brushwork, keeping it from really going out of control. His work has been described as striving "for a good understanding between the emotional and the rational or, should that not prove possible, a confrontation between the two opposite poles."[83]

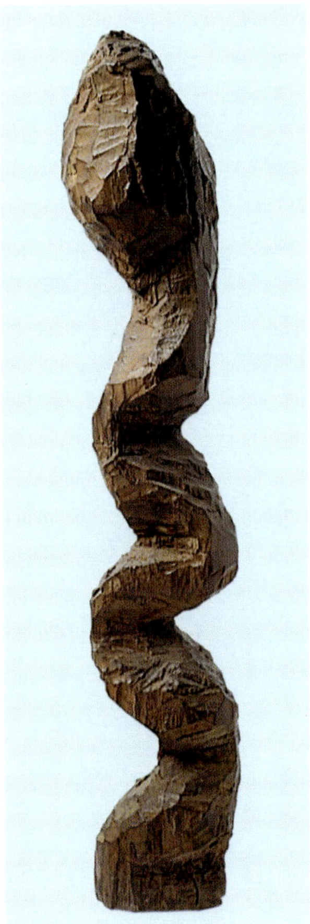

FIG. 102

Freijmuth has made sculptures in wood, bronze and clay. The bronzes, such as *Big Head (Portrait of D. v/d K.)*, fig. 102, a thick, brown coil three feet tall that could be described as worm-like except for its large, phallic head and its gravity-defying vertical posture, often have heavily worked surfaces that suggest the carving of blocks of clay or plaster. *De schrik* (Fright) (fig. 104) is a ceramic work about two feet tall that has a bulbous and irregular yet vase-like body. It is topped by a flaring neck where three holes have been cut in an arrangement

83. Gijs van Tuyl, "a Smack in Your Eye," in Alphons Freijmuth, Appeldoorn: Gem Van Reekummuseum, 1982, unpaginated.

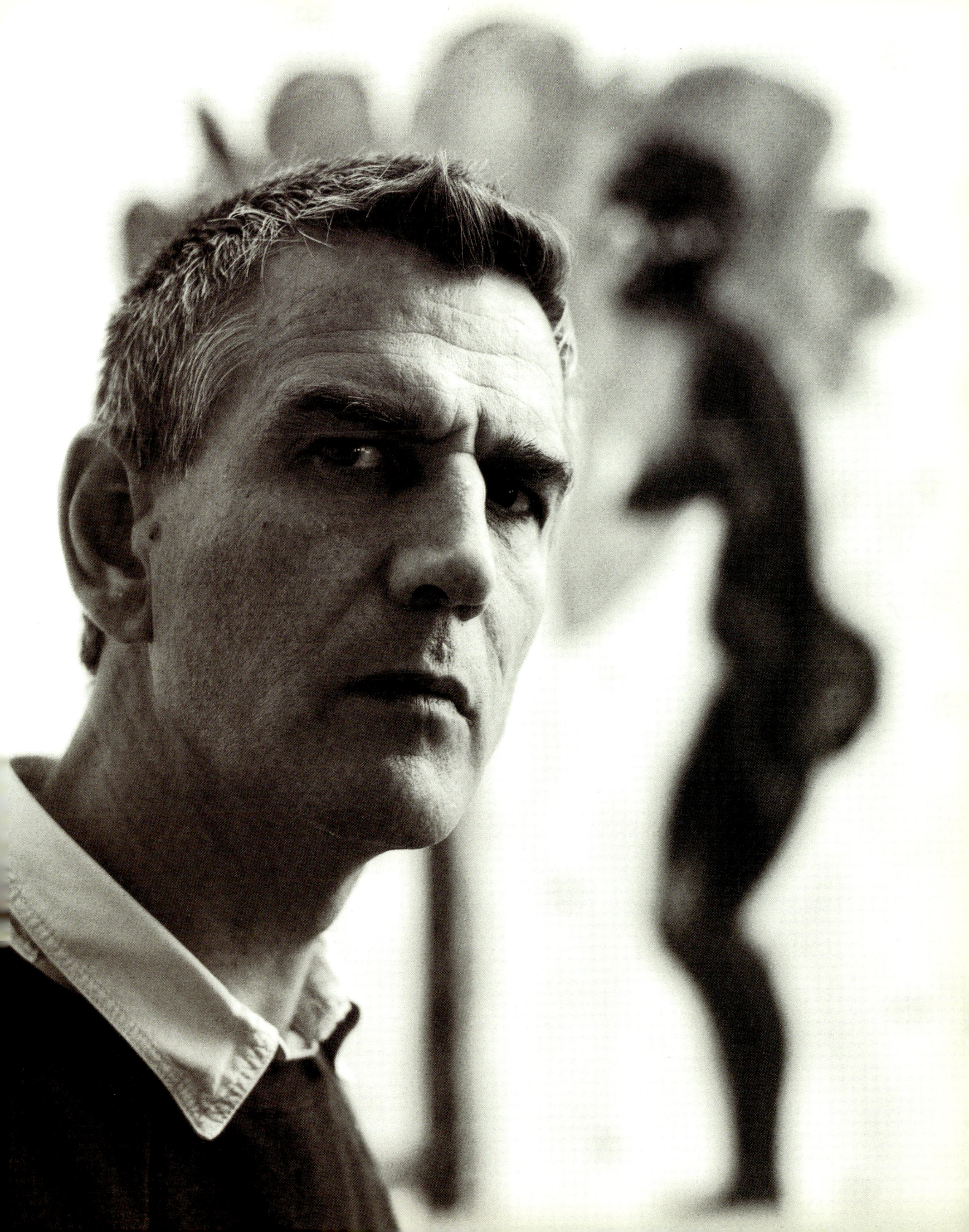

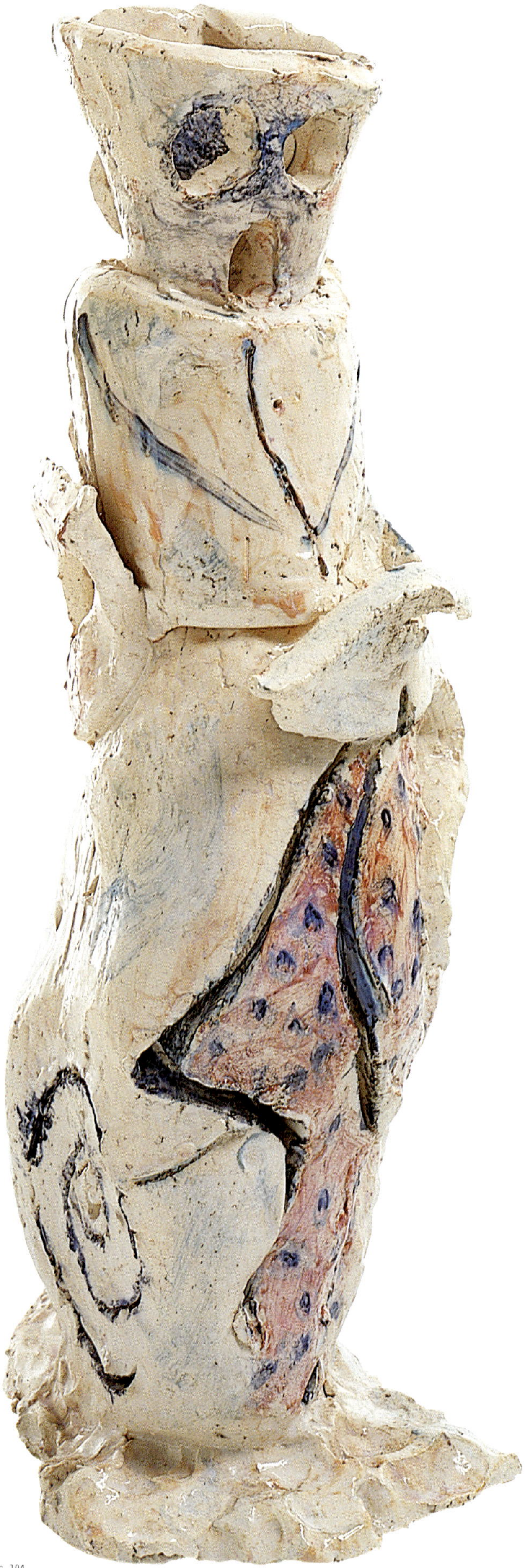

FIG. 104

FIG. 104 ALPHONS FREIJMUTH
DE SCHRIK 1991
sculpture/vase; 68 x 24 x 30 cm
COLLECTION MUSEUM HET KRUITHUIS

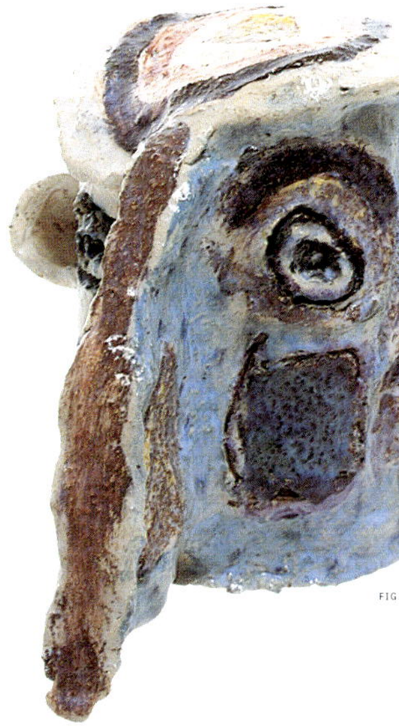

FIG. 105

FIG. 105 ALPHONS FREIJMUTH
NEUS 1991
sculpture; 22.5 x 16.5 x 18.7 cm
COLLECTION MUSEUM HET KRUITHUIS

that suggests a screaming face like that in Edvard Munch's famous painting. The vase is mostly a bland tan. It has both incised and painted blue lines that are sinuously organic, as well as rosy-red patches with blue spots and rough appendages that from different angles suggest a cat's paw, an arabesque or an alphabetic letter. Once again Freijmuth's work combines opposite effects, this piece being both rawly gestural and voluptuously undulant.

The Dutch painter **Jan van den Dobbelsteen** (b. 1954 – fig. 106) has made an installation of 10 ceramic jars, standardized in form but each treated differently on the surface (fig. 108). The 2 1/2-foot-tall jars have octagonal caps. Dobbelsteen's use of a cast, standardized form keeps his presentation coherent despite the fact that its parts fractiously call attention to themselves. Consistent with the historic ceramic attention to surface, he has been exotic in coloring and glazing his elements.

The vases are reminiscent of the white plaster jars used in vast quantities by the American artist Allan McCollum, in installations by which he asks questions about originality and commodification. Dobbelsteen, on the other hand, seems to be looking at the individuation of mass production in ceramics: the blank is, like a canvas, available for personal touch. It's just an accident or curiosity that these robust vase forms, when grouped in rows, recall soldiers with their chests thrown out. That image is inconsistent with other observations of this work.

Dobbelsteen is interested in Asian philosophies. His paintings take an enormous range of appearances, but often involve balanced parts, grids, mirror-inversions, overlaps that obscure vision, and sequences of shape that suggest infinite continuity. The paintings give a sense of pointing to something that they will not speak about, or of symbolizing conditions so basic that to name them would be to trivialize them (fig. 107). He has also made sculptures that use bowl-like forms – again sometimes in inverted relationships, or in situations where empty space balances substance. His concerns in an installation of vases, then, probably have to do with macro and micro, with invoking the vast but reveling in the particular.

His ceramic material allows him great latitude in particularizing the surface. One vase, for example, is a checkerboard consisting of squares made by applying white glaze over blue. -

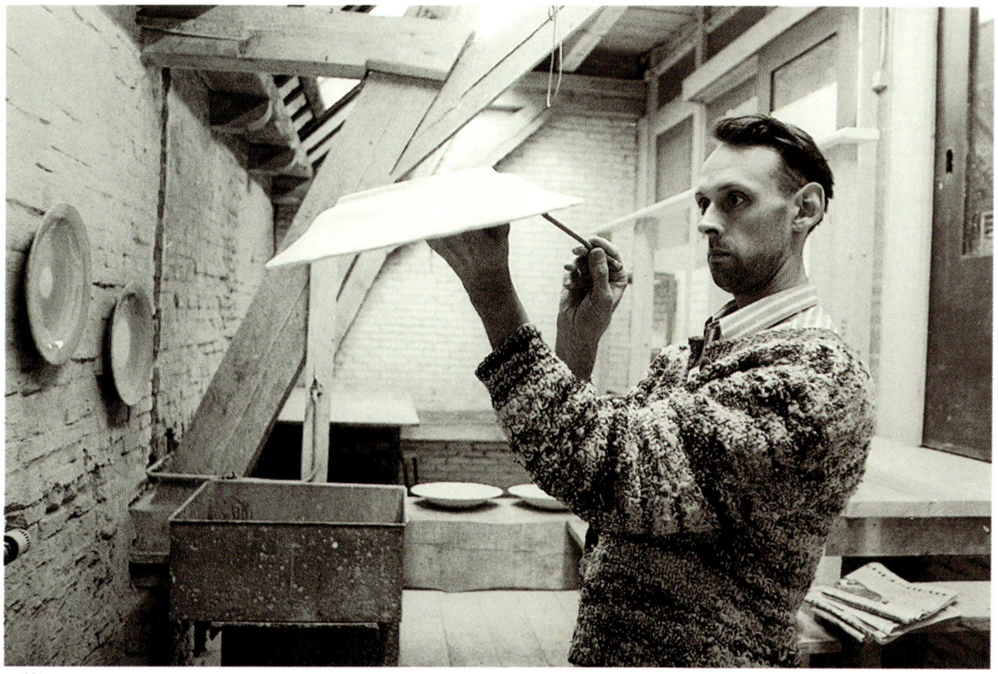

FIG. 106

FIG. 106 JAN VAN DEN DOBBELSTEEN

FIG. 107 JAN VAN DEN DOBBELSTEEN
UNTITLED 1990
painting; 100 x 140 cm

On one half, the white is brushed to give patterns of a whirlwind or wave. On the other half, the checkerboard is of the same warm white color but the surface is furrowed so the white is like pastry fingers. The top of this side is black only, but in various places it's fizzy, bubbled or pitted. Fluid tones of blue cascade down the lid in channels of color reminiscent of millefiori glass. Blue has dripped onto the black parts of the shoulder, even making a tiny stalactite/stalagmite. The fluidity of substance obviously appeals to Dobbelsteen, as well as the richness and variability of the colors (over one another they contrast or mix, and the black seems to soften to blue in some places).

A second vase from the installation is all black and white. Here the decoration is more uniform: vase and cap are entirely grooved. The black seems horizontally wiped and darkness is revealed under the blue in the square parts. These areas contrast strongly to the look of brushwork where the creamy white is thinly spread over the dark surface to make the checkerboard. We can see the artist's process (although with glazes, the contrast might not have actually looked like this as he applied it – it's a challenge of ceramics is that firing changes the colors and surfaces). Particular ceramic effects are seen at the stem of the cap as well as on the white shoulders: the glaze has pulled apart, the surface is fragmented, rather like mud that cracks as

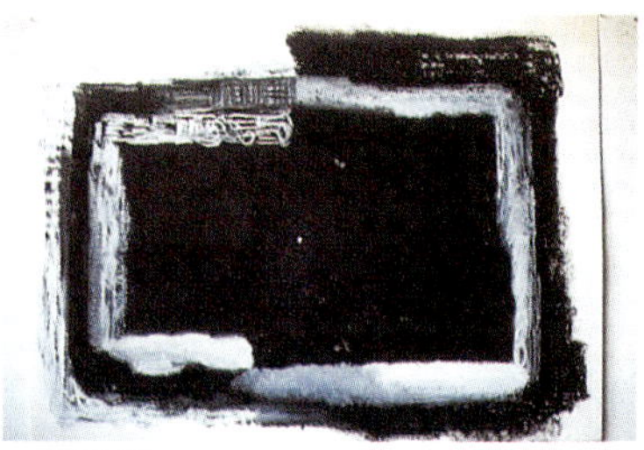

FIG. 107

it dries. On this vase the checkered design doesn't meet perfectly; it wasn't measured and, unlike a skilled production craftsman, Dobbelsteen can't "eyeball" the space and divide it accurately. The interesting result is that the piece seems unfinished, unconnected: there is a void across which sparks (namely vision and imagination) can jump. If the pattern were perfectly resolved, visual participation in this form would be different: viewers would have a sense of hovering in space amid a perfected structure, and would have a surer sense of position.

This rich variety in specific marks upon each vase is, of course, only one aspect of this work, which was conceived as an assembly with a cumulative effect. The grids, inversions and overlaps of Dobbelsteen's paintings have been multiplied here to an almost baroque complexity, which balances the succinct form and simple arrangement of the parts.

FIG. 108 JAN VAN DEN DOBBELSTEEN
UNTITLED, INSTALLATION 1989
10 vases; 80 x 45 cm
COLLECTION MUSEUM HET KRUITHUIS

FIG. 108

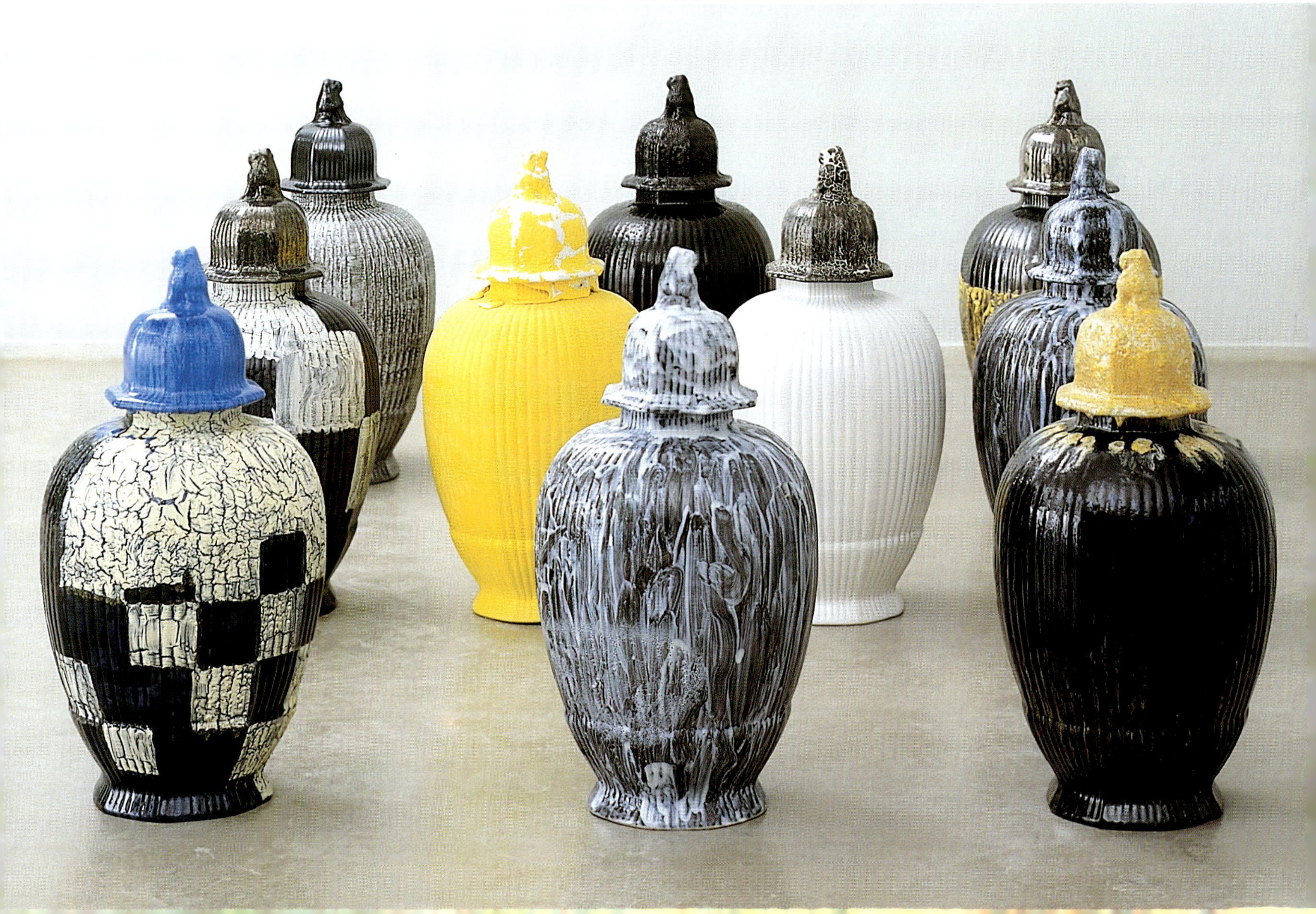

The British artist **Bruce McLean** (b. 1944 – fig. 110) might be expected to approach ceramics with a conceptual regard. McLean is a painter and sculptor who from his earliest days has responded skeptically and with humor to artistic orthodoxies. Early works concentrated first on arranging objects and then on posing the artist himself solely to be photographed. The most famous of these works were parodies of traditional reclining sculptures, with the artist less-than-comfortably perched atop pedestals (fig. 109). Beginning in the early 1970s, McLean performed with his Nice Style Pose Band, whose performances played out the concept of pose, "with all its connotations of gesture, posture, proximic positioning relative to persons and things within a given room, the stance, the glance, the look, the attitude, etc."[84] Nice Style's uniqueness was in "its consistent ironic exemplification of what it attacked, maintaining its pose with an impenetrable rigour of self-awareness."[85]

FIG. 109 BRUCE MCLEAN
POSE WORK FOR PLINTHS 1971
DOCUMENTATION OF PERFORMANCE AT SITUATION

FIG. 110 BRUCE MCLEAN

When McLean returned to painting, his compositions often consisted of athletes or dancers or circus performers in configurations that might be called pose-on-paper, with implications of other meaning: "McLean realised that acrobatics – the apotheosis of pose, being the outcome of extreme artifice and *signifying nothing but itself* – presented a richly allusive vocabulary of metaphor for political behavior."[86] These simple emblems on fields of color often brought flags to mind.

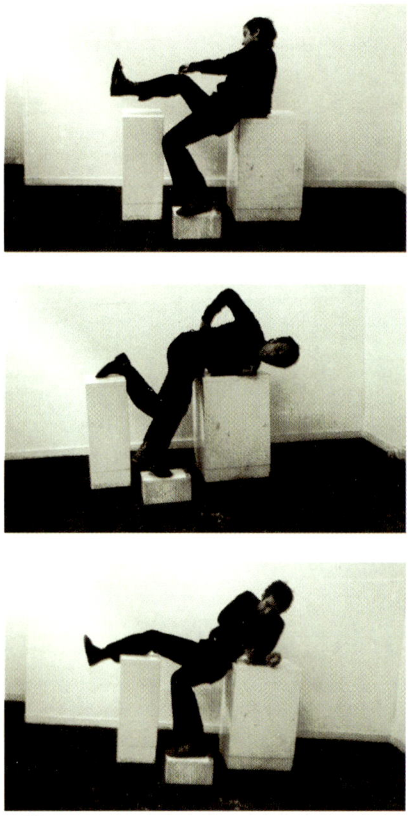

FIG. 109

McLean has done considerable work in ceramics, starting in 1986 at the Fulham Pottery in England. The Kruithuis in 1988 invited him to make pieces at the Ceramic Work Center, then located in the town of Heusden. He seems to be interested in contradictory understandings of space that arise simultaneously from his painting and the ceramic form it appears upon. Among the most striking of his works, by virtue of its size and the drama of its form, is a large pitcher (fig. 112). It has a warped vitality, and is another illustration of a ceramic vessel's ability to evoke human qualities of posture with even in forms defined by

84. Mel Gooding, Bruce McLean, New York: Phaidon Universe, 1990, p. 64.
85. Gooding, p. 64.
86. Gooding, p. 76.

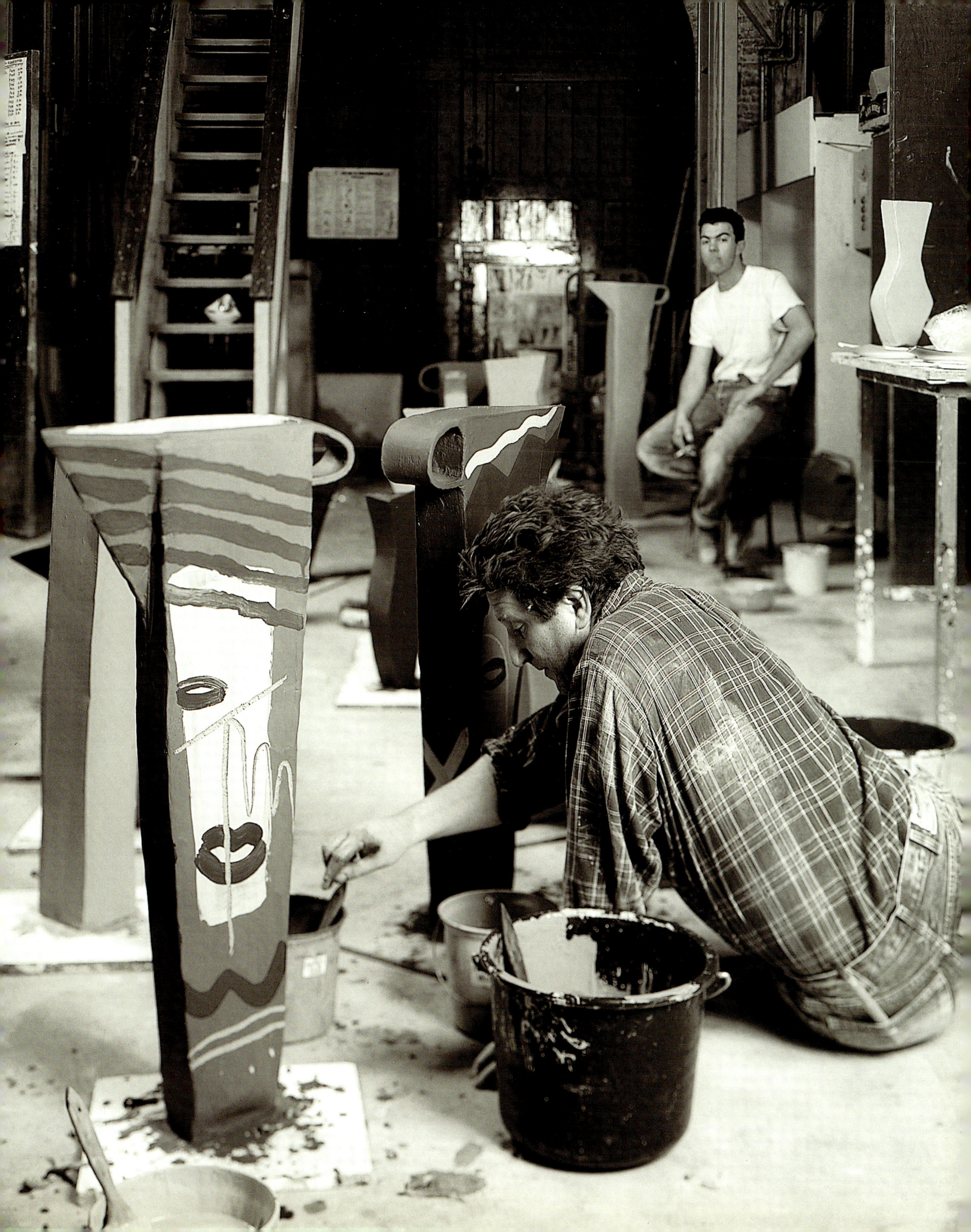

functional considerations – although, of course, a vessel this size is not literally usable. The pitcher's erect stance and large scale evokes inflating or inhaling – that sort of expansion – which is a further link to humanity.

McLean treats the inside of the pitcher celestially, making it a bright blue field with a random assortment of star-like brush splats. He responds to the details of form, stroking his brush across the handle and making an X below it, like a structural support for this functional element. On one side of the pitcher, near the top, a greenish band is embellished with a snake (black with whitish dots) that ends in a forked tongue. All the dots and the tongue are gouged through the glaze to the clay underneath. Then a simplified face: broad white strokes for head, black outlines for eyes and mouth, a zigzag line that makes brows and nose, two ocher strokes for ears. An incised hand, one finger pointing up, is carved over that painted face. A blue zigzag is painted at the bottom.

On the other side of the pitcher, McLean's painting may bring to mind Brancusi's famous *Sleeping muse* sculptures of abstracted heads. This head has blond hair indicated by a brush stroke at the top . The mouth, one eye and a simplified open hand are gouged into the clay. There are also two broad brush strokes of green and two snakes. It's interesting to compare this reductive visage with Penck's primitive figuration on his vase. The head here, being close to life size, seems more intimate, like another person in direct contact with us. Yet at the same time the detailing is so cursory that it's an emblem, like Penck's figures. Here the sharp compressions of the vessel form have no relationship to a real head shape – far less than we saw in the Picasso vase/head or even the Cocteau piece, since McLean has simply opted for two independent treatments on the two sides, not making the volume of the vessel equal the volume of a head, as his predecessors did. Regardless, the sharpness and drama of the form are very much in keeping with the imagery.

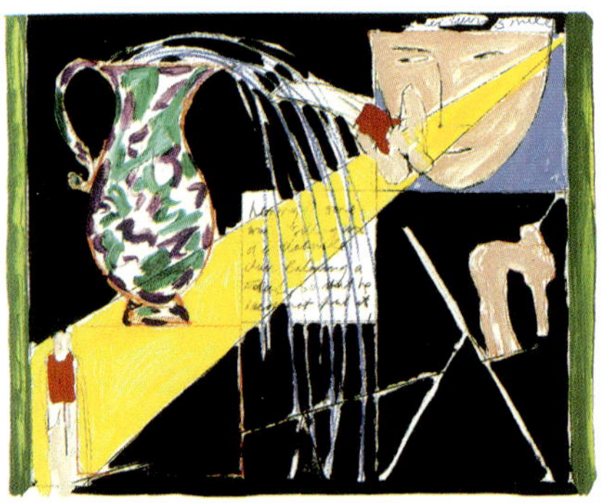

FIG. 111

FIG. 111 BRUCE MCLEAN
A CERTAIN SMILE 1978
acrylic on photographic paper; 115 x 140 cm

One of McLean's ceramic plates (fig. 113) is painted with a hat, its brim defined by a line gouged into the clay. There is also one eye, and a simplified mouth. The open hand is indicated with a painted black outline. The face is a couple of gray strokes and a white brushed rectangle at the eye (under the black outline and the scrape that

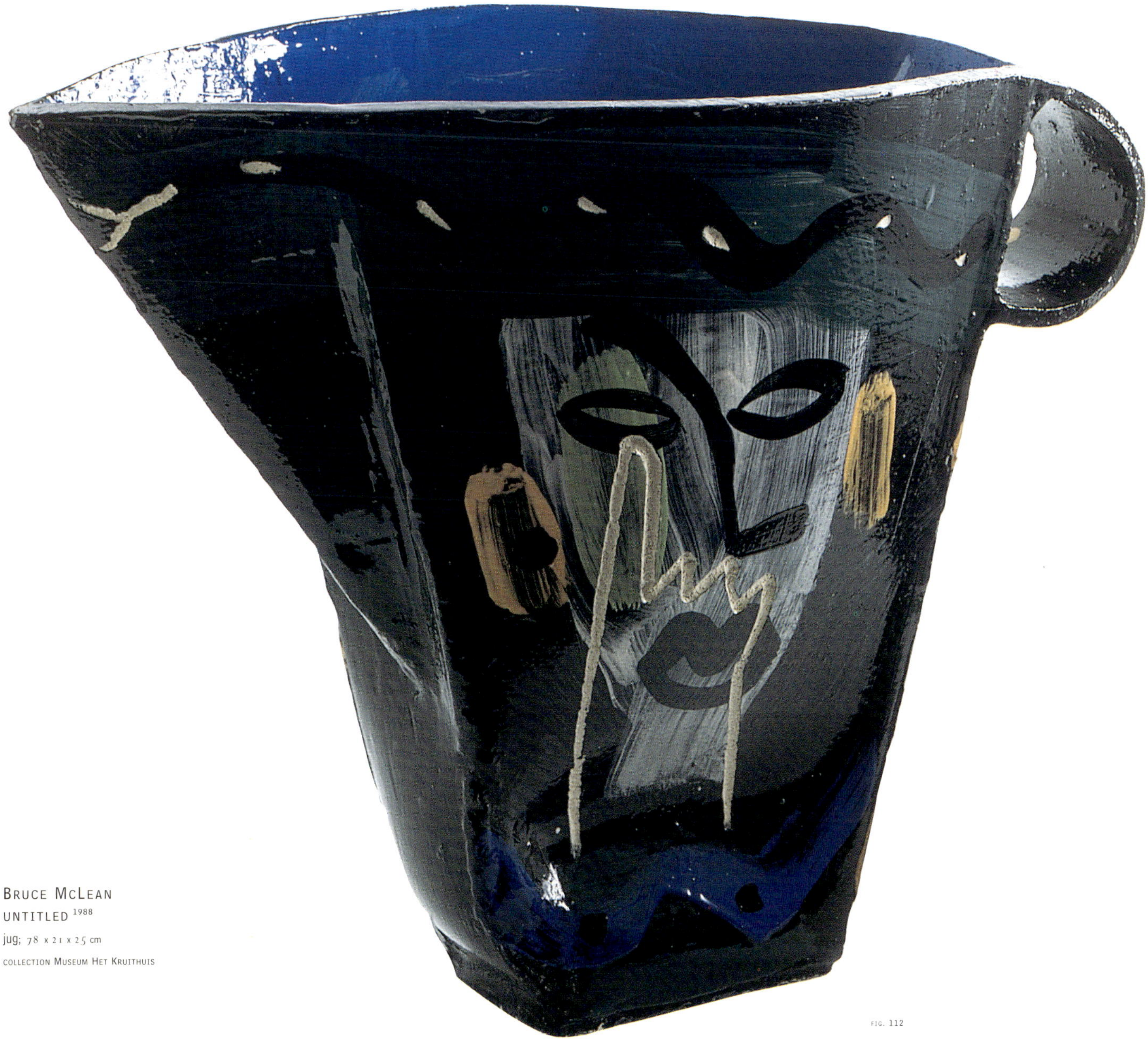

FIG. 112 BRUCE McLEAN
UNTITLED 1988
jug; 78 x 21 x 25 cm
COLLECTION MUSEUM HET KRUITHUIS

FIG. 112

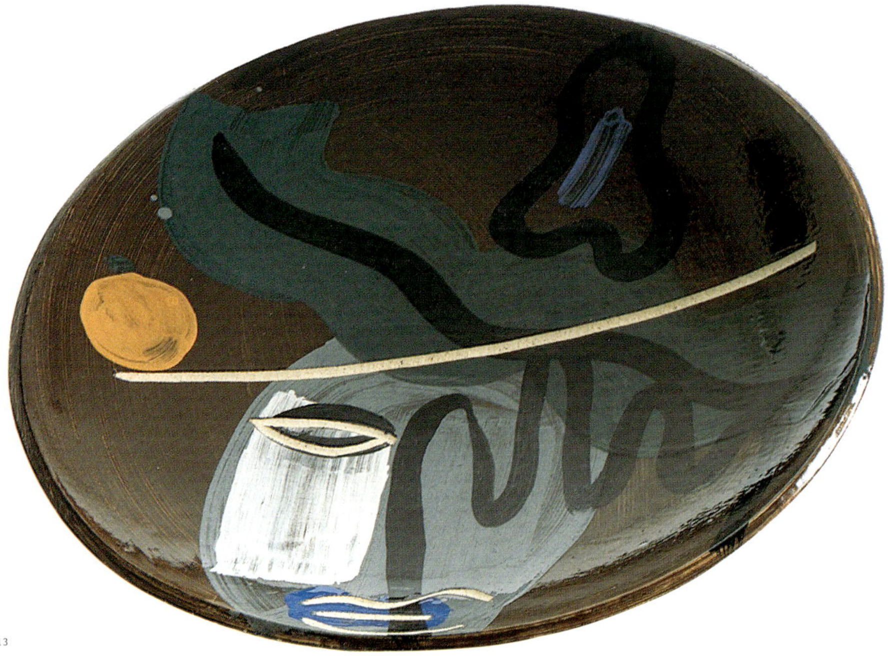

FIG. 113

define the eye). This looks mannered because the head and hand are an assembly of unrelated parts. It lacks the engaging primitivism of the pitcher. Because the plate is glazed all over, even over the gouges, it seems smooth and therefore more refined than the pitcher, where the gouging violates the glaze.

Other plates he has made are somewhat smaller but play with the same vocabulary of elements: gouged or painted; hand or eye; brush strokes as broad as fields or narrow and rudimentarily descriptive. McLean's imagery looks so quickly executed that it might make us think of cartooning, yet its color, its loose balance and its very nonchalance are so graceful and accomplished that we might think instead of Matisse or of design from the 1940s and '50. The plates have an ingratiatingly retro sophistication, like something out of a nightclub.

FIG. 113 BRUCE MCLEAN
UNTITLED 1988
plate; ο 48 cm
COLLECTION MUSEUM HET KRUITHUIS

It might seem quite a stretch to move from performance and painting to ceramics, but several features of McLean's earlier works clearly prefigure the ceramics in the Kruithuis collection. The spatial configurations of the imagery – a simplified figure in an indefinite space – is very like his paintings on canvas from the mid-'80s. He has always preferred the provisional and improvised, and has since the late '70s made installations in which "figures, faces and common objects are magnified and configured in enigmatic relations in ambiguous space"[87] – which sounds like an accurate description of the ceramic imagery. Domestic pose was a subject of several of Nice Style's performances, and McLean's drawings of the late '70s often feature a tulip-shaped face (sans cranium, ears or neck) that has been described as a "tea-cup face": "The

87. Gooding, pp. 28, 88.

conflation of the quizzical face – half ironical, half approving – of the spectator of domestic stylistics with the vessel that features at the heart of the ceremonies of middle-class politeness is one of McLean's most brilliant comic inventions."[88] The sgraffito technique of drawing by incising into a field of color was also McLean's method in fluid paintings on photographic paper that he made in the '80s (fig 111). A description of his painting – "The paint is brushed on with great speed and vigour, pushed and pulled across the surface, colour layered over colour, applied overall with an expressive gestural *élan*"[89] – exactly describes the impression his ceramic surfaces evoke.

In addition to the tea-cup face, ceramics also figures in images he developed for a 1988 book called *Apropos the jug* (Knife Edge Press) in which a female face or nude torso is conflated with an amphora or vase. At that time he was making ceramics and developing the work for an unusual exhibition entitled "The Floor, the Fence, The Fireplace." This 1987 London exhibition consisted of drawings for imagined interiors, ceramics, and furniture-sculptures that took the form of tables, fireplaces and mantelpieces featuring the same kinds of faces seen on the ceramics in the Kruithuis collection (fig. 114 and 115). The exhibition led to an invitation for McLean to design a bar for the Arnolfini Gallery in Bristol – "to create a place for seriously playful posing in a context of art."[90] Furniture

FIG. 114 BRUCE MCLEAN
UNTITLED 1988
plate; ø 32 cm
COLLECTION MUSEUM HET KRUITHUIS

FIG. 115 BRUCE MCLEAN
UNTITLED 1988
plate; ø 32 cm
COLLECTION MUSEUM HET KRUITHUIS

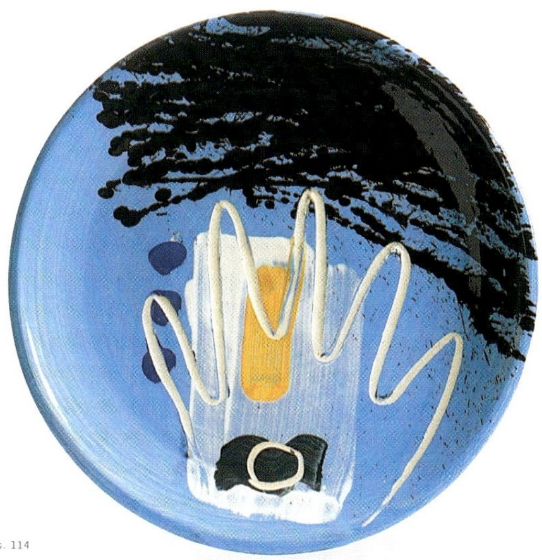

FIG. 114

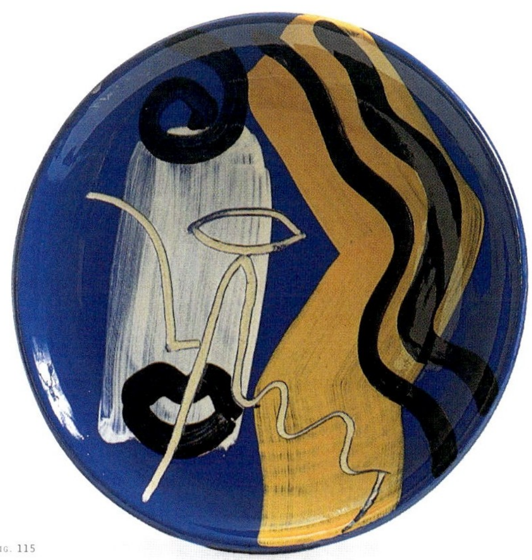

FIG. 115

88. Gooding, p. 100.
89. Gooding, p. 105.
90. Gooding, p. 158.

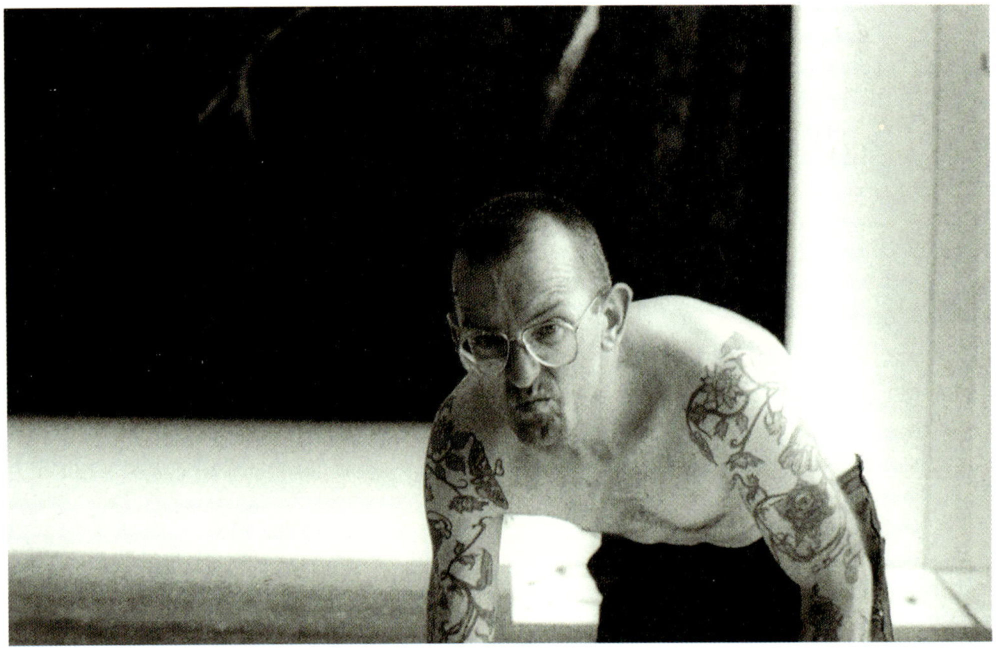

FIG. 116

FIG. 116 HANS VAN HOEK

FIG. 117 HANS VAN HOEK
DOOP 1996
relief; 70 x 35 cm
COLLECTION MUSEUM HET KRUITHUIS

and pots are said to interest McLean "as objects of use and decoration and at the same time metaphors for the immanence of art in life."[91]

The quick sophistication of McLean's art is a far cry from the unrefined directness of reliefs by the Dutch painter **Hans van Hoek** (b. 1947 – fig. 116). These are about baptism by the holy spirit (fig. 117, 118, 119, 121 and 122). Van Hoek's touch, in the lineage of his countryman Van Gogh (who, we might remember, once had religious aspirations) express almost throbbing physicality. What Van Gogh did with the build-up of paint, Van Hoek does by building up and digging into clay. His colors are surprisingly garish, as if this were a Caribbean vision, and the brightness is intensified by the glossy transparent glaze over all. The imagery is clearly symbolic and symmetrically orderly, and yet at the same time it is uncertain and disorienting.

It's surprising that such a metaphysical event would be represented in something so visually thick and weighty. In addition, the use of clay has a connotation of earth, not the spiritual, and that association is only made more palpable by the edges of the reliefs, poked and crimped with fingers. A flower-like form at center in fig. 119 and 122 is both the sun and a coronaed head of the believer, whose body is yellow,

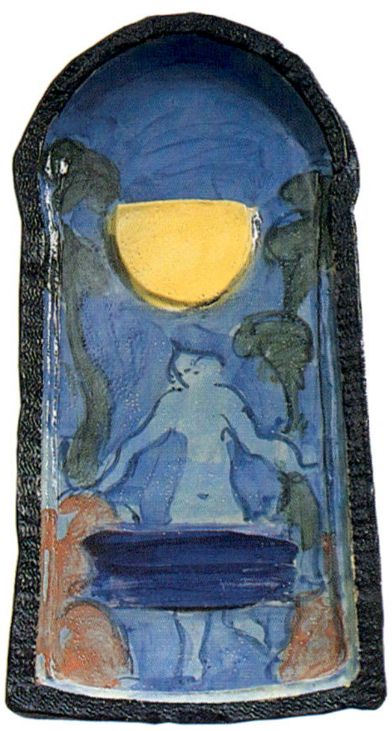

FIG. 117

91. Gooding, p. 164.

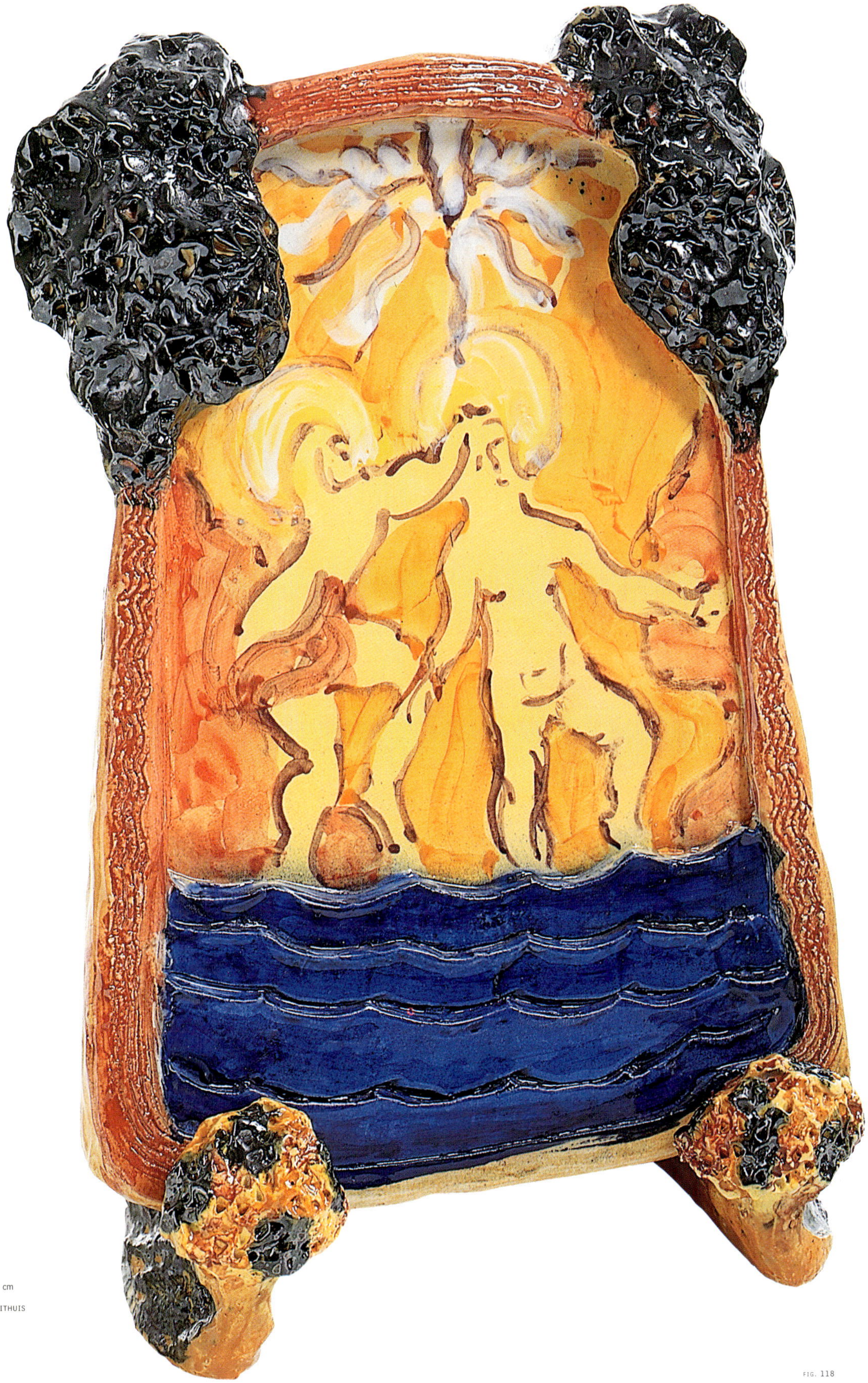

FIG. 118 HANS VAN HOEK
DOOP 1996
relief with base; 43 x 30 cm
COLLECTION MUSEUM HET KRUITHUIS

FIG. 118

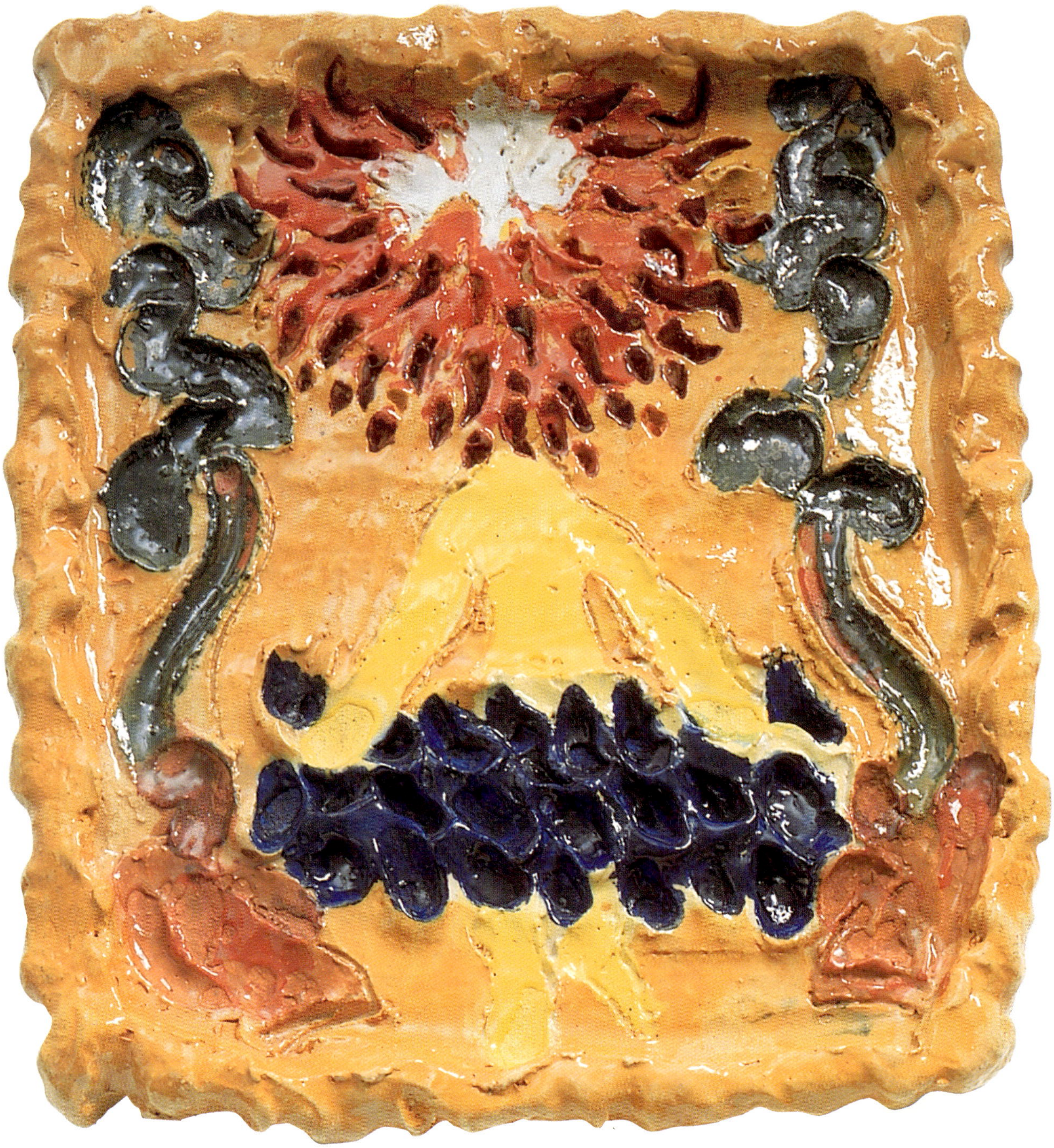

FIG. 119

FIG. 119 HANS VAN HOEK
DOOP 1996
relief; 48 x 44 cm
COLLECTION MUSEUM HET KRUITHUIS

perhaps with the radiance of the spirit descending in the form of a dove. The sinuous forms at the sides presumably represent trees, and the bubbly, grape-like blue clusters across the midsection of the figure symbolize the baptismal waters. Van Hoek has taken advantage of the clay's plasticity; his primitivism, reminiscent of COBRA paintings, may be surprising for this subject matter but communicates an affecting fervor.

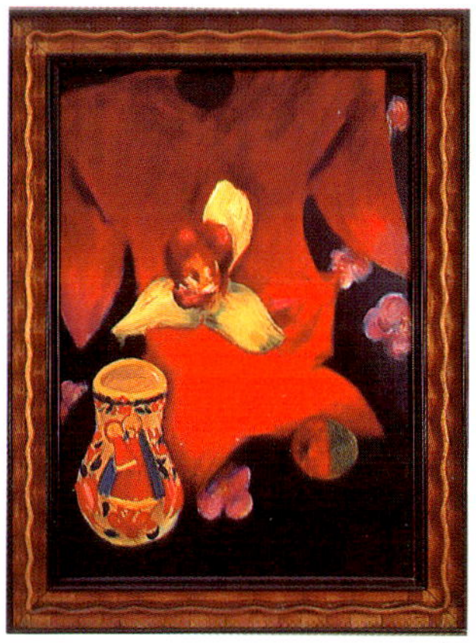

FIG. 120

His paintings also have a physical presence, not just illusion. Although his subjects are the classic themes of painting – landscape, floral still life (fig. 120), the nude – he typically encases the paintings in a frame that by its soberness or by its strange extravagance adds to the painted statement. His landscapes are often executed in dark, Rembrandtesque tonalities, which could seem surprising considering the openness of the Dutch landscape and the vaunted light in skies that are obscured by neither mountains nor deep forests (nor skyscrapers). Van Hoek may use that darkness to set off the light that is generated within his landscapes or within the very figure of the nude in some works. His patches of paint sometimes seem to be poised between the faceted substance of Cézanne and the colored etherealness of Signac, conveying both earth and air in a trembling, near-visionary manner. But Van Hoek does not look to the heavens or to some metaphysical existence; paint and frame as well as viewpoint all work to embed the experience of his painting in the palpa-

FIG. 120 HANS VAN HOEK
RODE KIMONO 1975
oil on canvas; 218 x 168 cm

FIG. 121 HANS VAN HOEK
DOOP 1996
relief with base; 40 x 28 cm
COLLECTION MUSEUM HET KRUITHUIS

FIG. 122 HANS VAN HOEK
DOOP 1996
relief; 55 x 43 cm
COLLECTION MUSEUM HET KRUITHUIS

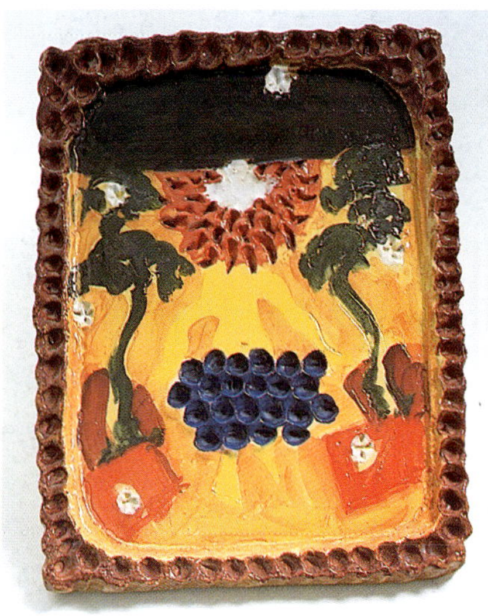

FIG. 122

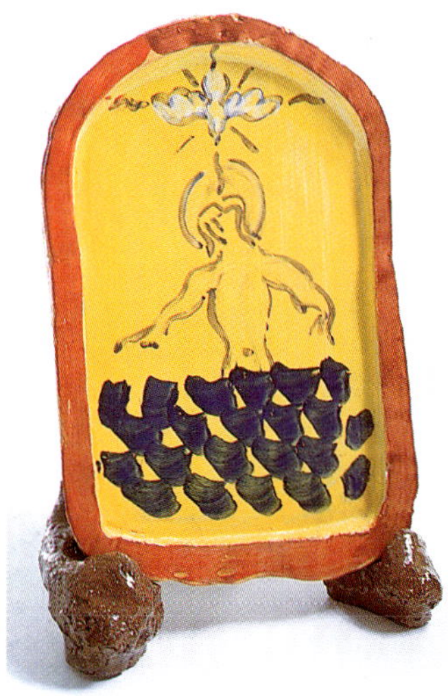

FIG. 121

bility of the here-and-now. Even when he paints a Christian cross in the landscape, that symbol is expressed in a familiar and human-scale context. Looking back to Van Hoek's reliefs, one recognizes the same physical power.

Ceramic dishes decorated with crabs, by **Erik Andriesse** (1957-1993 – fig. 125), are just as much relief as Van Hoek's large slabs, but Andriesse's use of the clay is playful. An Amsterdam painter who died unexpectedly of a cerebral hemorrhage at the age of 35, Andriesse made large and exuberant flower paintings for a few years in the '80s, then added skulls and skeletons and, after a trip to the Caribbean, tropical sea creatures and shells. His works, too, have a spiritual quality, but are not so tied to Christianity as Van Hoek's reliefs.

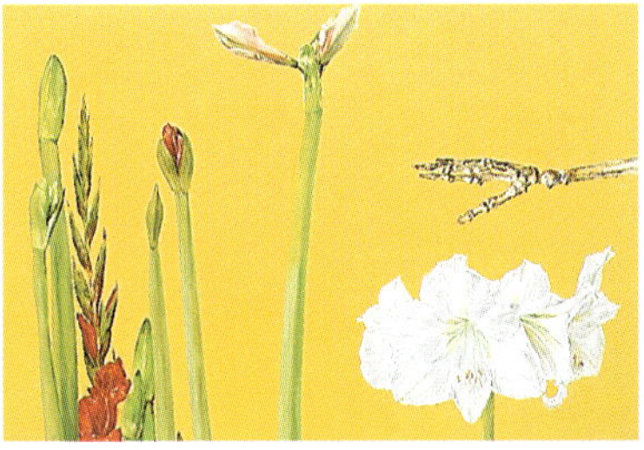

FIG. 123

Andriesse painted on the theme of death: the erotic profusion of his flowers represents their ephemeral peak. The flowers "open their petals, expose their heart and when the innocent stoop to worship their beauty with a kiss they are lured into the kingdom of death and decay," one critic wrote.[92] (fig. 123) The paintings are not morbid: he is subtler than that. One might almost read into his work the Japanese philosophy that ephemerality makes a thing more precious, or the Tao's continuous and therefore unfrightening flow of births and deaths.[93] In his work, Andriesse seems to relish life precisely because it is short for everyone, though he could not have known how short it was to be for himself. Yet there it is, running through his work. "When you see these paintings you experience at once, and to the marrow of your

FIG. 123 ERIK ANDRIESSE
AMARYLLIS, KNOPPEN + KNOOK 1992
oil on canvas; 80 x 120 cm

FIG. 124 ERIK ANDRIESSE
UNTITLED 1992
plate; 26 x 41 cm
COLLECTION MUSEUM HET KRUITHUIS

FIG. 125 ERIK ANDRIESSE

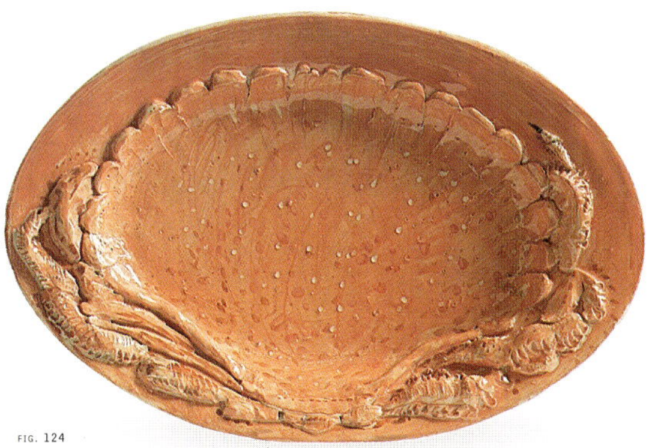

FIG. 124

92. Els Hoek, Erik Andriesse, New York: Jack Tilton Gallery, 1989, unpaginated.
93. Geurt Imanse, Erik Andriesse, Amsterdam: Galeries Paul Andriesse, 1987, unpaginated.

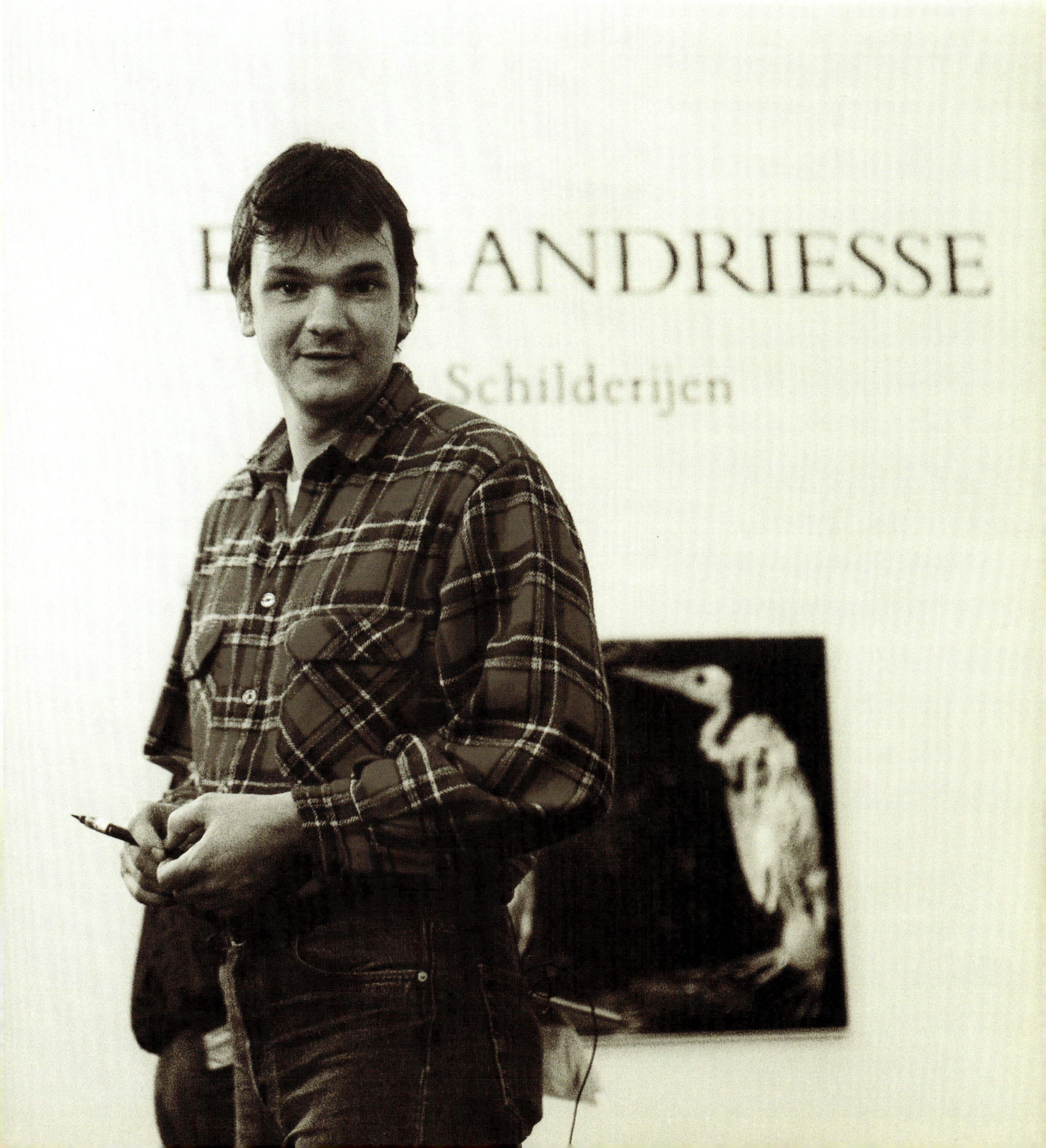
ANDRIESSE
Schilderijen

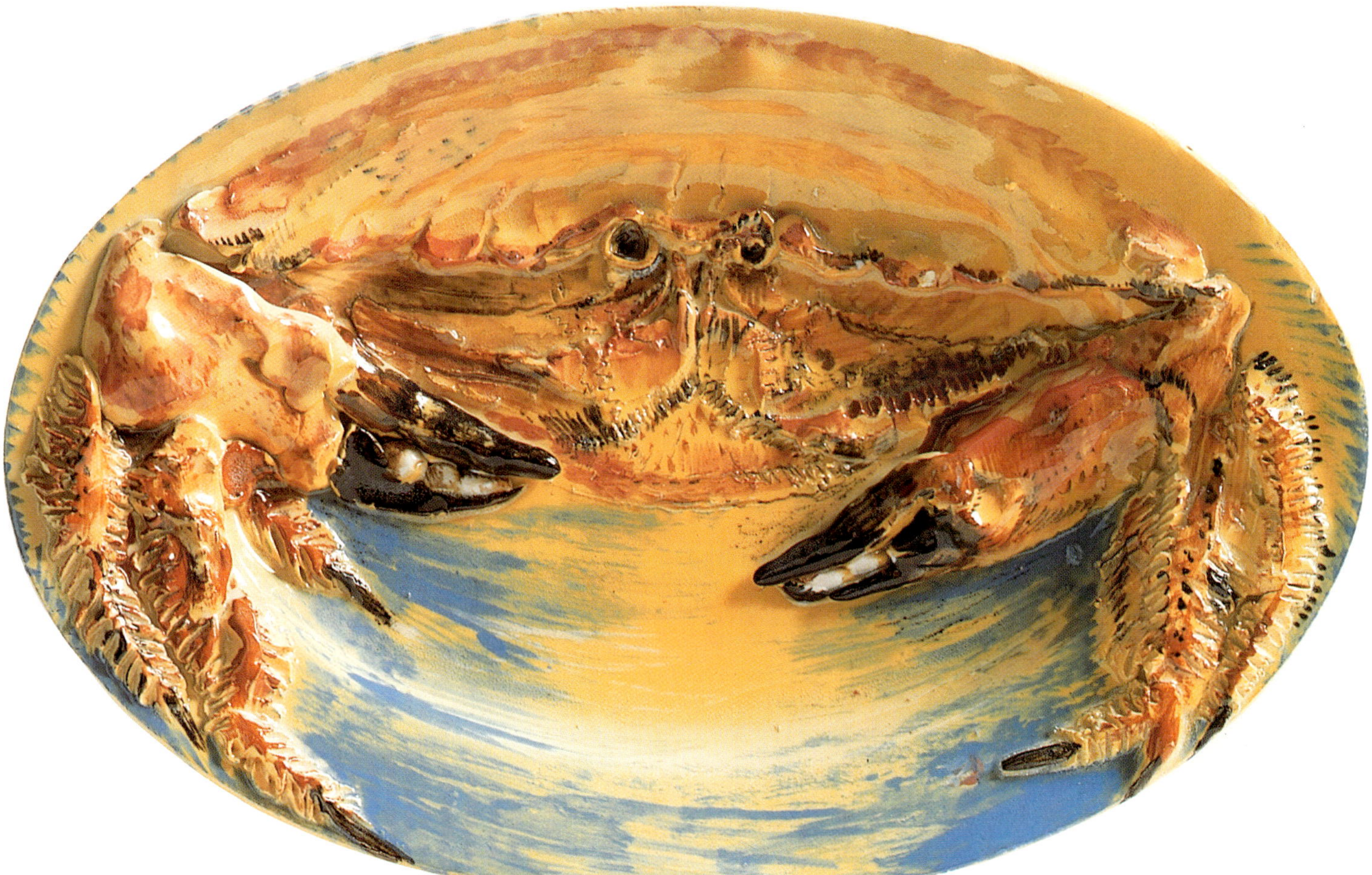

FIG. 126

FIG. 126 ERIK ANDRIESSE
KREEFTESCHAAL 1992
plate; 26 x 40 cm
COLLECTION MUSEUM HET KRUITHUIS

bones, how the depths of longing – be it for beauty or for ecstasy – are inextricably intertwined with terror of that beauty or that ecstasy. And how deeply beauty and ecstasy are bound up with death."[94]

Andriesse had begun working in ceramics only shortly before his sudden death. At the European Ceramic Work Center in 's-Hertogenbosh he made vessels embellished with skeletons or skulls. His ceramic representations of crabs (fig. 124 and 126) might seem mundane by contrast. In fact, however, there is a strangeness to these works, and although they are less direct they are no less interesting. The claws are probably an inch deep, while the rest of the crustacean's body subsides in relief to the point that the shell is "completed" on the rim of one oval dish by a painted line that has no relief at all. The other dish has the same effect, only with less relief and it's pinkish instead of mostly golden with just a little pink. Andriesse plays very effectively with ceramic space. The dish curves in a way that we know and expect; a pattern would simply follow that curve, but this relief works against it to make an ambiguous and alive space, rising against illusion into reality.

Another work by a young Dutch artist, and one of the most provocative and innovative works by a "visitor to clay" in the Kruithuis collection, is *Schaalman* (Bowlman – fig. 129) by the Dutch artist **Rob Birza** (b. 1962 – fig. 127). This is not a functional pedestal bowl because a column of empty space runs down the middle of it. The base is treated like a bronze – it looks like an Art Nouveau object sculpture. At the front are two legs in relief. They give the piece its human character, although only in a very cartoony way. Two dents and a bulge suggest the eyes and nose of a simplified face attached to these legs. Around the legs, the dish flares out into a skirt with a web-and-vein pattern that looks a little like a gingko leaf. This skirt appears to be held out by six stays. The clay is simply worked and the glaze is barely satiny and full of bubbles and pitting. The clay is wonderfully draped and cloth-like (or just generally membrane-like). The color is a '50s kitsch aqua green that incorporates the memory of the verdigris we would expect had it been made in bronze.

The bowl part of Birza's object, almost an inch thick, is shallow like a the Olympic flame's basin. There are two aqua

94. Hoek.

lugs, as if the leg-and-head figure were holding up the bowl like Atlas holding up the globe. The rim of the bowl is painted a nice pastel-sky blue, which, in combination with the outside, gives a peaceful feeling. But then the temperature changes: the inside of the bowl is visually pure lava, glowing hot. The thick surface is red-orange and appears to have heavily, sluggishly flowed. Hot color coats the "vent" running through the base, to extend this volcanic association. The vent is slightly off center in the bowl, so glaze-lava pools to one side of it. This tactile excess, both inviting and repelling touch, has a glossiness that could be associated with volcanic glass. Little rivulets of darkness (perhaps from the blue of the rim, or the thin line of purple at the inside edge of the blue) creep down into the inferno.

FIG. 127 ROB BIRZA

On first thought, the triple association of human and bowl and volcano seems unsustainable. But the linkage of vessel and human body is very old, as we know, and the volcanic evocation seems to be an inchoately emotional one. A person's feelings might burn up his insides and sometimes come spewing out lethally. This is not spelled out, and the piece is better for that. Birza's *Schaalman* is a marvelously effective piece on its own idiosyncratic terms.

Birza rapidly became known in Holland for his early paintings, which show Pop imagery extracted and adapted from newspapers, television and advertising in all its forms, and a humor that seems to coexist with a certain melancholy. He looked as well at previous art, in a proper postmodernist fashion, but executed his paintings in the decidedly old-fashioned and demanding technique of egg tempera rather than a casual contemporary method. His works always seem to exist on two levels of regard. His painting *Strawberries, pistache, peach and banana* (1990 – fig. 128) is a grid inevitably reminiscent of Mondrian, yet shifted from primaries to pastels, from brisk rigidity to the soft geometry of textiles (it looks like a dishcloth), and linked to consumption of sweet, pleasing, hedonistic things rather than being associated, as Mondrian's grids were, with syncopated traffic and jazz. Birza's paintings always seem to convey an acute sense of self-awareness of an artist's ambiguous position in the contemporary world. He has been described as dabbling in the modern stream of reproduced images: "There is no longer any question of hierarchy or hierarchical ordering... Birza takes the promiscuity of visual images

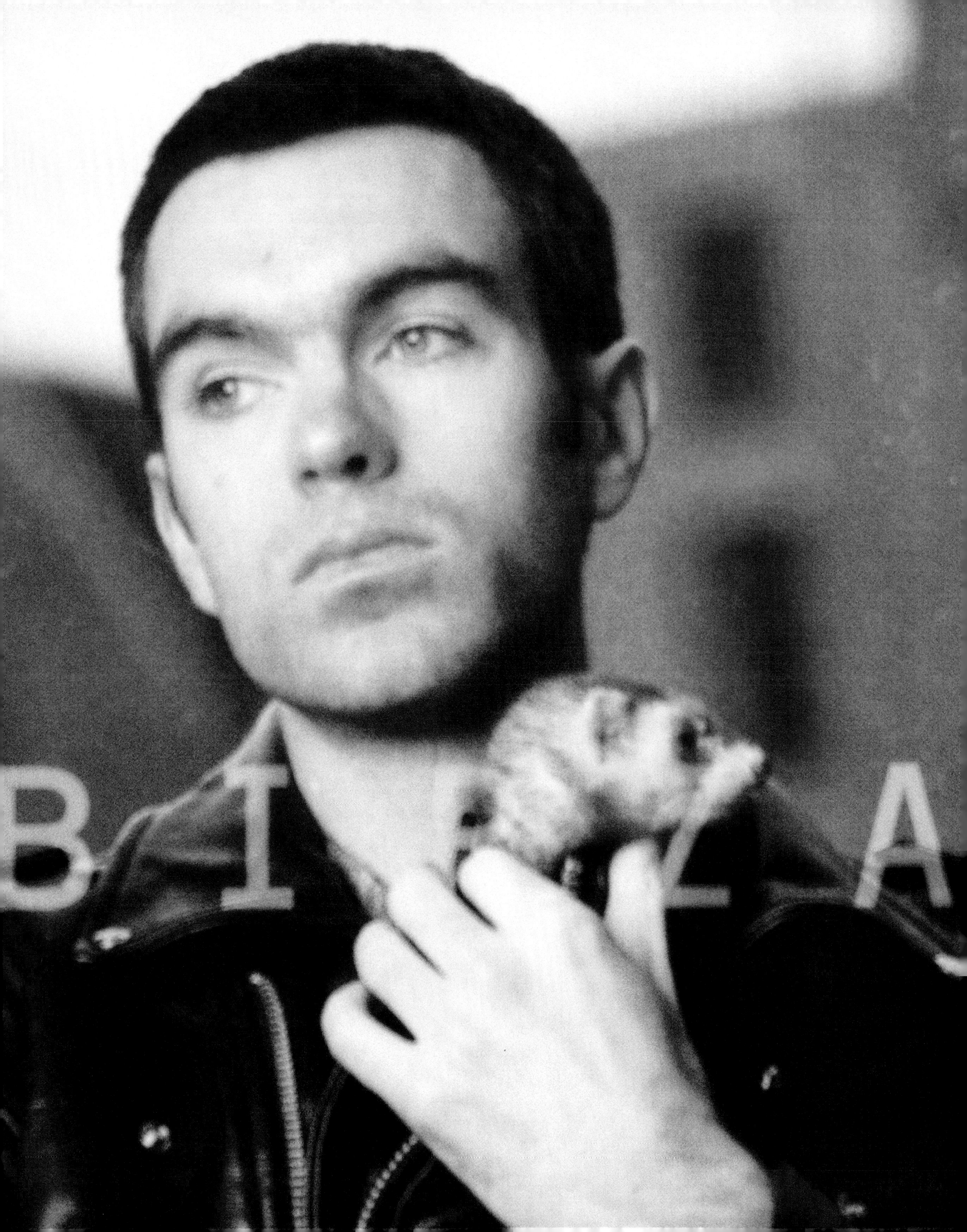
B I Z A

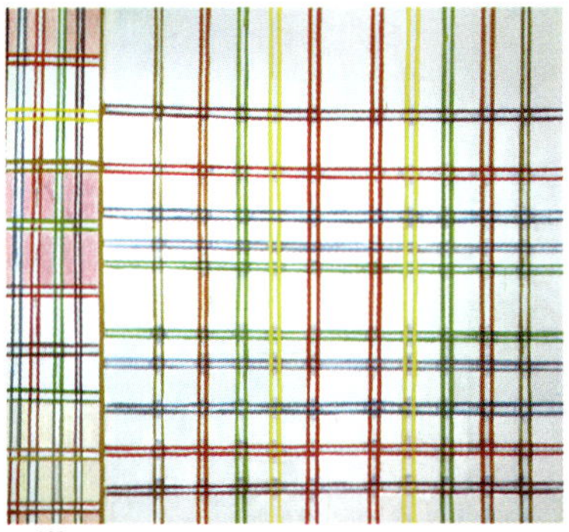

FIG. 128

as a fact, is inspired by it and responds via selection and playing along with the *Umwertung aller Werte* (reversal of all values)."[95]

His more recent work further distorts the convention of painting by incorporating lighting elements, shag carpeting and furniture, and drawing on the taste of the '50s and other boundaries of kitsch. He communicates not exuberance but a sense of dislocation and uneasiness. One critic concluded that his "attempt to break out of the pictorial space, added to the withdrawn, dull materiality of the egg tempera he uses, creates an enormous tension."[96] In his ceramic work, the materiality is anything but dull. Nevertheless, the separation and distinctness of the colors and surfaces support a mood of uncertainty by their lack of integration. There seems to be a message in that.

These many examples from the Kruithuis collection of artists' pottery make clear that ceramics, like any artistic medium, offers extraordinary opportunities to those who take the time to know it. Some may start by transferring what they already do to the different medium, but the best works are fresh realizations that take advantage of the age-old yet ever-new capabilities, character and symbolism of clay.

Thanks to Nora Brodnicki for research assistance on this essay.

FIG. 128 ROB BIRZA
STRAWBERRIES, PISTACHIO, PEACH AND BANANA 1990
egg tempera on canvas; 250 x 275 cm
COLLECTION STEDELIJK MUSEUM, AMSTERDAM/NL

95. Wim Beeren, Rob Birza, Amsterdam: Stedelijk Museum, 1991, p. 13.
96. Toine Ooms, "This is not a Birza," in Rob Birza, p. 48.

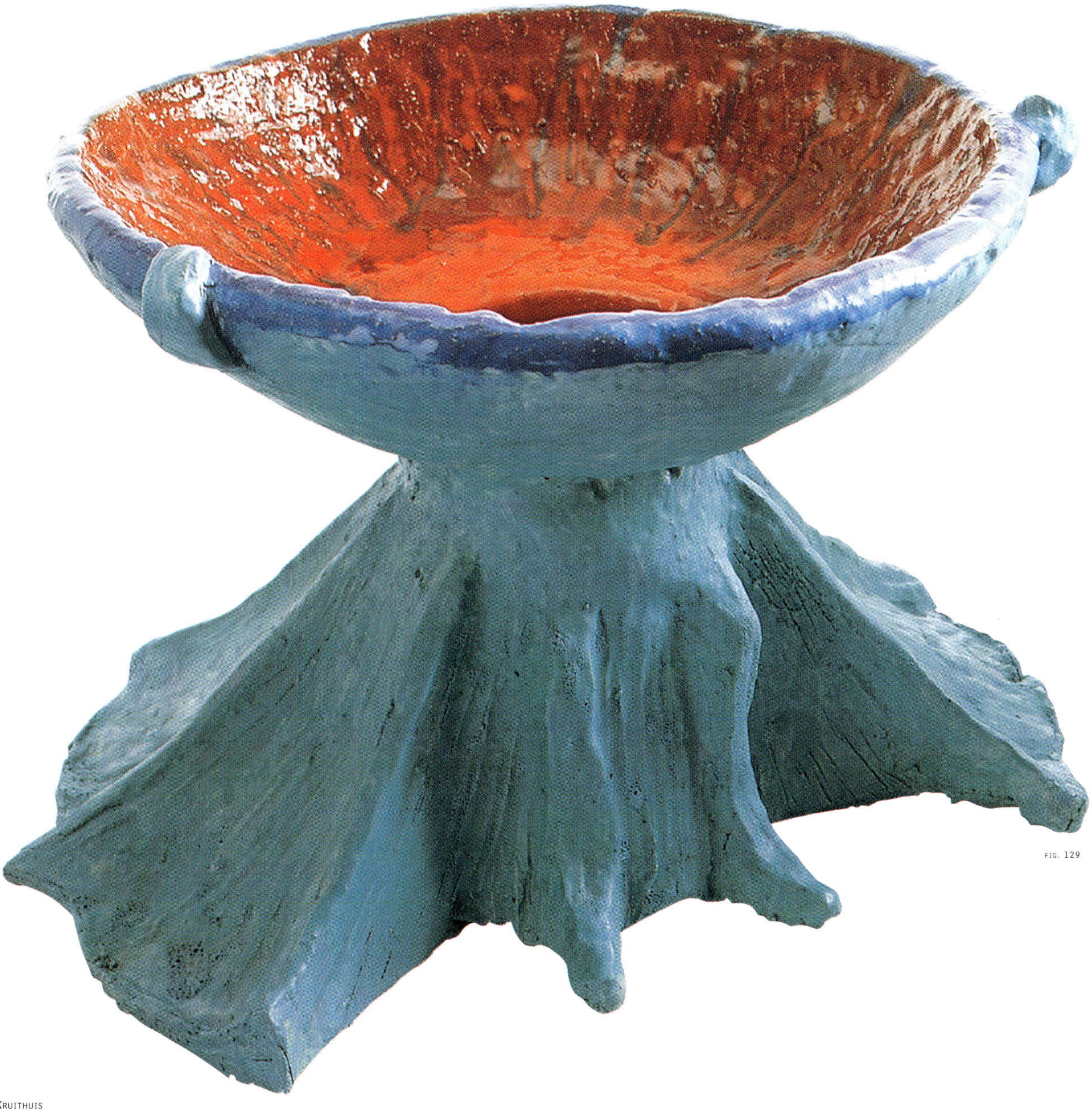

FIG. 129

FIG. 129 ROB BIRZA
SCHAALMAN 1993
sculpture; 37 x 53 cm
COLLECTION MUSEUM HET KRUITHUIS

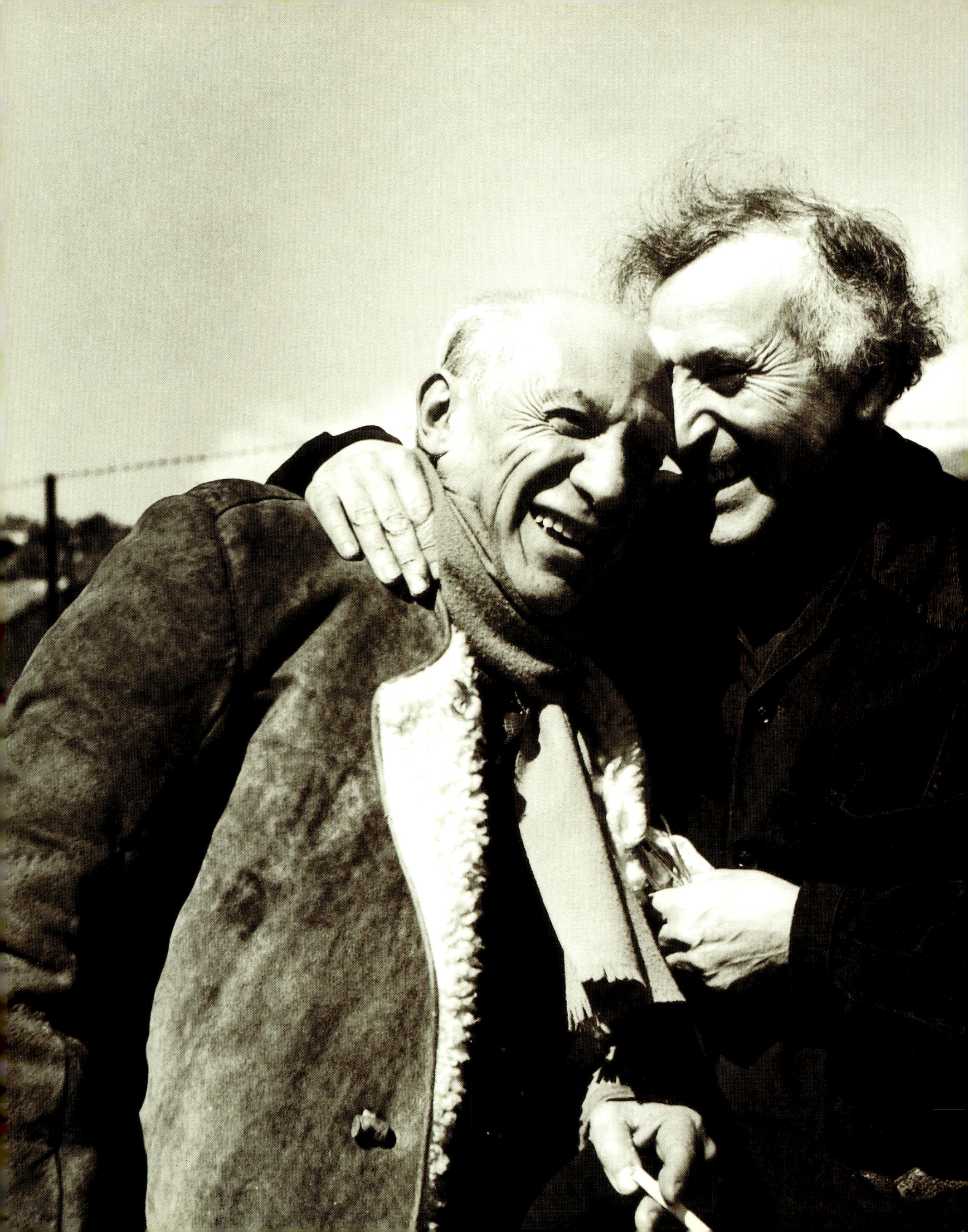

Picasso and the picassiettes

by Max Borka

"If it's anecdotes you're looking for, you've come to the wrong place," warns Alain Ramié. "Sometimes it's hard to reveal personal feelings." In other words he doesn't want to talk to us. We have driven all the way from Belgium to the south of France to ask Ramié about the Madoura workshop his parents Suzanne and Georges set up in 1938 in Vallauris, a stone's throw from Antibes and Cannes. And about his memories of Picasso, who brought the workshop instant international fame when he began to experiment there with pottery in 1946, sparking what was probably the key development in twentieth-century ceramics.

Alain was seven years old at the time. Picasso came back to Madoura regularly until his death in 1976. Until now anyone wishing to know more about the golden years of Madoura and Vallauris had to make do with a few hundred pages written by Georges Ramié – an endearing but unreadable paean of praise. The memoir says nothing about the relationship between Picasso and the many other artists who descended on Vallauris in the 1940s, breathing new life into a more or less defunct local ceramic industry. Nor does it mention their reasons for settling in this unprepossessing village or the fashionable crowd who followed in their wake, led by Gary Cooper who was to present Picasso with a gun. The reader also seeks in vain for less cheerful details, such as the poor quality of the material used to make pottery in Vallauris or the part Suzanne Ramié played in the marital tensions between the Picassos.

Pablo Picasso and Marc Chagall 1955

Historians agree that a great deal of research still has to be done into this period – and quickly, while the last witnesses are still around. As Alain Ramié sits in the Madoura workshop's showroom however he shows little inclination to contribute. When I ask him whether he ever felt the urge to work as a potter in his parents' workshop, he replies "Never". He trained as a nurse before returning to Vallauris in 1976 to take over the commercial management of Madoura after his mother and father died in quick succession, a couple of years after Picasso himself. With Alain at the helm, the workshop continued to produce Picasso's work, even though the master was dead. According to Ramié, it was agreed with the artist that some 600 of the estimated 4,000 pieces Picasso produced via the workshop would be issued in numbered series. The project required so much time that the work was far from complete when Picasso died. The master's death was followed soon after by the departure of two of his three surviving collaborators. The late Jean Ramié left when his half-brother Alain assumed control, followed by Dominique Sassi. "Because it just wasn't Madoura any more. The things that had made it different from other workshops for all those years – the inspiration, the spirituality, the sense of a sacred place – all that had gone." Picasso's widow Jacqueline held the next major exhibition of Picasso's pottery at Sassi's showroom rather than Ramié's.

Ten years ago, Alain Ramié prepared a catalogue of the numbered editions. There is still no sign however of a complete *catalogue raisonné* of Picasso's output at Madoura, capable of fixing the precise number of pieces once and for all. "It's a task I would gladly have undertaken," confesses Dominique Forest, curator of the "Musée de Céramique et d'Art moderne de Vallauris", "but it proved impossible to find a publisher. Picasso has yet to find his way into the public domain and so there are a lot of copyright holders who have to be paid. And his ceramics are spread all over the world, which means tracking them down would take years and cost a publisher a fortune. There is a lot less interest in ceramics in France than the northern European countries. We do have a hard core of collectors, but the public isn't interested. What publisher is going to risk investing in a project like that? It's a shame because in the meantime we only have a very rough idea of what Picasso produced at Madoura. I mentioned a figure of 4,000 pieces, but that's not based on research, it's just the most frequently cited estimate."

FIG. 130 PABLO PICASSO
PICADOR 1960
tile; 15.2 x 15.2 cm
COLLECTION MUSEUM HET KRUITHUIS

FIG. 131 PABLO PICASSO
EL PICADOR 1960
tile; 15.2 x 15.2 cm
COLLECTION MUSEUM HET KRUITHUIS

Dominique Forest was appointed curator of the Vallauris museum four years ago, since when she has staged the exhibitions "Artists and Sculptors' Ceramics" in 1995 and "Pots and Pans. Culinary Pottery from Vallauris" in 1996. The more recent show focused on the many generations that from time immemorial had turned the village on the Mediterranean coast into one of the world's leading centers for the production of earthenware for the kitchen. The 1995 exhibition explored the rebirth of the old cookware industry just after the Second World War, when its survival prospects were starting to look bleak. It was rescued by a generation of artists who made soup bowls from which people no longer wanted, dared or indeed were able to eat. Artisanship became art. The exhibitions led to the publication of a few modest books and Forest already has another show in mind for the year 2000. "So much research still needs to be done. For instance, we have to study the more decorative kind of pottery that was already being produced in Vallauris alongside purely functional goods at the end of the last century. This work has not received the attention it deserves."

In her award-winning *L'Age d'Or de Vallauris* (1995) Anne Lajoix expresses surprise at the fact that no basic works have yet been written about developments in Vallauris before the "golden age" that she explores in her book, which was in turn the first major publication to look at the period. *L'Age d'Or* includes a biographical list of the other artists who, less famously than Picasso, helped revive the ceramic industry in Vallauris. Despite the hundreds of witnesses she interviewed over a four year period, Lajoix is the first to admit that her encyclopaedia of forgotten souls is not complete. Unfortunately it is also occasionally sloppy. She gives the impression for instance that Georges Ramié, who has been dead for a quarter of a century, is still with us.

Suzanne Douly studied decorative art and ceramics at the "Ecole des Beaux-Arts" in Lyon in 1922-26. She was working as a designer for the Gilet silk factory when she met Georges Ramié. The silk industry was badly hit by the general economic crisis at that time and so in 1936 the couple moved to Vallauris, where Suzanne became assistant to a ceramist called Chiapello. Two years later Douly and Ramié set up their own workshop, which they called "Madoura" (a combination of their names). Suzanne began to make pottery of her own.

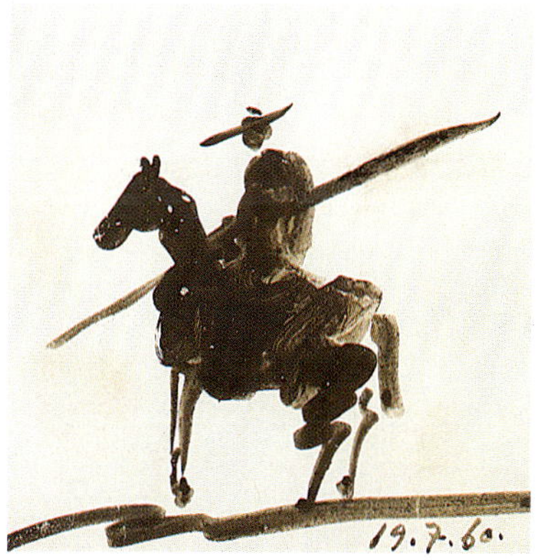

FIG. 130

FIG. 131

Her early work was highly traditional and *provençal* but she subsequently began to rethink everyday utensils in a considerably more modernist idiom. There wasn't exactly a fortune to be made in Vallauris when she set out on her own. The focus in the village was still on industrial ceramic production, which was halted by a strike in the year of the Ramiés' arrival. The newspaper *L'Eclaireur* was in no doubt as to the cause of the trouble: "Our once-flourishing pottery industry is withering rapidly. No fewer than 25 of the 33 factories that used to operate here have closed their doors and things are going from bad to worse for the remaining eight." *Les Echos de Vallauris* recorded 60 workshops in 1887 – a spectacular increase on the number half a century earlier. The growth in the average workforce of these operations was no less startling. In 1850 Vallauris' 30 workshops had employed around 180 workers. A quarter of a century later the total workforce had risen beyond the 900 mark.

As competition from metal cookware steadily intensified the manufacturers of Vallauris banded together in conglomerates like "Les Fabricants réunis", the "Société Industrielle" and the "Société Générale." Unfortunately, the revival that occurred during the metal shortage in the First World War proved short-lived and the conglomerates too eventually had to call it a day. The Société Générale went out of business in 1932.

The problems experienced by Vallauris' ceramic industry were not helped by the quality of the local clay, which contains a lot of gypsum, limestone and iron pyrites. These have to be carefully removed before firing as they can cause cracks. Mechanical removal is extremely complex and so the industry in Vallauris was doomed to continue in the old style, with the impurities removed by hand.

What possessed the Ramiés to set up as young artists in the village? Perhaps it was the very fact that the traditional methods were on the brink of dying out, taking the soul, memory and identity of the craft with them. The "Musée National des Arts et Traditions Populaires" opened in Paris a year after the Ramiés' arrival in Vallauris. Georges Henri Rivière was the driving force behind the new institution and a year later he also founded the "Commission Nationale des Arts et Traditions Populaires", complete with an "Office de Documentation Folklorique". According to Anne Lajoix in *L'Age d'Or de*

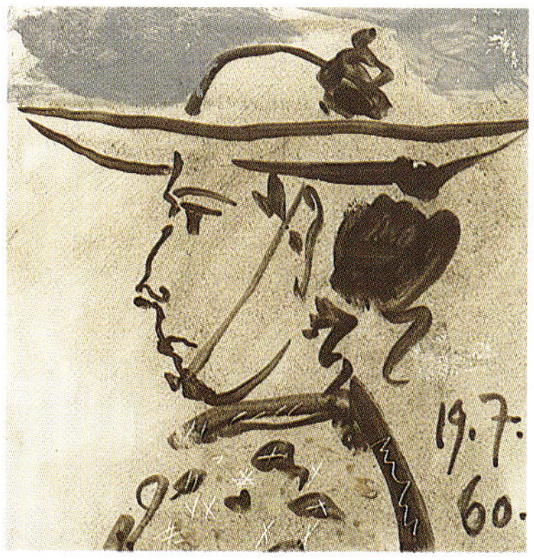

FIG. 132

FIG. 132 PABLO PICASSO
PICADOR 1960
tile; 15.2 x 15.2 cm
COLLECTION MUSEUM HET KRUITHUIS

Vallauris, these developments reflected a broad political movement in pursuit of more far-reaching objectives. Rivière – by no means the first or only one to do so – campaigned for urgent research into a whole range of agricultural and craft traditions threatened with extinction throughout France. Moves towards political centralization and cultural uniformity merely accelerated the process. The first steps to preserve France's rural and craft heritage had been taken by René Guillère, who founded a society for decorative artists in 1901 and artists like Paul Beyer, who settled in Vallauris in as early as 1905. Others moved to Saint-Amand-en-Puissaye, Dieulefit and La Borne. It was only with the approach of the Second World War however that the cult of ruralism and the "terroir national" reached its peak. The organization "Témoignage" (Testimony) for instance was founded in 1936 with Marcel Michaud at its center. Its purpose was to encourage young people to develop an interest in "materials, folklore and provincial mysticism".

Nationalism, centralization and uniformity – fascism in other words – were very much in evidence that July in Picasso's native Spain, where civil war had broken out between the republican government and Franco's fascists. "They kill people here as if felling trees," Saint-Exupéry wrote. Picasso fled Paris and the commotion sparked by news of the war in Spain. He drove his Hispano to the little town of Mougins, near Cannes, and took up residence at the Hôtel Vaste Horizon. He also found his way to Vallauris for the first time, accompanied by Paul and Nush Eluard. The move marked the beginning of a politically charged period in which Picasso was to produce his masterpiece *Guernica* a year later. It culminated in October 1944, a month before the Liberation, when he joined the Communist Party.

To what extent was his conversion to ceramics connected with that to Communism? As far as I am aware no-one has previously linked the two developments. The fact remains however that the ideology of the French Communist Party, which had won the majority of seats on Vallauris' municipal council, still adhered strongly to the notion of the "terroir national" and its attitude towards art remained dominated by the cult of the artisan. Picasso was received with great honor, even though his work had broken every rule of the Socialist Realism art preached by the Communists. "If the artists of the

Soviet Union, the Anglo-Saxon countries and the Latin nations were asked who is the most important artist," wrote *L'Humanité*, the official organ of the French CP, "they would unanimously select Pablo Picasso as the greatest master of contemporary painting." A sudden passion for ceramics, a genre viewed condescendingly by the contemporary avant-garde, provided Picasso with an ideal opportunity to demonstrate how seriously he took his new political allegiance. After all, quite a few people remained to be convinced on that score. There were even persistent rumors that Picasso was a supporter of Franco.

In 1953 Picasso experienced at first hand just how narrowly the leaders of the French Communist Party viewed the principles of Socialist Realism when his *Portrait of Stalin* sparked a furore. He may have wished to make art for the proletariat but he never lost sight of the principles of capitalism. "He once told me about a dream he'd had," recalls Yvan Oreggia, who worked alongside Picasso in the Madoura workshop from 1953 onwards. "He dreamt that he loaded his work onto a donkey, like they did years ago, and traveled from market to market selling his art to ordinary people. To a certain extent that was the motivation behind his serial work. In reality of course everything turned out very differently. The pieces were bought up by dealers and immediately resold in New York for ten times the price. If Picasso caused a revolution it was in the fact that pottery, which used to be sold for pennies, now changes hands for millions."

FIG. 133 VALLAURIS CELEBRATES WITH PICASSO

Picasso wasn't the first artist to settle in Vallauris after the war. He was preceded there by Roger Capron, who studied textile and wallpaper-making at the "Ecole des arts appliqués" in Paris. He had moved to Vallauris in February 1946 – "a year before Jesus Christ", as he put it – together with his classmate Robert Picault. Capron organized birthday parties for Picasso right up to the artist's death, turning the village upside down once a year (fig 133). For Picasso's last party but one he staged a fully-fledged *corrida*, in which bulls were fought and killed in the marketplace, breaking every local bylaw in the book. It was the first and last time, Yvan Oreggia recalls, that a bullfight was allowed in Vallauris. In 1996 it was Capron's own turn to be feted on the fiftieth anniversary of his arrival in the town. He points out that he is probably the longest-serving ceramist of his generation in Vallauris. What's more, he had the largest

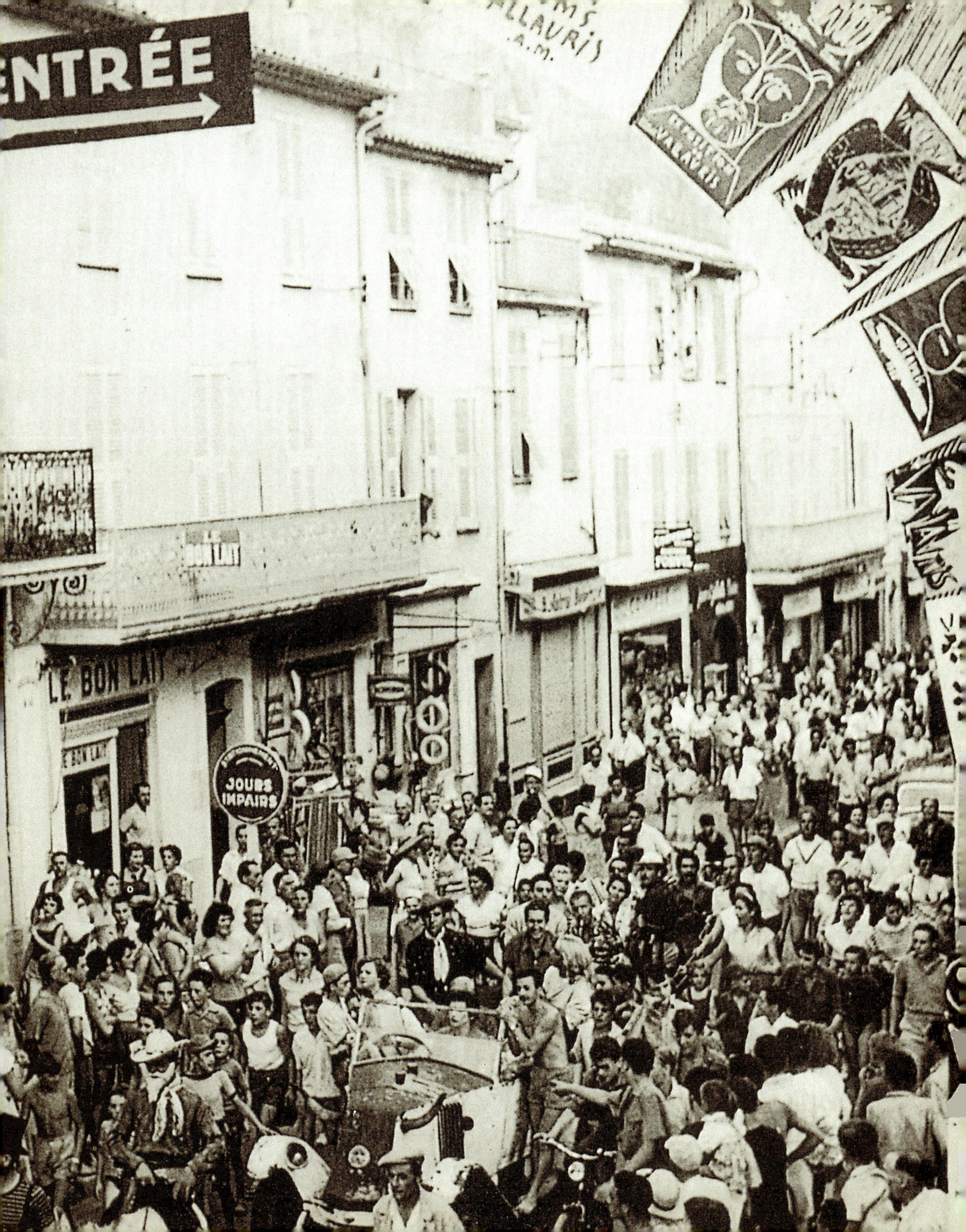
ENTRÉE
LE BON LAIT
LE BON LAIT
JOURS IMPAIRS

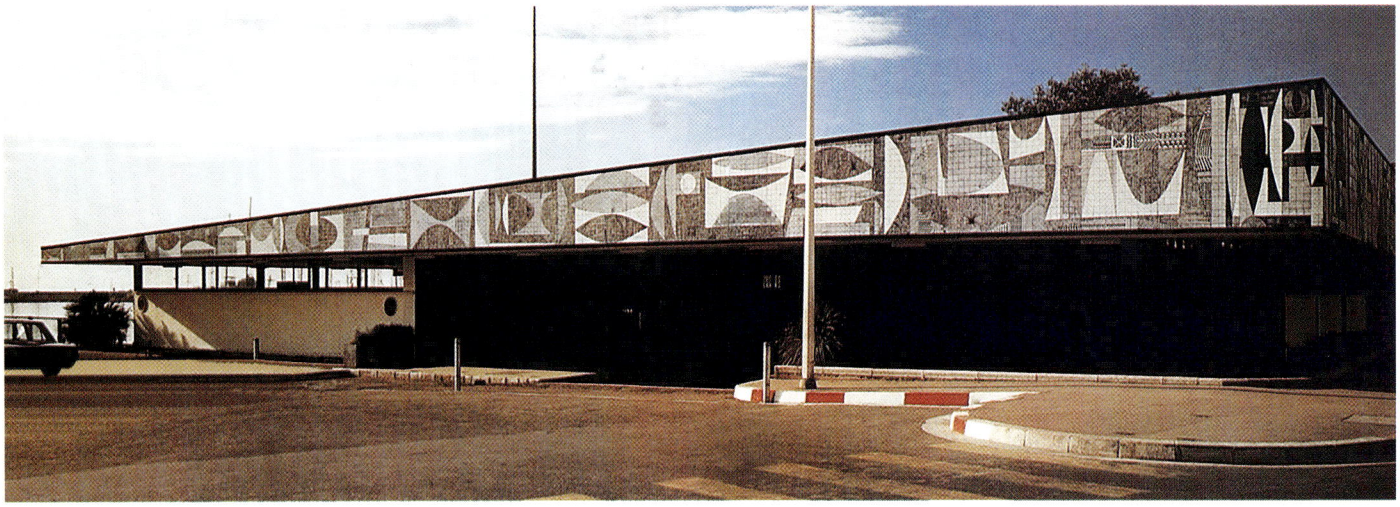

FIG. 134

FIG. 134 Roger Capron
Gare Maritime de Cannes

ceramic business in the village, employing 125 people. And he truly produced art for the people, including 150 square meters of tiling for the eaves of the Gare Maritime railway station in Cannes (fig. 134). When you talk to Capron in person he plays down the noble political explanations put forward for his move to Vallauris: "We just wanted to get away from Paris, to the sunny south of France," Capron confesses as he shuffles over to the table where his assistant, Jean-Paul, is busy working on his next project – tiles decorated with New Year greetings.

Françoise Gilot, Picasso' girlfriend at the time he began working at Madoura, paints a dismal picture of the state of Vallauris' pottery industry immediately after the war. Less than a dozen of the old guard were still at work and these were sorry individuals with nowhere else to go. As Picault recalls they were not quick to welcome the innovators, whom they saw jettisoning long-established traditions without an afterthought. Capron and Picault for instance had brought an electric kiln from Paris. "They'd never seen anything like it in the village," Capron recounts. "If it broke down, we had great difficulty finding someone to repair it." Yvan Oreggia remembers how Capron took twenty girls into the woods to pick flowers. The blooms were rolled into tiles ready for firing, leaving their imprint in the clay. But this kind of novelty was nothing compared to the way Picasso overturned the rules of the potter's craft. "Picasso once made a plate for Suzanne Ramié," Oreggia says, "which he humbly signed: *your pupil Pablo*. But the roles were soon reversed. He did things that we'd been taught to avoid at all cost and they turned out to work extremely well."

Picasso, who was born in Malaga, a town with a long tradition of Hispano-Moorish pottery, was hardly a beginner when he started to work as a ceramist in the Ramiés' workshop. The Kahnweiler collection for instance included a terracotta female mask bearing the date 1908 and there are two vases with the signatures of both Jean Van Dongen (brother of Kees) and Picasso. There is also the story of the 20 ceramic pieces Picasso once showed to the Catalan ceramist Llorens Artigas, who considered them so mediocre that the artist immediately destroyed them.

Artigas had been one of the first ceramists after the First World War to persuade famous artists like Miró, Dufy and Braque to collaborate with him. Picasso's dealer Daniel-Henry Kahnweiler wrote an analysis of the artist's ceramic work in which he argued that since Caravaggio and the seventeenth century painters had lost interest in achieving any kind of synthesis with sculpture and architecture. With one or two proverbial exceptions they preferred to concentrate almost exclusively on the painted canvas. In Kahnweiler's view their mentality arose from a thematic shift. Light, hitherto only a means to an end, now became the painter's ultimate goal.

It was not until the nineteenth century that artists like Renoir, Degas, Gauguin and Daumier began to show a renewed interest in sculpture. The impressionists, by contrast, stuck resolutely to their paintbrushes. Van Gogh, Seurat and even Cézanne experimented with optical perception rather than tangible forms. Only when they were succeeded by the Fauves and the cubists – Matisse, Derain, Braque, Gris and Léger – did a generation arise that viewed ceramics as a medium in which painting and sculpture could be set against one another. The driving force on this occasion was the ceramist André Metthey, who moved to a suburb of Paris in 1903. Matisse, Rouault, Derain and Vlaminck were all encouraged to collaborate with him by their dealer, Amboise Vollard. Like the painters who would subsequently work with Artigas their intervention was limited to painting objects made by the ceramist. The same can be said about the artists who came to work at Vallauris for shorter or longer periods, often at Picasso's urging. Victor Brauner and Amédée Ozenfant for instance restricted themselves largely to decorative work.

That was not the case with Picasso. Although the actual turning was done by the late Jules Agard, until his

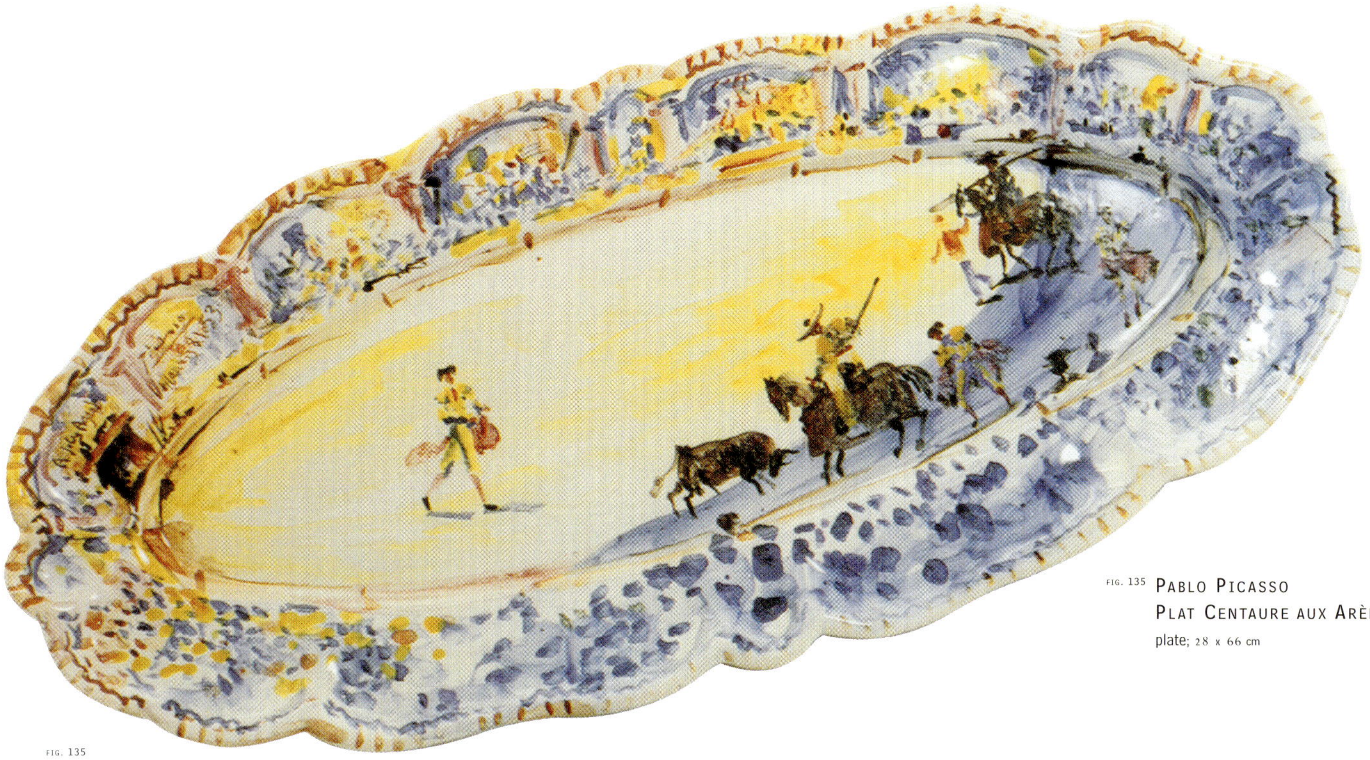

FIG. 135

FIG. 135 PABLO PICASSO
PLAT CENTAURE AUX ARÈNES 1953
plate; 28 x 66 cm

retirement in 1970, and then by his successor Francis Medicis, once this initial stage was complete, Picasso would carve and shape the piece to his heart's content. "His great strength," Yvan Oreggia says "was the way he immersed himself in the volume of the object. He didn't look at a ceramic as just an alternative canvas – a background for another little painting. He could turn a flat plate into a bullfight. The edge became the stand and the middle part the arena (fig. 135). You were drawn into the plate like a spectator. You felt you were inside it rather than just looking at it."

Viewed from a different angle a simple dinner plate becomes a miniature battlefield, a stage for three daily performances of the Theatre of Cruelty. There could hardly be a more apt support for a painting of a bullfight – the perfect metaphor in Picasso's work for the Sadistic Universe. Certain death awaits both the bull and the food on the plate (fig. 136). It isn't the only moment in Picasso's ceramic work when it strikes you that he could not have chosen a better form or material.

There are several widely differing versions of how Picasso first came into contact with the Ramiés. Françoise Gilot recounts in *Life with Picasso* that the artist found his way to their workshop in 1946 virtually by chance. The results of his experiments that July day had no more value to him, she adds, than the doodles he left on restaurant napkins. She implies that it was sheer boredom – even a tour of the *corridas* had failed to spark his interest – that prompted him to accept Suzanne's invitation to return to the workshop a year later to view the results of the first session. Picasso was also keen to keep out of Monsieur Fort's house, where they had also stayed a year earlier, as he was not only accompanied by Françoise this time but by their son and a nanny.

Gilot's account is difficult to square with the fact that between the two visits Picasso produced a great many preparatory drawings for future ceramics. Whatever the reality, Gilot too recalls that what began as something to pass the time soon became a genuine passion. We have already mentioned a few possible motives for this – Picasso's membership of the Communist Party and the widespread craft revival in France. Not to mention pottery's legendary claim to be the oldest of all the arts and the semi-magical powers attributed to it because of its fusing of the four primary elements: water, fire, air and earth. Or the near-alchemy with which it conjures up

FIG. 136 PABLO PICASSO
COGIDA (ED.) 1959
plate; ⌀ 42 cm

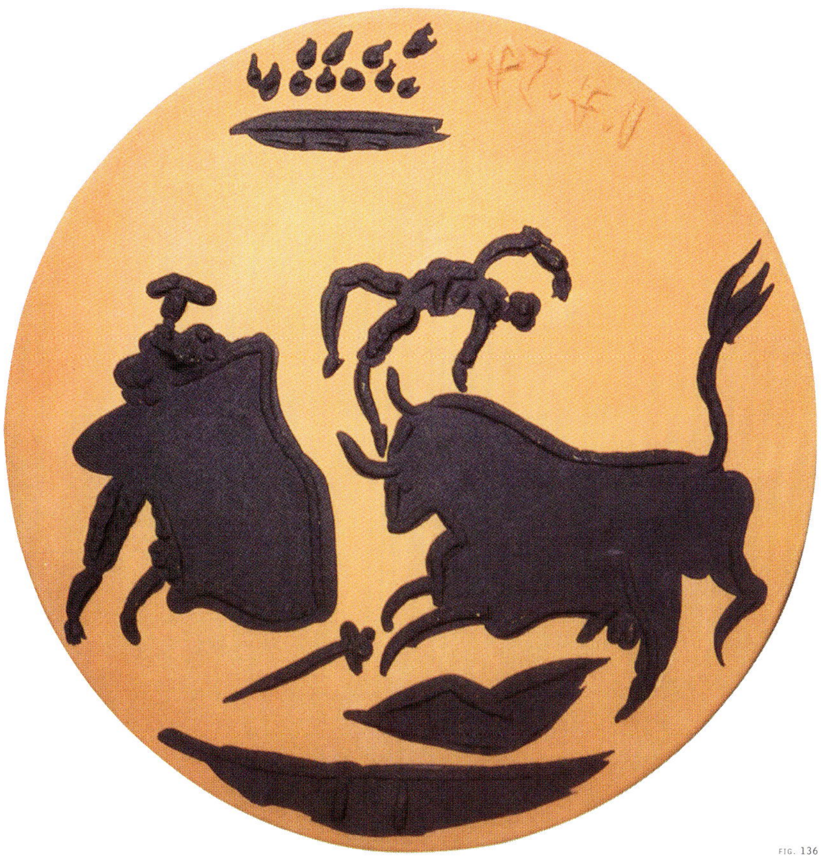

FIG. 136

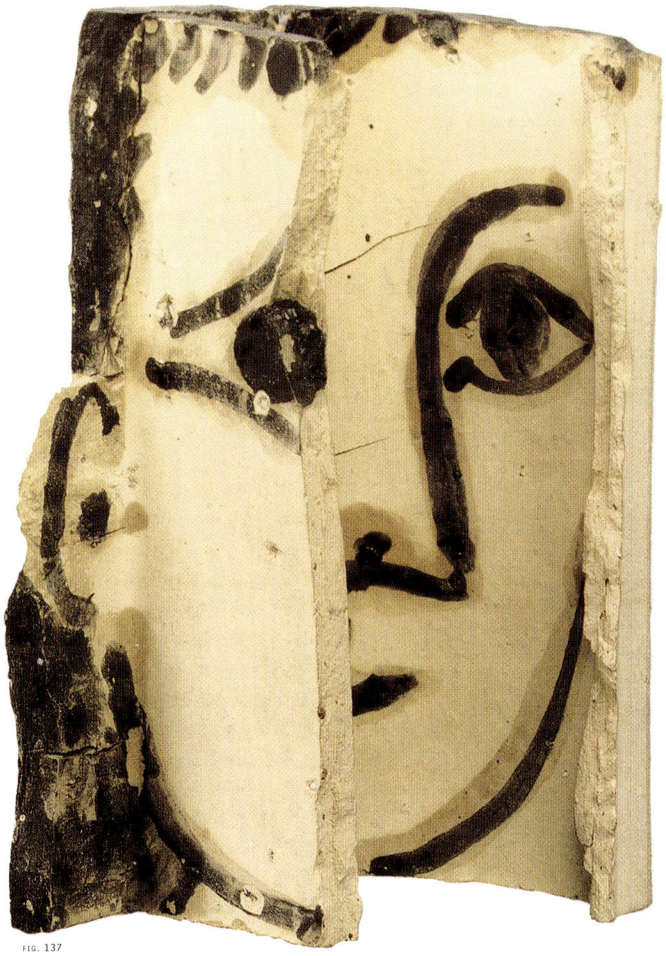

FIG. 137

FIG. 137 PABLO PICASSO
FRAGMENT DE BRIQUE
TÊTE DE FEMME 1962
sculpture
COLLECTION MUSÉE PICASSO, PARIS

colors where none had been before. All of this must have appealed strongly to Picasso, who was fond of working in the heroic jargon of ancient myths and archetypes. Then there was his cubist's passion for translating the Theory of Relativity into practice by setting several views of a single object against one another. Ceramics seemed to offer a more convenient medium with which to achieve this than the abstract white canvas. A sun on a plate can never be interpreted purely as a cosmic force – at the end of the day, it also remains a simple piece of tableware.

Picasso habitually shattered the illusion of verisimilitude embodied by the two-dimensional plane of his paintings by adding three-dimensional objects. Conversely he gave sculptures a deceptive appearance of two-dimensionality. Thanks to its merging of painting and sculpture ceramics was the ideal medium in which to continue this joust with the eternally misleading image. Picasso had barely begun work at the Madoura workshop when he told the sculptor Henri Laurens: "You have to get into ceramics. It's marvelous! I made a head that you can view from any angle and it always stays flat. I painted it and it's the paint of course that makes it seem flat (fig. 137). What do people actually look for in a painting? Depth and as much space as possible. What you should try to achieve in a sculpture is to make it seem flat from every angle."

"What you're asking isn't very nice, *monsieur.*" A little more wrangling however and Alain agrees to take us from the showroom to the actual workshop. He brings out a large photograph in which Picasso and Chagall are shown fraternally engrossed in some ceramic problem. The pieces in the photo have gone as has the atmosphere of panic that used to grip the workshop whenever Picasso drove up and Chagall had to be hustled out through the side door. Otherwise, nothing seems to have moved a millimeter. Even the layer of grayish dust that has settled on everything in the picture, under the watchful eye of Saint Claude, the patron saint of potters, seems to have been carefully preserved.

Picasso continued to work at Madoura with virtually the same team until his death – Suzanne Ramié, Agard and a team of three assistants, the most important of whom were Dominique Sassi, Yvan Oreggia and Jean Ramié. "Without wishing to brag it wasn't just any old potter who was chosen," Yvan Oreggia points out. "The same goes for the artists who wanted to work with us. They had to pass a kind of exam. I was selected at the 'Ecole de céramique', where Madame Ramié chaired the jury. And it is safe to say that there has never been a better turner in Vallauris than Agard."

Numbered, serial work was just one of the innovations Picasso introduced to the field of ceramics. "The series were partly intended as a kind of compensation," explains Dominique Sassi. "During his visits, Picasso often helped himself to pieces that Suzanne Ramié had produced for herself. He took the newly turned, malleable ceramics and reshaped them as he saw fit. It meant we ran into difficulties from time to time with our own production. Picasso worked extremely fast and could easily use up 50 pieces in the space of a few hours. Chagall was totally different (fig. 139). He sometimes spent hours brooding over a single piece. Chagall had a tendency to keep on adding, even though the essence of good ceramics is actually spontaneity and simplicity. I always felt Chagall was afraid of fixing the definitive form of a piece. He also had problems with colors, which are transformed during firing. You have to be something of a visionary. That was no problem for

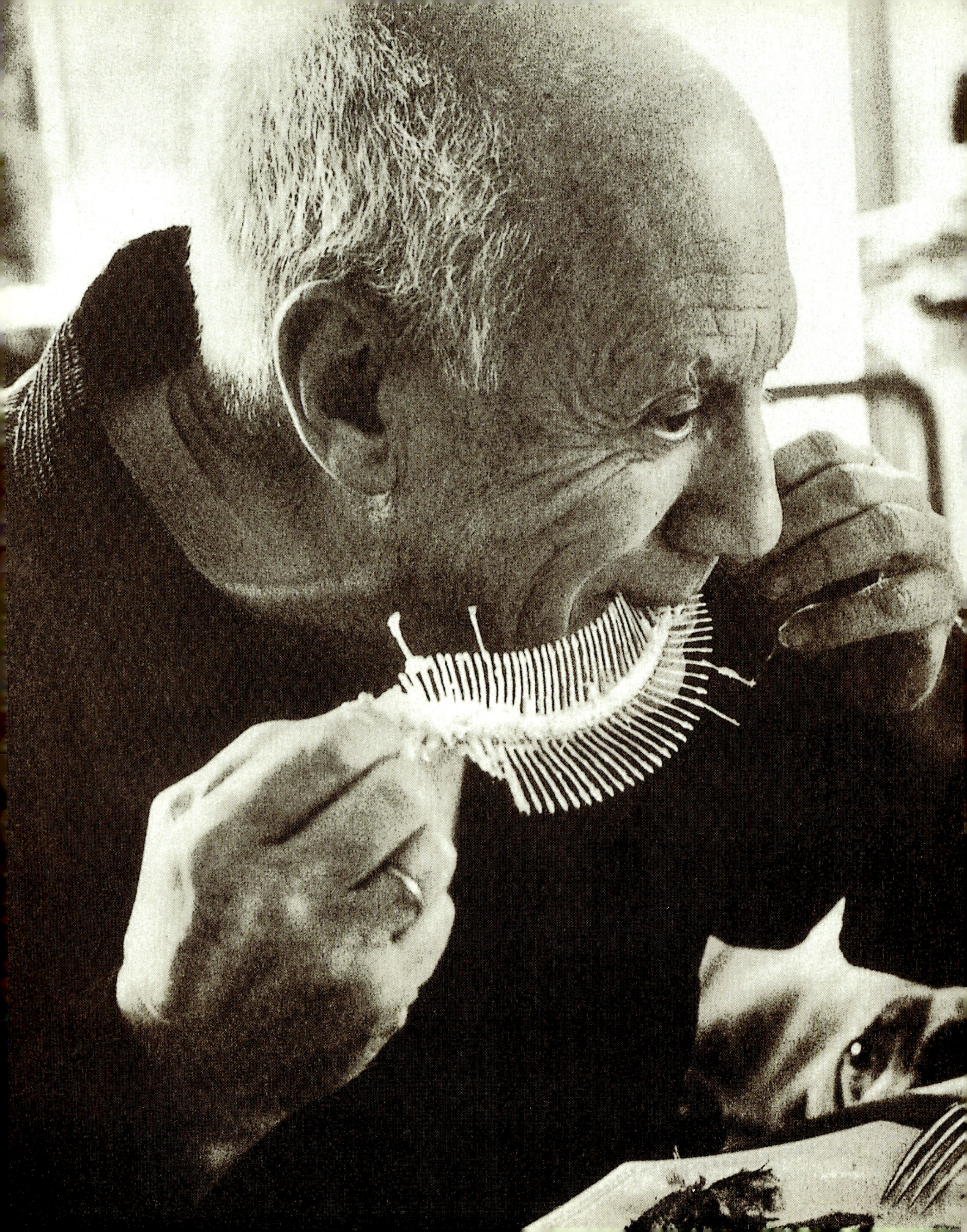

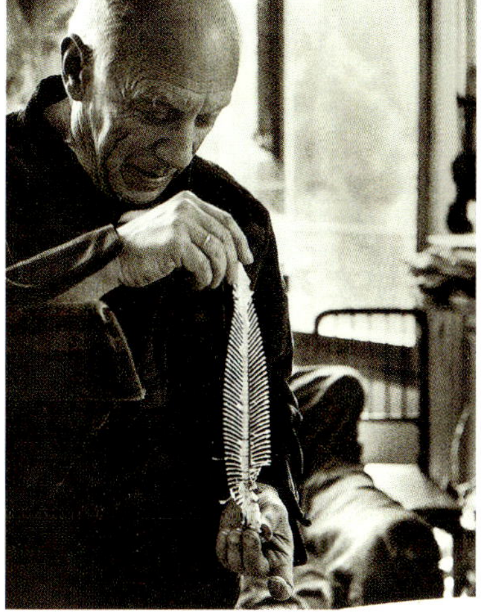

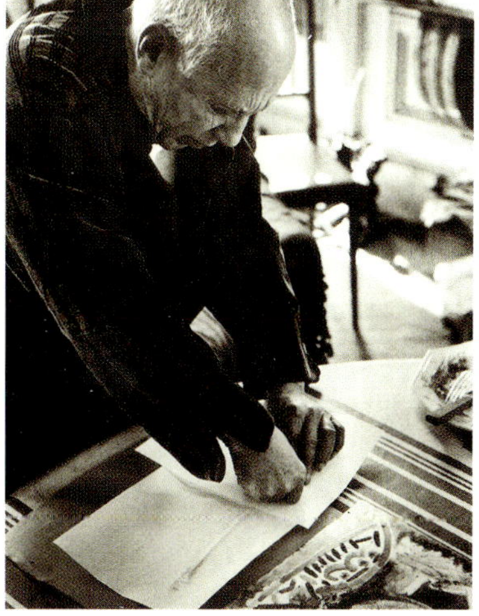

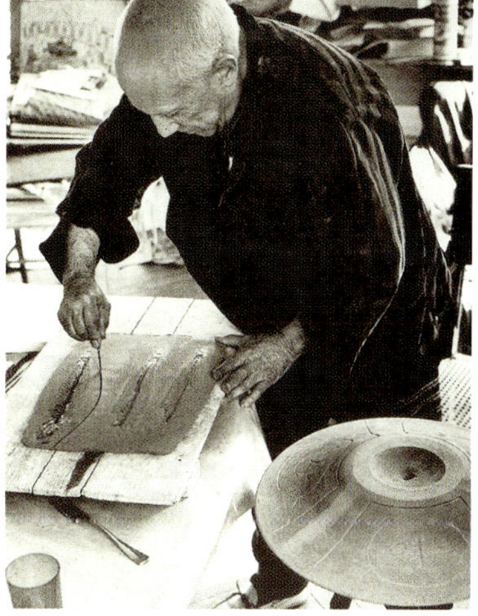

FIG. 138 PABLO PICASSO

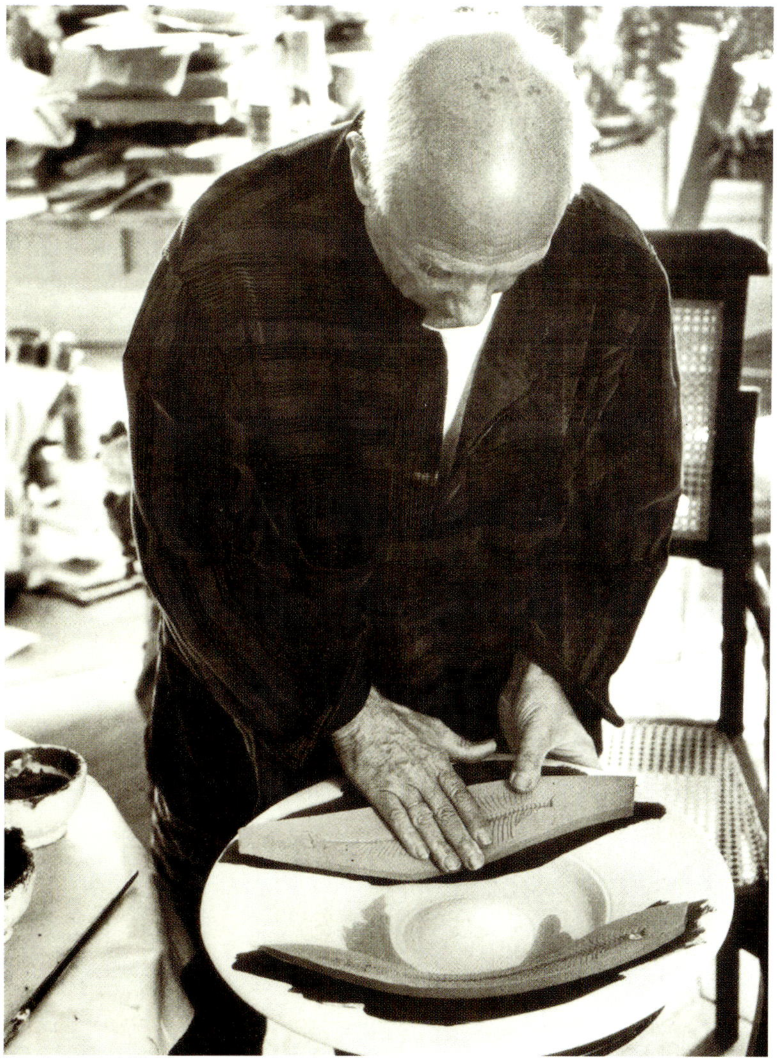

Picasso. No matter how experimental he got he always seemed to have a clear idea in his mind of the final result. When Chagall was here we constantly had to explain what the colors would do. He always forgot things like that, which is obviously a problem for an artist who was first and foremost a colorist."

Some series were made by placing fresh sheets of clay onto a hardened plaster mold. In other cases however there was no option but to make one replica after another of the original figure. It was a hellish task in which Sassi and Oreggia had to transform themselves into Picasso clones. "Only by carefully imitating his cutting and shaping movements could we produce the best possible duplicate of the original work," says Sassi. "We had to try to work with the same speed and aggression as Picasso, which is virtually impossible." (fig. 138)

Picasso had his moods, Yvan recalls, like the time he "accidentally" dropped a particularly attractive plate made by another artist. Otherwise, he doesn't have a bad word to say about the master. It is telling however that according to Sassi even Jacqueline, whom Picasso met when she was working as a saleswoman at Madoura and who was to take Francoise's

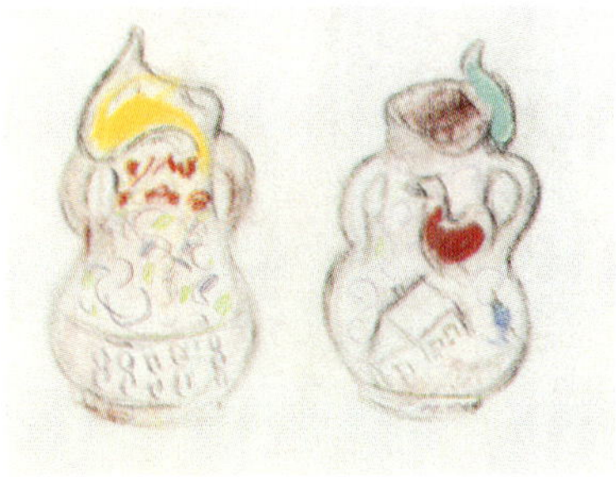

FIG. 139

FIG. 139 MARC CHAGALL
L'ANE BLEU (+ SKETCHES) 1954
vase; 31.5 x 22 cm

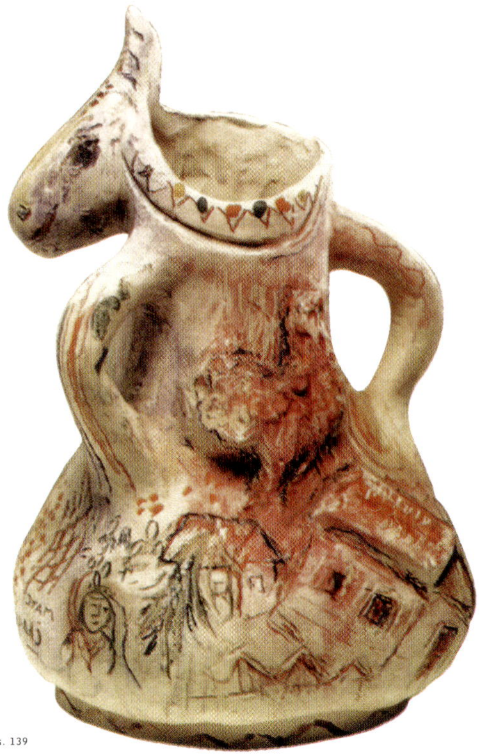

FIG. 139

PABLO PICASSO AND MARC CHAGALL 1955

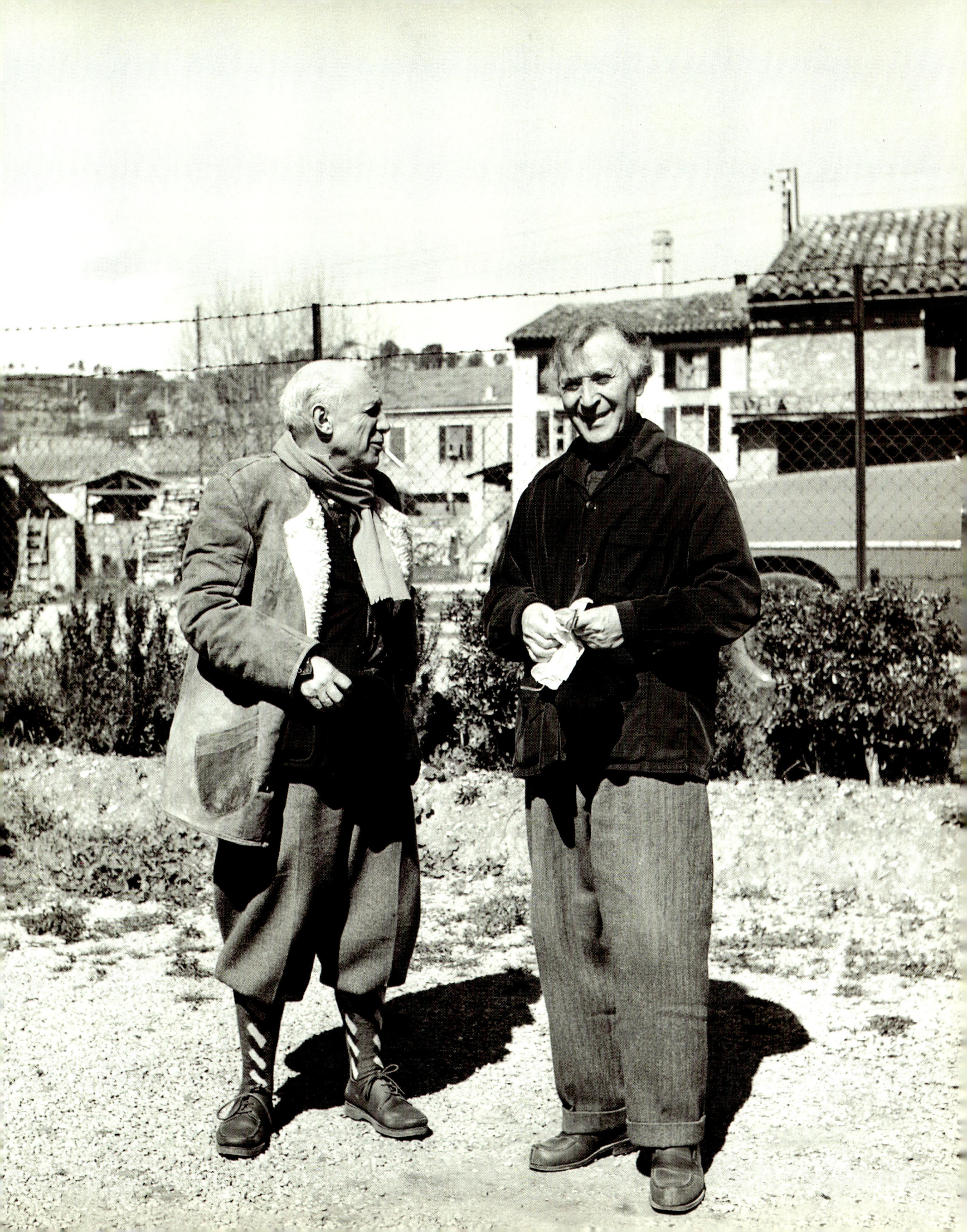

place, habitually addressed him as "Monseigneur". "Collaboration of that kind can only work if everyone knows their place. Things start to go wrong the second a craftsman tries to take the artist's place or to work as his equal. There were crazy Spanish scenes every time Picasso arrived. But then it was time to work – in silence – until he'd had enough after a few hours and headed down to the beach. He asked our advice from time to time, but we all knew his decisions didn't really depend on it."

Picasso died in 1972 and was followed two years later by Suzanne Ramié. Georges died in turn in 1976. It was as if they suddenly had no reason to go on living. These days Roger Capron works in a small studio accompanied only by his faithful assistant Jean-Paul. His business, which once employed 125 people, was forced to close back in 1982. He still has a fair number of exhibitions, he says, including one in Germany, and a few years ago he received a commission from Saudi Arabia for a ceramic panel covering an area of 100 square meters. At the age of 75 he is still one of the few artists in Vallauris whose name is mentioned from time to time outside the village. Most of the ceramists who came to settle in Vallauris in steadily dwindling groups have since been more or less forgotten – a situation not entirely undeserved. The style of their work is *picassiette* at best. It is almost impossible nowadays to find a piece with even a modicum of quality in the boutiques along Avenue Georges Clemenceau. The large flowerpots that line the avenue were made in another village – yet another sign that the inhabitants of Vallauris have lost faith in local production.

It is not entirely clear how often Chagall returned to Madoura after his initial collaboration with the Ramié family in 1947. What we do know is that he exhibited work in Madoura's gallery in Cannes in 1962. Dominique Sassi estimates that he produced around 500 pieces. Most of the well-known artists, among them Victor Brauner, who came to Vallauris to produce ceramics, some of them at Picasso's invitation, stayed for considerably shorter periods. In 1948, when Matisse was looking for a workshop to help him decorate the Chapelle du Rosaire in Vence, he was quick to scratch Madoura from his list. Artists like André Verdet and the Algerian Baya worked there, as, briefly, did poets like Pierre Reverdy, Paul Eluard and Jean Cocteau, who left behind a few plates bearing a poem or a profile. Apart from Madoura, artists without workshops of their

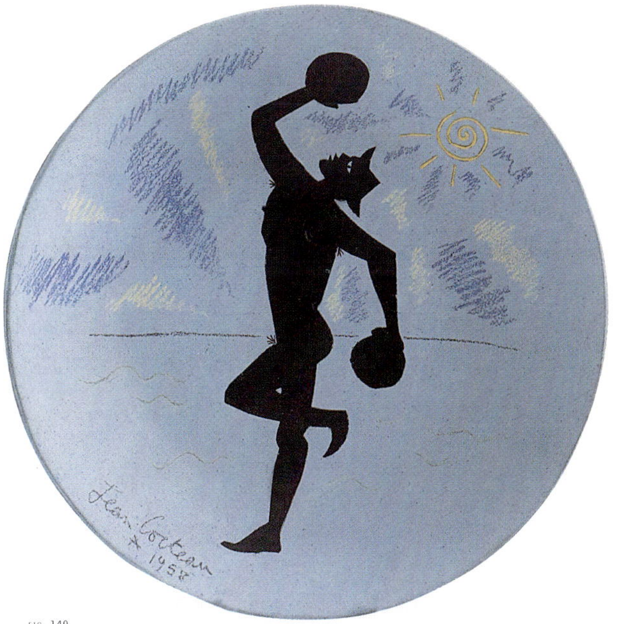

FIG. 140

FIG. 140 JEAN COCTEAU
CONTRE-JOUR (ED. 11/30) 1958
plate; ○ 32 cm
COLLECTION MUSEUM HET KRUITHUIS

own headed mainly for René Batigne and Claire Voight's "Ateliers du Tapis Verts", which operated from 1950 to 1965. The Romanian transvestite Anton Prinner used that workshop to incise the Tarot and other motifs on plates. When it closed down, he returned permanently to Paris.

Dominique Forest certainly hasn't lost heart. She is about to embark on a project to bring an international group of young artists to come and work for a while in Vallauris. "It's really striking how the name 'Vallauris' still has a kind of mythical resonance for young people." Others are somewhat less enthusiastic, among them Alain Ramié. His workshop recently ceased production – permanently he says. He then adds, as if he had a score to settle with a past that had made him a hostage to ceramics for so long, "I'm going to sell it. And I promise you I'm going to make absolutely sure the buyer has nothing to do with pottery." The little smile that plays on his lips means you never know whether he's being serious. "Am I sorry? Not a bit. Everything has to come to an end, *monsieur*, even a sacred place."

BIBLIOGRAPHY

Daix, Pierre, *Dictionnaire Picasso*, Robert Laffont, Paris, 1995
Forest, *Dominique et al., Vallauris, Céramiques de peintres et de sculpteurs*, Réunion des musées nationaux, Paris, 1995
Forest, Dominique *et al., Pignates et Poêlons, Poterie culinaire de Vallauris*, Réunion des musées nationaux, Paris, 1996
Gilot, Françoise and Carlton Lake, *Life with Picasso*, Anchor Books, New York, 1989.
Kahnweiler, Daniel-Henry, "Picasso als Keramiker" in: *Picasso-Keramik*, Stadtmuseum Siegburg-Rheinlandia Verlag, Siegburg, 1992
Lajoix, Anne, *L'Age d'Or de Vallauris*, Les éditions de l'amateur, Paris, 1995
Ramié, Alain, *Picasso, catalogue de l'oeuvre céramique édité 1947–71*, Madoura, Vallauris, 1988.
Ramié, Georges, *Céramiques*, Verve, 1951, vol. iii, no. 25–26
Ramié, Georges, Picasso: *céramiques*, Hazan, Paris, 1962
Ramié, Georges, *Ceci est notre témoignage*, Madoura, Vallauris, 1971
Ramié, Georges, *Céramiques de Picasso*, Cercle d'art, Paris, 1974

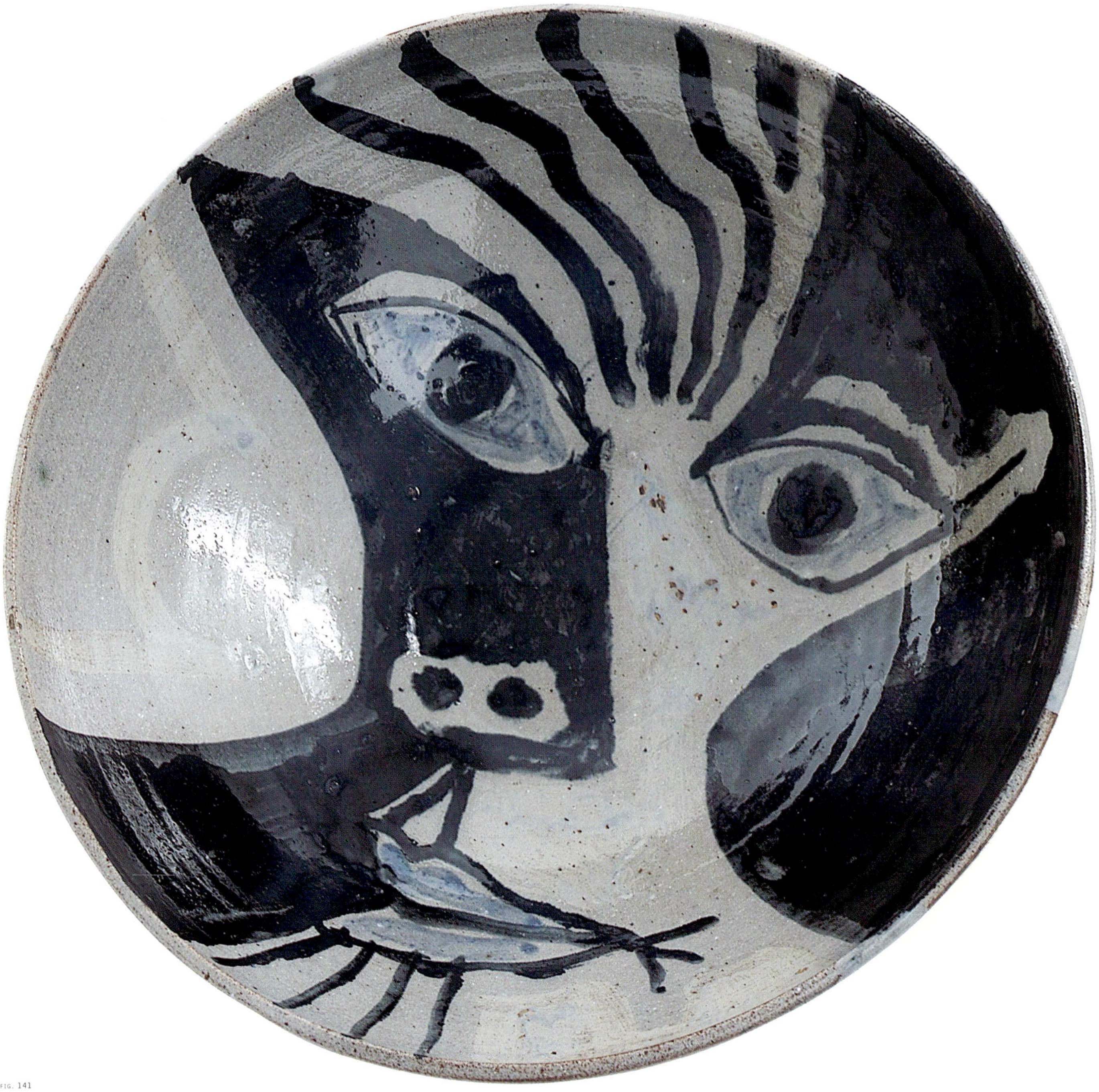

FIG. 141

FIG. 141 LUCEBERT
UNTITLED CA. 1951
plate; ø 26.5 cm
COLLECTION MUSEUM HET KRUITHUIS

COBRA and ceramics

by Willemijn Stokvis

Those familiar with the ideals and spontaneity of expression of the so-called "experimental artists" who formed the international COBRA movement will not be surprised to learn that they produced (and in some cases continue to produce) ceramic work. After all, they recognised no limits to the means and materials through which they sought to express themselves. These Danish, Belgian and Dutch artists put their names to the founding manifesto of the newly-formed group at the café Notre Dame in Paris on 8 November 1948. Their most important stated aim was to collaborate with one another in practice. They were motivated by the desire to clear a path not only for their own creative drive, but also for that of ordinary people, or humanity in general. A Marxist vision of the future ran through their ideas and actions like a thread.

The old wish, first expressed in Great Britain in the middle of the previous century by John Ruskin and William Morris, that every person should be involved creatively with their environment, and should surround themselves with self-made objects rather than industrial products, seemed to have taken on a new shape in this movement[1]. Like their nineteenth-century forebears, the COBRA artists – or rather those who acted as the movement's theoretical mainspring – longed to revive

1 The Dane Asger Jorn, the prime mover behind the Cobra movement, felt a very direct attraction to Ruskin's ideas. He expressed this in articles like: 'Forme et structure – sur le culte du "nouveau" dans notre siècle' and 'Misère et merveille – sur le role de l'extrémisme dans le développement culturel', pp. 33–42 and 43–48 respectively in Pour la Forme - ébauche d'une méthodologie des arts, Ed. Internationale Situationniste, Paris, 1958, (a publication that will be referred to several terms in the context of this article). See also in this respect: Graham Birtwistle, 'From Ruskin to Jorn', in ANUS QUADRIGA MUNDI, Opstellen over middeleeuwse kunst opgedragen aan Prof. dr. Anna Esmeijer, Walburg Pers, 1989, pp. 31–48.

popular creativity. However, their enemy was not so much industry, as the straitjacket of academic convention in western art. In words that echoed Jean Jacques Rousseau's "back to nature" call, they wished to return "to the fountainhead, the natural state, in which every person decorated their surroundings as they saw fit". Certain COBRA members have filled many pages with the theories of a movement that ostensibly wished to have none.

To my mind, however, the most immediate source of the immense vitality that characterised the COBRA group is not to be found in this theory. It derived instead from the fact that the movement happened to bring together a number of highly talented individuals at a moment when immense expectations were still cherished with regard to the future. As far as their desire to practise "all branches of art" was concerned, the COBRA artists had numerous predecessors in the immediate past. Not only had painting, sculpture and poetry been closely interwoven in the twentieth century's various avant-garde movements prior to 1940, the applied arts too had been given plenty of attention. And not merely in the form of "better design" for industry, but also in a more innocent and spontaneous way, as in the case of the French Fauves. These were the first generation of twentieth-century artists to become involved, at the behest of a ceramicist in around 1907, with the painting of pottery[2]. Similar activities were also engaged in by members of the German Expressionist group "Die Brücke".

It was precisely these avant-garde movements that enjoyed a strong revival in interest in the immediate postwar period because of the freedom of expression that they represented, in sharp contrast to the traditional, hidebound character of the recently defeated enemy. At the very pinnacle was the dazzling talent of Pablo Picasso, who was, perhaps, also the most direct inspiration for the explosion of spontaneous creativity on the part of the COBRA artists, who "devoured every material". His reputation as a potter spread quickly after 1947 when his prolific output helped breath new life into the old Vallauris pottery on the French Riviera. Even before Picasso, though, Miró – a crucial influence on the COBRA artists – had embarked on the same path. Both of these artists, and Léger too in subsequent years, fashioned in clay the forms that they

2. See Daniël-Henri Kahnweiler: Picasso, Keramic/Ceramic/Céramique, Hannover, 1957, p. 14.

later painted. Their nineteenth-century predecessor in this was the great French artist Paul Gauguin.

Poets painted and painters wrote poetry in the COBRA movement. They made objects and sculptures, and it is thus unsurprising that when the opportunity arose, they also produced pottery.

First principles

Before discussing the ceramic work of COBRA artists, I would first like to present a specific vision, to justify the application of the term "COBRA ceramics". As it had been for the Surrealists, theory was an important element for COBRA, probably forming the key impetus behind the initial foundation of the group and its subsequent unity. Another element was the style which the artists developed in their work, and which is considered "typically COBRA". In my view, it is above all this individual manner of expression that lends COBRA its weight in the history of twentieth-century art. This approach – a principal characteristic of which is the free rein given to the imagination, allowing fantastic creatures to arise from the interplay of lines and spots, with the art of "primitive" and naive artists, children and the mentally-ill serving as a key source of inspiration – was already visible in the work of several Danish artists in around 1938–39. In the COBRA years 1948–51, it took the form of an international experiment, before subsequently evolving into a grand style, from which the childlike, fairy-tale element gradually disappeared. Spot and line merged into dramatic movement in the paint, through which demonic beings were now invoked. This later development of the "COBRA jargon" in particular was to have a deep influence in many countries.

Having briefly sketched out the evolution of this "jargon" – created by associated artists during COBRA's international zenith, 1948–51 and afterwards, but also to a significant extent in previous years – I now feel justified in using the term "COBRA art"[3].

The highpoint of what might be called "COBRA ceramics" occurred in 1954, a few years after the disbanding of the movement, at the Italian craft centre Albisola. In the context of a collaborative ceramic experiment, earlier COBRA ideals were,

3. For a fuller account of this "Cobra jargon", see my dissertation "Cobra, geschiedenis, voorspel en betekenis van een beweging in de kunst van na de Tweede Wereldoorlog, Amsterdam", 1974, pp. 155–164.

in a sense, put into practice once again. This was not, however, the first time that COBRA artists had experimented in this field.

Dutch "Experimentalists" and pottery

In the early autumn of 1948, shortly after they had set up their "Experimentele Groep in Holland", and just before the foundation of COBRA, the painters Appel, Constant, Corneille and Rooskens were given the opportunity of trying their hand at pottery at the "Russel-Tiglia" ceramic factory in Tegelen. The manager of the factory's pottery department, G. Goossens, was a childhood friend of Anton Rooskens (originally from Limburg), and enjoyed giving artists the chance to experiment with pottery. Rooskens had done so before with the artists Frieda Hunziker, Ger Gerrits and Harry van Kruiningen, fellow associates of "Vrij Beelden" – a rival avant-garde movement to the "Experimentele Groep in Holland" – which had been founded in 1947[4]. "The workers at the factory used to call our department 'the circus'", Rooskens has said of this early "COBRA project" in around September 1948[5]. Between 23 October and 4 November that year, an exhibition of drawings and pottery by Appel, Constant and Corneille was held at the Van Lier gallery on Amsterdam's Rokin. The three "figureheads" of Dutch COBRA visited Tegelen again separately a little later, probably in the course of 1949. "They spent a fortnight working there, and it was then that they made the best stuff", Rooskens recalls[6].

Although the artists themselves refer to "ceramic experiments", their contribution consisted primarily of the painting of plates, vases and dishes that had already been made in the factory. They only ventured to produce a very few clay objects themselves. Constant, for instance, turned a small vase. For the most part, these ceramic products are not dated, and, in my view, the rare publications that reproduce any of them often give incorrect dates. The plates and a number of vases with more abstract motifs are likely to have been produced in 1948. Sixteen items by Appel, including a teapot, are

4. See op. cit. (note 3), p. 74 and p. 74, note 9; also Isabel Brouwer and Willemijn Stokvis, 'De kunstenaarsgroep Vrij Beelden', in W. Stokvis (ed.), De doorbraak van de moderne kunst in Nederland, Amsterdam, 1984, pp. 148 and 154; Mieke Spruit-Ledeboer, Nederlandse keramiek 1900–1975, Assen/Amsterdam, 1977, p. 37, and Arjan Moscoviter, Schilderskeramiek in Nederland - Een onderzoek naar het ontstaan, de aard, de receptie en de betekenis van de Nederlandse keramiek in deze eeuw, (unpublished doctoral thesis, Leiden, 1991), p. 26.
5. See Anton Rooskens, 'De a van Cobra', in the catalogue Anton Rooskens 1949 Cobra 1951, Galerie Delta, Rotterdam, Dec. 1963–Jan. 1964, (not numbered), p. 4.
6. He told me this in 1965. See op. cit. (note 3), p. 74, note 9.

reproduced in the book *Karel Appel, street art, ceramics, sculptures, etc.*, published in New York in 1985, which states that they were created in 1947–48. The imaginary figures that so characterised COBRA will first have appeared on plates painted for the most part in 1949, just as they were being developed at length in the artists' free work[7].

Appel again worked in Tegelen during the summer of 1954. In addition to painting a number of plates, there he also managed to produce a series of terracotta sculptures - variations on the human head, partly painted in black and white and partly left without color[8].

Lucebert, whose brief involvement with COBRA was primarily as a poet, and whose paintings drew unmistakably upon the "COBRA jargon", especially after 1960, came to paint pottery in the years 1950–52 via a wholly different route. He was closely involved at that time with the poet Bert Schierbeek, whose wife, Frieda Koch, was a ceramicist. Lucebert was quickly smitten by Frieda, who had christened her studio "U.R.N." and signed her ceramic products on the base with the initials F.S.K.U.R.N. He dedicated several of his hand-made poetry anthologies from that period, illuminated with his own drawings or collages, to her[9]. He also focussed his urge to draw and paint onto dishes and vases made by Frieda. For the most part, the motifs with which he decorated her pottery are clearly influenced by Picasso and Miró. He also made his own small clay figures on one occasion: an example of this often difficult-to-trace pottery is a coloured and glazed relief by Lucebert dating from 1952, that depicts a little owl[10].

Freestanding, imaginary creatures in clay or plaster were produced by a variety of COBRA-related artists, even during the movement's existence. Appel, for instance, began to make little figures in 1950, in both clay and plaster, painting the latter with patches of colour[11]. Corneille had been making

7. Not all the plates were dated.
8. Some of this work was reproduced in Karel Appel, street art, ceramics, sculptures, wood reliefs, tapestries, murals, villa el Salvador, (texts by Pierre Restany and Allen Ginsberg; interview by Frédérique Towarnicki), New York, 1985.
9. See the catalogue Lucebert in het Stedelijk, Stedelijk Museum Amsterdam, 1987, p. 81 under: I Unica. (Two are dedicated to 'Fried and Bert', one to 'Fried' and two to 'f.d.', or Frieda Diotima (the name of the beloved of the German poet Friedrich Hölderlin, whom Lucebert admired so much). The joint prose experiment Chambre-Antichambre, which Lucebert and Schierbeek published under the pseudonyms 'Oog van Gol' and 'Lilithoog' in the course of 1950 in the magazines Braak and Podium, and which was subsequently reprinted by BZZTÔH in The Hague in 1978, clearly takes their mariage à trois as its starting point.
10. Some documentation regarding this little owl and a number of Frieda Koch ceramic pieces painted by Lucebert, can be found in the archive of the Lucebert expert and collector, C. Groenendijk in Amsterdam (which is now - after his death - in the Stedelijk Museum in Amsterdam)
11. See op.cit. (note 8), ill. 155, 159 and 160.

plaster figures since 1948[12]. However, these forms of artistic expression in plaster or clay are better categorised as "COBRA sculpture". Clay was the most important medium of expression in those years for the sculptor/painter Lotti van der Gaag, who joined the COBRA circle in late 1950. Her uncoloured terracotta figures were actually intended for casting in bronze, which occurred in some cases, but only many years later, when the opportunity arose. (The precise location of the borderline between ceramic work and sculpture is a problem that I will not attempt to solve in this article, in which I have been asked to discuss COBRA ceramics. It ought to be stressed, however, that a good deal of this pottery work could be placed equally well under the heading "COBRA sculpture").

FIG. 142 ASGER JORN, ALBISOLA 1954

JORN, THE "COBRA POTTER" PAR EXCELLENCE (fig. 142)

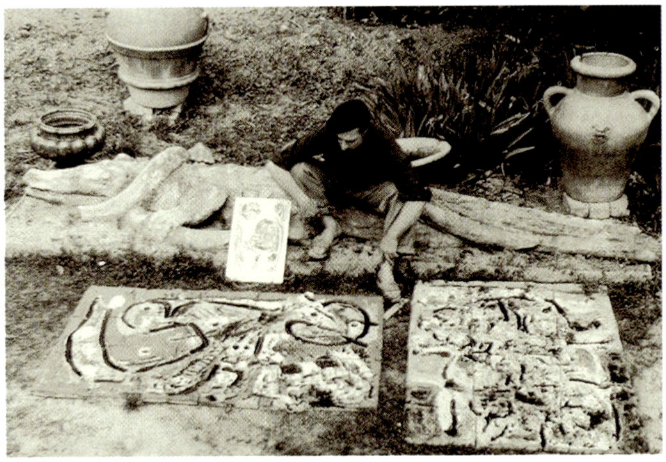

FIG. 142

The COBRA artist most intensively involved with ceramic work – which was to become an important part of his total oeuvre – was also the man who may be viewed as the great inspirational force behind the movement: the Dane Asger Jorn. He began to produce pottery in the years after the dissolution of COBRA, a period in which he was confronted by ill-health, and had to spend seventeen months in the sanatorium at Silkeborg, the small town where he spent his youth.

He had been active in the workshop of the famous Danish potter Niels Nielsen as early as 1933, where he produced, amongst other things, a small female nude that recalls the early sculptures of Matisse[13]. During the war, he made six imaginary figures in clay or plaster that may be compared to the mythical creatures that his Danish sculptor colleagues Ejler Bille, Henry Heerup (both of whom were also to become COBRA members) and Robert Jacobsen had been creating in plaster or

12. Corneille found three plaster pieces, two of which date from 1948 and one from 1951, in his sister's attic in the early 1980s, and cast them in bronze at the behest of gallery-owner Herman Krikhaar. Six copies of each were cast (reported by Krikhaar, 18.2.1985).

13. See Asger Jorn 1914–1973, (a catalogue of works in the Silkeborgmuseum), Silkeborg, 1974, ill. 46; also Ursula Lehmann-Brockhaus, 'Chapter 4: Sculpture', in Guy Atkins, Asger Jorn: The final years 1965–1973, London, 1980, p. 77.

stone since the mid-1930s[14]. Jorn was inspired by the free, improvisational way in which his good friend, the ceramicist Erik Nyholm, used colours and glazes, and began to work with clay very intensively from 1953 onwards[15]. He had discovered a field in which he could apply his love of spontaneous working in three dimensions too, thanks to the pliancy of the material, which could be formed into all kinds of textures, and the wealth of opportunities for unleashing colour. He used Nyholm's kiln in Funder, near to Silkeborg, for his *Varyl*, which he made as early as 1952. ("Varyl" is an invented word, consisting of a combination of werewolf and snake). Jorn mastered the craft under Nyholm's teacher, Randlev Pedersen, and went on to produce a great deal of pottery in the workshop of Niels Nielsen in Silkeborg and that of Knud Jensen in Sorring, a small town that has long been Jutland's pottery centre. Jorn was interested above all in the old handicraft, such as he encountered in Jutland. He recorded its methods in his notebooks, and praised it in an article he wrote in 1953 entitled "Indtryk af Silkeborgegnens pottemageri" (Impression of the art of pottery in Silkeborg)[16].

In this period, sponsored by the now enthusiastic Silkeborgmuseum, Jorn covered hundreds of vases, pots and dishes, which Jensen produced from his designs, with coloured sludge. This was on top of the many dishes he decorated at Nielsen's workshop. As his sense of liberation increased, he began to combine added layers of clay (engobes) with the glazes, and to work the surface of his products by scraping, moulding and scratching it.

The Silkeborgmuseum has much of the ceramic work produced in 1953, together with the design sketches. With the

14. For information on Ejler Bille, see: Poul Vad, Ejler Bille, Copenhagen, 1961, and Ejler Bille, 'Kommentar til mine skulpturer' and Ejler Bille and Poul Vad, 'Fortegnelse over skulpturer af Ejler Bille'. Both of the latter articles appeared in Signum, volume one, no. 3, 1961, pp. 3–6 and 7–20; for Henry Heerup see: Preben Wilmann, Henry Heerup, Copenhagen, 1962, and Virtus Schade, Henry Heerup, Copenhagen, 1967; and for Robert Jacobsen: Ernst Mentze, Robert Jacobsen, Copenhagen, 1961.
15. See Ursula Lehmann-Brockhaus in Atkins 1980, op. cit. (note 13) p. 82; also Guy Atkins, Asger Jorn, The crucial years 1954–1964, London, 1977, p. 17 and 18 (it is stated here that Jorn had already experimented with this technique at a pottery workshop during a stay in Djerba, Tunisia, 1947–48). Unless stated otherwise, further details on Jorn's career as a ceramicist are also drawn from the aforementioned books edited by Guy Atkins and published in 1977 and 1980, and from the recent catalogue, Asger Jorn: Keramik, with texts by Erik Nyholm, Troels Andersen and Ursula Lehmann-Brockhaus (ed. Troels Andersen), Badisches Landesmuseum/Silkeborg Kunstmuseum, Karlsruhe/Silkeborg, Aug.–Oct. 1991 (the article by Troels Andersen, 'Das Bild aus Ton – Die Keramiek Jorns 1953–54', pp. 63–75, looks in detail at his early ceramic output). For the ceramicist Erik Nyholm, see also: Erik Nyholm, Arbejieder gennem 40 aar, texts: Per Hojholt, Robert Dahlmann Olsen and Troels Andersen, Silkeborg Kunstmuseum Forlag, 1981.
16. Asger Jorn, 'Indtryk af Silkeborgegnens pottemageri', in the magazine Dansk Kunsthaandvaerk, Copenhagen, XXVII, 1 Jan., 1954, pp. 11–15.

exception of a few freestanding, imaginary figures, like his *Man in the moon*, Jorn remained as faithful as possible to traditional potter's forms, to which he simply applied his "modifications": such as his *Vase-man, Jug-women, Jug animal* and a *Portrait* on an inverted pot[17]. His great example in this enthusiastic outpouring of pottery (which drove Nielsen and Jensen to the brink of exhaustion), was Picasso. He hoped to breathe new life into the old pottery centre in Jutland, just as Picasso had done at the French coastal town of Vallauris[18].

The ceramic event at Albisola (fig. 143)

Shortly afterwards, elsewhere in Europe, and in a wholly unexpected manner, Jorn drew on his now considerable ceramic experience to achieve hitherto unparalleled results. He departed for Switzerland for reasons of health in the autumn of 1953, where he immediately began to develop an entirely new range of activities. He was rendered indignant by the indifference of his new acquaintance, the Swiss architect Max Bill, towards the free arts. Bill denied these a place at his "Hochschule für Gestaltung" in Ulm, Germany, which was instead to concentrate entirely on the "industrial and productive"[19]. As a reaction against this so-called "new Bauhaus", oriented exclusively towards the functional, Jorn set up a "Bauhaus of the Imagination" (un Mouvement International pour un Bauhaus Imaginiste, M.I.B.I.)[20]. The initiative met with great enthusiasm on the part of the Italian artists Enrico Baj, with whom Jorn began an intensive correspondence, and Sergio Dangelo, both members of the avant-garde movement "Arte Nucleare", founded in Milan in 1952, and partially inspired by COBRA. Former members of COBRA, Pierre Alechinsky (Belgium), Karel Appel (the Netherlands), Karl Otto Götz (Germany) and Anders Österlin (Sweden) also supported Jorn's latest venture[21].

17. The first three works referred to here are depicted in Atkins' book (1980) (note 13), namely figs. 102, 104, 105 and 107. The Portrait, which according to Troels Andersen (op. cit. note 15, p. 73) is not a self-portrait, but a depiction of the Italian sculptor Marino Marini, is reproduced in the article by Jorn (note 16) dating from 1954, p. 11.
18. As he enthusiastically explained in the 1954 article (note 16), p. 14 and 15.
19. Op. cit. (note 3), p. 168.
20. His dislike of functionalism had already formed by 1937, when he assisted Le Corbusier in Paris with the decoration of the 'Palais des temps nouveau', at that year's World Exhibition. He dedicated several articles to this dislike during the war: 'Arkitektuur er ikke kunst' (Architecture is not art), in LP & Co. Nyt, volume 2, no. 19, March, 1943, pp. 147–151, and 'Ansigt til ansigt' (Face to face), in A5, Meningsblad for unge arkitekter (Magazine for young architects), vol. 2, no. 5, Copenhagen, Jan./Feb. 1944, pp. 3–26. See also op. cit. (note 3), p. 20 and p. 20, note 5.
21. See Tristan Sauvage (pseudonym of Arturo Schwarz): Art Nucléaire, ed. Villo/Galleri Schwarz, Parigi-Milano, 1962, pp. 23–27.

It was Enrico Baj who first suggested to Jorn the idea of settling at the little coastal town of Albisola, not far from Genoa, which had been a centre of pottery-making for hundreds of years. In this Italian counterpart to Vallauris – with which it had long maintained contacts, exchanging potters and types of clay – Jorn found a house with an old kiln at number six, Via Isola. Jorn was able in Albisola to experiment at length with ceramics, though this occurred not so much at his own kiln, as at the ceramic factory of the leading potter (and poet) Tullio Mazzotti, who called himself "Tullio d'Albisola". The townspeople at that time were more willing than those elsewhere to accept different approaches to their traditional handicraft. Experiments had, after all, been carried out there since the late 1920s, initially by the sculptor Arturo Martini, then by the Futurists, to whom Tullio d'Albisola belonged, and by Agenore Fabbri, Lucio Fontana and Eliseo Salino. On a variety of occasions the potter's craft was effectively abandoned, and the results can only be classified as sculpture[22].

FIG. 143 Asger Jorn, Roberto Matta and a ceramist, Albisola 1954

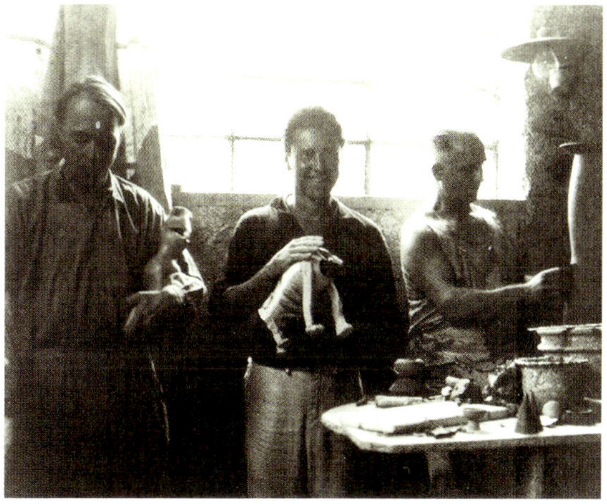

FIG. 143

In the summer of 1954, Jorn organised the first manifestation of his new international movement, the M.I.B.I., in this inspirational environment. It was called "Incontri Internazionale delle Ceramica" (International encounters in ceramics), and enabled participants to engage in collaborative ceramic experiments. The following artists took part in the event, which strongly recalled earlier "COBRA congresses": apart from Baj and Dangelo, the Italians included Emilio Scanavino and Lucio Fontana; Appel and Corneille came from the Netherlands; Matta (Echaurren) from Chile; the writer Theodor Koenig, who had also belonged briefly to COBRA, from Belgium; and from France, the (Canadian) poet and artist Roland Giguère[23] and the poet Edouard Jaguer and his wife (fig. 144). The participants gave their imaginations free rein, and in the "authentic COBRA manner", texts were written on the plates too. Tullio Mazzotti

22. See Ursula Lehmann-Brockhaus, op. cit. (note 15) p. 90 and 92, and the article by the same author entitled 'Incontri internazionale della ceramica, Albissola, Sommer 1954', in the 1991 catalogue cited in note 15, in which the events at Albisola are examined in detail; also Tullio d'Albisola, Amore del 'gran fuoco', Milan, 1963.
23. See Tristan Sauvage, op. cit. (note 21), p. 225.

organised an exhibition of the results of this collective exploration of clay and colour, as a demonstration of the possibilities of his factory. Entitled "Incontro Internazionale dei Ceramisti", it featured work by Appel, Baj, Corneille, Dangelo, Fontana, Jorn, Matta and Scanavino, and was also to be seen in October that year at the tenth Triennale d'Arte in Milan[24]. It also provided Jorn with ammunition for his contribution, entitled "Contre le fonctionalisme", to a debate at the first International Congress for Industrial Design held during the Triennale, where he spoke against Max Bill[25].

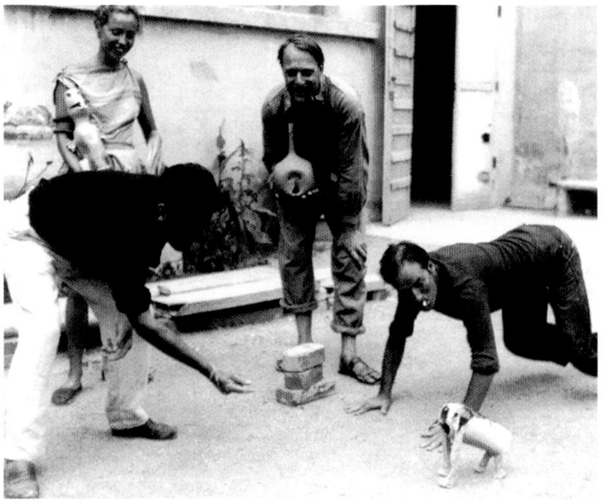

FIG. 144

Karel Appel gave his views on the events at Albisola to Simon Vinkenoog in 1963: "It was like opening the floodgates. We were allowed to make pottery at Mazzotti's factory. Everyone was busy painting pots and plates and vases, but I preferred to hit the bits of clay I pulled out of the dirt with an iron bar. I beat relief animals into the material, and once I had hammered out the shape, I painted it before firing the piece in the kiln. Jorn observed all this, and – you know how he is – had to go and lie down on a plank for half an hour, then a bit longer, to have a good think about it. Then he got up and shouted: 'that's it!' and came out with this big speech about how spontaneity is all that counts in this century, art only exists because of the spontaneous, and so forth. I went back later to pick up my work, although Martha (Jackson) wanted to buy it. It was lying in the dirt again, in a lean-to outside. It was raining, and the piece had almost merged into the earth. Only then did I notice what Jorn had made: reliefs in the same style as I had discovered. So I went to see him, and asked him precisely what he was up to. We had a bit of a row about it."[26]

FIG. 144 ROBERTO MATTA, MALITE, ASGER JORN AND CORNEILLE, ALBISOLA 1954

24. See Mirella Bandidi, 'Introduzione e catalogo', in exhib. cat. Pinot Gallizio e il Laboratorio Sperimentale d'Alba del Movimento Internazionale per una Bauhaus Immaginista (1955–57) e dell'Internazionale Situazionista (1957–60), Turin (Galleria Civica d'Arte Moderna), 1974, p. 45. Several of the ceramic pieces produced at Albisola, including work by Appel, Corneille and Matta, are reproduced in the magazine Eristica, (publication of the 'Laboratorio Sperimentale d'Alba del Movimento Internazionale per una Bauhaus Immaginista'), no. 2, 1956. See also the 1991 article cited in note 22 by Ursula Lehmann-Brockhaus, p. 102, and my article 'Cobra en Italië', in Jong Holland, vol. 4, no. 5, 1988, pp. 3–5.
25. Published in Asger Jorn, Pour la forme, op. cit. (note 1) (no page numbers) between pages 20 and 29.
26. See Simon Vinkenoog, Het verhaal van Karel Appel. Een Proeve van waarneming, Utrecht, 1963, p. 127.

A further experiment in ceramics was undertaken at Albisola in 1955. This recalled the interest in children's drawings that had also been manifested by other movements in which Jorn had once played a pivotal role, namely the group around the magazine *Helhesten* in wartime Denmark, and later COBRA. On this occasion, a hundred plates were decorated by a group of children, five of which were reproduced on the front and rear cover of Jorn's theoretical treatise *Structure et Changement* in 1956. The printed commentary on the rear states that: "The results [...] seem to reveal that any child, before it has reached school-age, is better able to apply modern techniques to bring a particular surface to life than all the professionals in the field of decoration, both in the artistic sense and in terms of handicraft, architecture and industry[27].

Several of the artists mentioned earlier must have continued or returned to work at Mazzotti's factory, because in the summer of that year an exhibition was held in Albisola of work by Appel, Corneille, Jorn and Matta, for which Matta designed the poster. Jorn included a general photograph of the exhibition and photographs of work by Matta, Appel, Corneille and himself in his 1958 article "Image et Form contre l'empirisme éclectique", in which he once again attacked what he saw as "Calvinistic purism" in architecture, which wanted to push free plastic art and handicrafts into the pigeonhole of specialism and to cut people off from their need to decorate their own environment themselves. He again chose Max Bill's "new Bauhaus" as his target[28]. The photographs reveal how exuberantly the participants at Albisola experimented during their creative releases in clay and glaze with the possibilities offered by ceramics. Apart from the enormous freedom apparent in the figures and colours created on dishes and vases, it is primarily the hilarious imaginary creatures, freestanding or in relief, produced by Appel, Matta and especially Jorn that stand out. Just how much of a highpoint this moment of collective creative expression must have been is evident from the photographic report of the event produced by the photographer Henny Riemens, Corneille's wife, in 1954 and 1955 (fig. 145).

27. Published (no page numbers) in Asger Jorn, Pour la Forme, op. cit. (note 1) between pp. 48 and 65.
28. This is, in fact, also a brief summary of the theme of his earlier publication Pour la Forme, op. cit. (note 1), which opened with this article, pp. 9–20.

A final ceramic activity mounted by the M.I.B.I. was a "retrospective of Futurist ceramics", held in September 1956 at Alba, further inland. The exhibition included work dating from around 1930 by Tullio d'Albisola. The exhibition catalogue features an extract from a "Manifesto Futurista della Ceramica", that had been compiled in 1938 by Marinetti and Tullio d'Albisola under the title "Ceramica e aeroceramica"[29]. A photograph of the two authors' heads appears above it. All in all, it was a remarkable initiative, not least because in its later stages, under Marinetti's leadership, Futurism had taken on strongly fascistic overtones, while the M.I.B.I. overtly espoused Marxist ideals. What's more, the aforementioned extract immediately makes clear the Futurists' preference for machine-aesthetics, a concept which Jorn fiercely opposed, especially through his M.I.B.I.[30]

The M.I.B.I. was renamed the "Internationale Situationniste" in 1957, and the centre of experimentation shifted to the Alba "laboratory" of Pinot Gallizio – a like-minded artist with whom Jorn had become acquainted[31]. The focus of attention was, however, no longer pottery.

Nevertheless, Jorn remained true to Albisola. He returned regularly until 1960 and then for the final two years before his death in 1973, and built up an impressive ceramic oeuvre. Reviewing his development, it is apparent that from 1954 onwards – a year in which he began to use his own paintings and lithographs as the basis for a number of clay reliefs – his paintings and his pottery had a mutual influence on one another[32]. He came to feel so at home in ceramics that he allowed himself new liberties in this field. His improvisation conjured up mythical creatures in the clay – as it did with paint in his paintings – which constantly reveal new aspects as one walks around them[33]. Similar creatures are to be found in the garden and interior of the house in Albisola, which was declared a museum in 1974, and which he wholly redesigned, adding new walls and terraces. They form the mysterious,

29. See Ursula Lehmann-Brockhaus, op. cit. (note 13), p. 90. The manifesto is quoted in the catalogue to an exhibition of pottery made in Albisola in 1954: Asger Jorn keramik, Copenhagen, Industri-Museet, 5–20 Nov. 1955.
30. See also in this context my article, op. cit. (note 24), and the catalogue La Ceramica Futurista da Balla a Tullio D'Albisola, (a cura di Enrico Crispoliti), Albisola, May/July 1982; Faenza, July/Oct. 1982.
31. Idem. See also Mirella Bandini, L'Estetico / Il Politico – da Cobra all'Internationazionale Situazionista, Rome, 1977.
32. See Troels Andersen, op. cit. (note 15), pp. 74 and 75.
33. Ursula Lehmann-Brockhaus, op. cit. (note 13, p. 84 ff.), brilliantly describes the later development of Jorn's pottery.

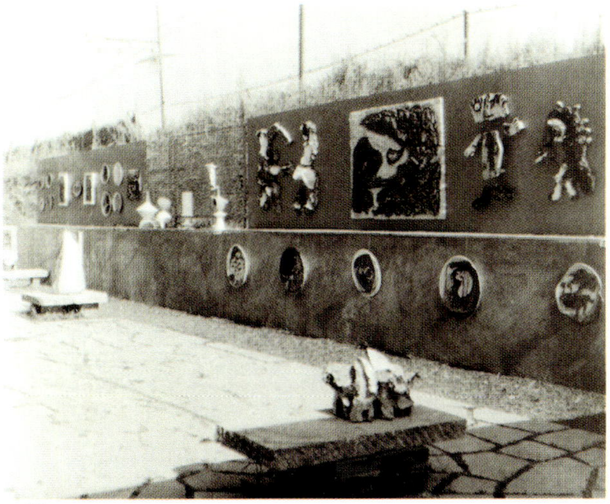

FIG. 145

three-dimensional population of the house and its grounds. He also invoked his misty, northern world through large reliefs inside and outside his house – here in the centre of Latin culture, with its penchant for clear form and colour[34]. Jorn reached a highpoint in his oeuvre and in Danish "mythic art" – which had so entranced the Dutch COBRA members when they first encountered it in Copenhagen in 1948 – in the giant relief (some three metres high and twenty-seven metres wide) that he produced in the San Giorgio pottery in Albisola for Aarhus Grammar School in Jutland in 1959[35]. The relief was cut up into rough, irregular pieces and then reassembled, before being thoroughly worked over, giving it a heavily furrowed structure. He even rode over it on a motor-scooter. The mythical creatures, in beautiful, mixed up and diffuse colours, stare out of the Aarhus mural at the viewer. They are immersed in the mystery of a hidden world that glows and seems constantly to change shape in the shining and stirring surface of the ceramic relief.

MONUMENTAL "COBRA CERAMICS" (fig. 146)

Other former COBRA members also produced ceramic work in later years, some of which was on an even bigger scale than Jorn's Aarhus work. None, however, was as engaged with the craft as Jorn. The Danish painter Carl-Henning Pedersen, who also produced a whole series of fantastic creatures cast in bronze, executed a number of colossal ceramic murals. Having already produced a large wall mosaic in Copenhagen in 1964[36], he painted a ceramic mural featuring gigantic dream-birds, that measures five metres in height and two hundred and twenty metres in length for the Angli factory in Herning, Jutland, between 1966 and 1968. The factory, whose manager, Aage Damgaard, had collected art and encouraged artists for many years, became a museum in 1976. Pedersen produced the work at the Elmental ceramic factory near Düsseldorf. The

FIG. 145 EXHIBITION IN ALBISOLA 1955

34. See also Ezio Gribaudo (ed.), Jorn, le jardin d'Albisola, Fratelli Pozzo, Turin, 1974.
35. See Erik Nyholm, Asger Jorn's Aarhus Mural, Guy Atkins (ed.), Kent, 1964; included with a few amendments in Atkins, 1977, op. cit. (note 15), pp. 75–87, and op. cit. 1991 (note 15).
36. See the catalogue Carl-Henning Pedersen 1964–1973, malerier-akvareller-bronzer, Den Frie Udstillings Bygning, Copenhagen, 15–30 Sept. 1973.

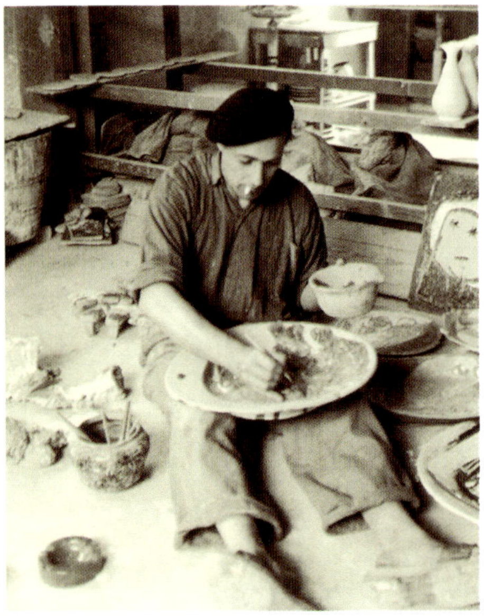

FIG. 146

overwhelmingly blue decoration, which he called "Fantasiens leg omkring levets hjul" (The play of imagination around the wheel of life), was applied to a wall made up of large square tiles around a circular grassy field laid out within a factory building that curls like the tail of a snake[37]. In 1976, he produced a similar wall, eight metres high and ninety metres long, at the same factory. This time it was designed to decorate the outside of a circle, namely the round museum near the Angli factory in Herning, dedicated to his work and that of his wife, the painter Else Alfelt[38]. For subsequent commissions of this type, Pedersen turned to the Dutch workshop "Struktuur 68", which had been set up in The Hague in 1968 to produce monumental ceramic work[39].

FIG. 146 ASGER JORN, ALBISOLA 1954

Karel Appel in particular produced a great deal of ceramic work, including both monumental murals and free-standing figures, in collaboration with Struktuur 68. Here the "Appel colors", so uncommon to ceramics, were developed[40]. Rooskens, Corneille and Lucebert also found their ways to "Struktuur 68". Lucebert moreover produced a lot of ceramic work in 1990–91 at the studio of Kattrin Kühn in Berlin (the Droysen Keramik workshop-cum-gallery), where he not only decorated dishes and vases, but made a number of fantastic creatures in clay[41].

Finally, "COBRA Belgium" has made an important contribution to ceramics, in that Alechinsky began to work intensively with the medium in 1981. Although he subscribed to the ideals expressed at Albisola in 1954, he chose not to try his hand at pottery at that time. In 1981, however, he was invited by Galerie Maeght (which changed its name to Galerie Lelong

37. See the publication Angli i Herning, Snekkersten, Denmark, 1969 and my article 'Kloosterlijke eenvoud en een curieuze zonnetempel – Nieuwe musea in Denemarken', in NRC Handelsblad, 2.4.1982.
38. See the catalogue Carl-Henning Pedersen og Else Alfelts Museum, Herning, Denmark, (at the time of the inauguration), Sept. 1976.
39. See Nederlandse monumentale keramiek, published by Struktuur 68, The Hague 1990.
40. See Elisabeth Reinhartz-Tergau, 'Het monumentale werk van Karel Appel', in the catalogue Karel Appel tentoonstelling t.g.v. zijn 60ste verjaardag, 2-31 May 1981, Galerie Nova Spectra, The Hague; and op. cit. (note 8).
41. I obtained this information from Tony Lucebert via a telephone conversation on 7.9.1993. See also the catalogue to the exhibition Lucebert Keramik, at Droysen Keramik-Galerie Kattrin Kühn and Galerie Springer in Berlin, Sept.–Nov. 1991, and Peter Bötig, 'Luceberts poetische Welten', in Neue keramik, volume 2, 1991, no. 11, Sept.–Oct., pp. 770–771.

in 1982) to experiment with ceramics. Since that time, he has produced many clay objects at the gallery's workshop in Grasse, and has painted plates, vases and tableaux by the ceramicist Hans Spinner. In 1985, two tile tableaux by Alechinsky were installed in a park at the University of Liège. He has also decorated crockery at the Sèvres porcelain factory on several occasions[42].

The traditional craft of the potter enabled the ideals of the COBRA movement to reach a new highpoint at the Albisola project organised by Jorn in the years 1954–55. Furthermore, at other, sometimes unexpected moments in the oeuvre of many COBRA-related artists, the vitality that so characterised the movement found an exuberant medium of expression in ceramics. This usually occurred when the opportunity arose, and it involved not only the painting of pottery but from time to time the actual moulding of the clay – a material so compliant to the imagination.

FIG. 147 ASGER JORN
VOGEL 1953
plate; ⌀ 21 cm
COLLECTION MUSEUM HET KRUITHUIS

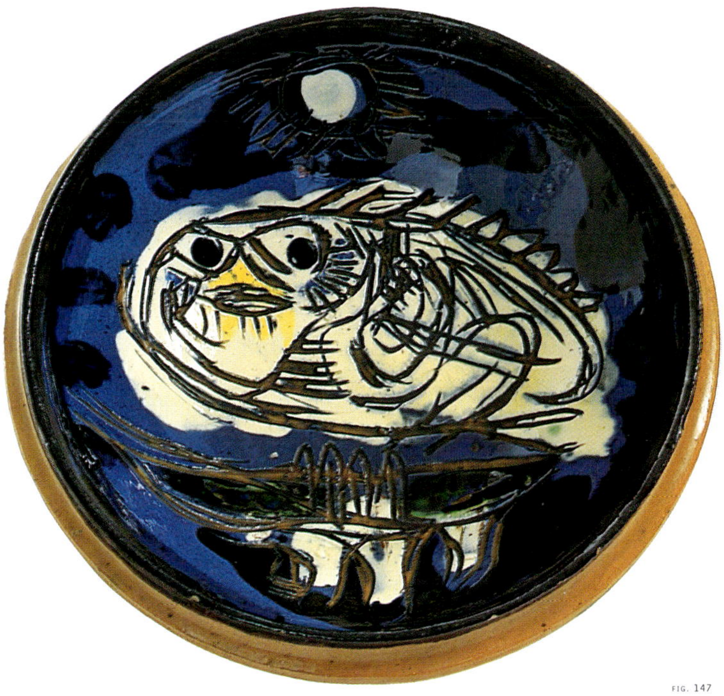

FIG. 147

42. Information regarding Alechinsky from a telephone conversation on 18.3.93. See also Pierre Alechinsky. Peintures et écrits, (Eugène Ionesco, Trois Approches), Paris 1977, pp. 233-234, the catalogues Pierre Alechinsky, Pièces uniques céramiques, May 1985, Galerie Birch, Copenhagen; the catalogue Alechinsky, Laves émaillées, (with an introduction by Jacques Dupin), Galerie Lelong, Paris, Zurich, New York, 1988; the publication Porcelaines 1990: la Manufacture Nationales de Sèvres, p. 6 ff.; and New Work: Pains de terre émaillés, Flora Danica Drawings, revalorisation, André Emmerich Gallery, New York, May 1991.

The tangerine test

by Jos Poodt

In 1990 the American minimal artist Dan Flavin produced a series of colorful neon works, each of which he dedicated to the grand old lady of ceramics, Lucie Rie. His admiration was underscored by the addition of the words "master potter". It is not uncommon for Flavin to show an appreciation or an affinity with a thinker or visual artist in this way. His precise reason for making these tributes, however, is left unexplained.

George Ohr, a figure totally ignored in his own time, has received a similar honor, albeit a posthumous one. His whimsically shaped ceramic work served as a model for the Jasper Johns painting *Ventriloquist* (fig. 148), from 1983. Johns, a great admirer of the "mad potter of Biloxi" along with Andy Warhol, owns a variety of Ohr's amazing creations. Neither Flavin's nor Johns's work has anything to do with ceramics, and it is perhaps this very distance which makes them admirers of the ceramists Rie and Ohr, respectively.

These are two examples of the proverbial exceptions that prove the rule, since ceramic work is generally only mildly appreciated among visual artists who do not work with clay themselves. It is striking how artists, even when they are used to employing a variety of materials and techniques, never – or only later and usually by chance or by invitation – come into contact with this medium. This delayed interest in ceramics applies not only to many of the "classic modern" artists, but also to many contemporary artists.

The material itself evokes not so much resistance, but rather associations with what has been done with it over the past century. "Ceramics can be so frumpy," says Rob Birza,

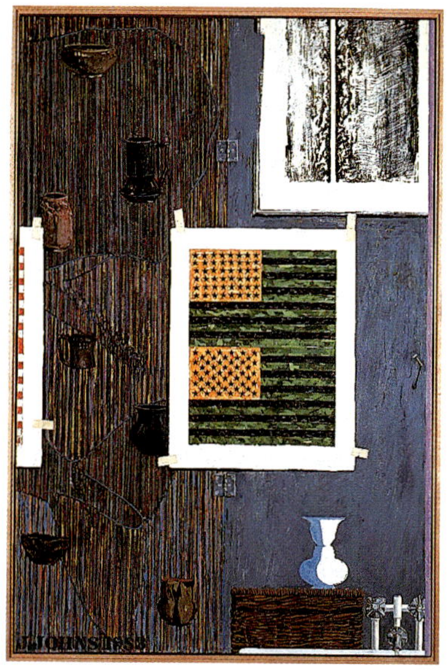

FIG. 148

voicing his own reticence and probably that of many colleagues. Once artists have touched clay, as he did, reticence usually turns into fascination: even kitsch and ceramic ugliness can be absorbing.

Hans van Hoek has also made a painted tribute. In one painting he honors a trio who form a close friendship with each other – the Japanese Soetsu Yanagi and, through him, his countryman Shoji Hamada and the founder of modern ceramics in the West, Bernard Leach (fig. 149). The first is valued for his profound theory of aesthetics, the second for the way in which he puts this into practice with his ceramics and the third for being the dedicated messenger of what appeals so much to Hans van Hoek in the work of these two Orientals.

As an artist he had never touched clay prior to that point. The hand of fate and the stimulus of a skilled ceramist set him on the track. Circumstances forced the painter Hans van Hoek to put his brush aside and of that necessity he made a virtue: an experiment with ceramics. Earth, water and fire suddenly appear like a gift from heaven. With almost childish ease he modelled a series of ceramic tableaux. The motif which he imagined – baptism – was clear to him. The theme had already appeared in paintings from 1992 and in a watercolor from that same time, titled *Doop door het vuur van de Heilige Geest* (Baptism by the fire of the Holy Spirit – fig. 150), seems to be a sketch for what he would like to bring about in ceramics. The edges of thick slabs of clay are kneaded into a low, upright rims. This simple intervention transforms each tableau into the most elementary form of a basin. The rest is variation, relief, decoration and – not least – painting.

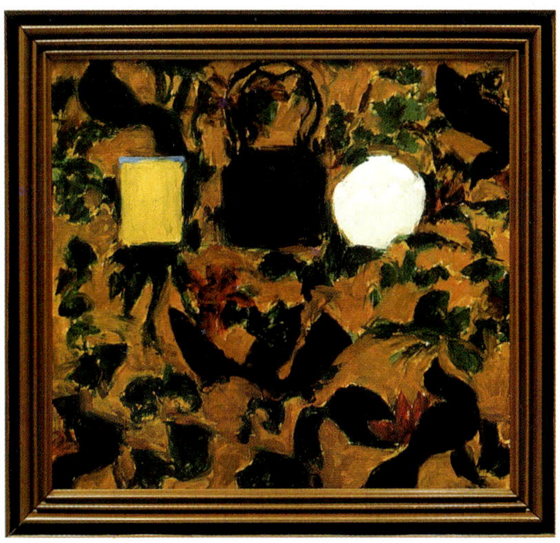

FIG. 149

The theme of baptism has more than symbolic meaning to Van Hoek. In reference to his painting *Doop onder de brug* (Baptism under the Bridge – 1992), he says, "Experienced emotions such as fear and doubt, pain, dying, the dead body and mourning for this, transposed into motifs such as the Crucifixion, the Resurrection, the Pietà, Lamentation, eventually brought me to the motif 'Baptism under the Bridge'. It is one which, through experience, has become

FIG. 148 JASPER JOHNS
VENTRILOQUIST 1983
encaustic on canvas; 190.5 x 127 cm

FIG. 149 HANS VAN HOEK
HOMAGE TO YANAGI AND LEACH 1990
oil on canvas; 173 x 187.5 cm

intrinsic to me, one in which I also recognize my own nature and in which my painterly instincts can unfold.

In the light of this confession, the tableaux are reminscent of forms of early Christian folk art – not so much due to the iconography as to the simple, intense and authentic way in which expression is given to religious feelings. Such feelings and experiences are more universal to Van Hoek than is generally presumed in the West. It is with this outlook that Van Hoek paints his images of baptism. He does this “blind” as he calls it, because the colors appear only after the firing process. Submission to the effects of the kiln and fire is experienced by him as a judgement upon his actions. “The fire was like a judge of my dreams, a merciful judge, as I see it this time.”

It is as though Van Hoek wishes to say that the result comes about in spite of him. This and the way in which he “lives through” the tableaux project a quality of that Oriental wisdom that appeals to him so much.

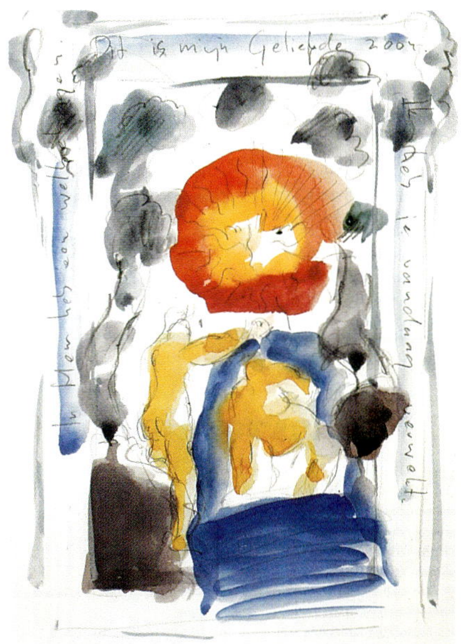

FIG. 150

FIG. 150 HANS VAN HOEK
BAPTISM BY THE FIRE OF THE HOLY SPIRIT 1992
aquarelle; 36 x 26 cm

In 1997 **Jan van den Dobbelsteen**, during a period working in the 6000-year-old heart of the Chinese earthenware industry, Ding Shan, produced a teapot that can laugh: a fantastic statement and a pithy summing-up of Van den Dobbelsteen’s artistry, in which he wishes to allow philosophical ideas and sensory experiences to coincide. It was the first time he actually experienced something that fascinated him for years: China and its ceramic tradition, into which thousands of years of cultural history have been instilled. Finally, in the home of the Chinese earthenware industry, he was in a position to investigate its ceramic secrets and to examine, at the source, what qualities the Chinese attribute to porcelain other than its sheer function. He came across the old handbooks, in which the beneficial effects of kaolin (the basic ingredient for porcelain) are discussed and it was here he found what most fascinated him: the fact that material consists not only of matter, but also of invisible energy, which spiritually influences man. The belief that Chinese culture still contains traces of this notion interested Van den Dobbelsteen and prompted him to seek similar sources in the West. He discovered that medieval alchemists sought, in the

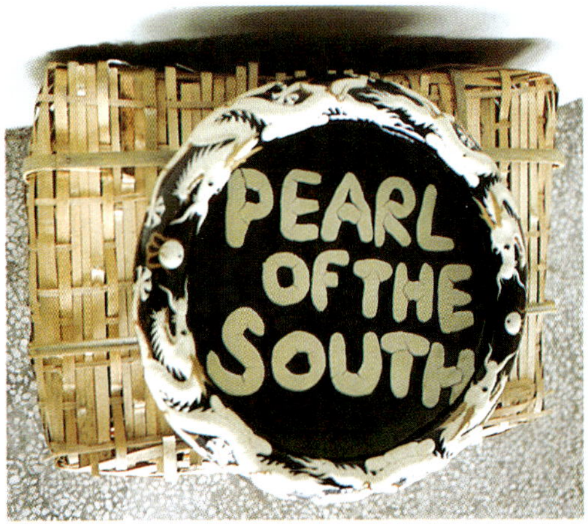

FIG. 151

same way, to invent the material from which they could produce porcelain. They, too, recognized the spiritual quality of the material.

In his installation with ten "lion vases", he managed to link the two traditions in a magnificent manner. It is based again on an orientation to the source: in this case, Holland's oldest earthenware factory "De Porceleyne Fles", famous for its delftware. History is not only present in the vase form, whose origins lie with the traditional Chinese storage jars, but is particularly evident in the reference to alchemistic endeavors to produce porcelain. In each jar he has hidden a porcelain pellet, the sound of which is reminiscent of "the philosopher's stone" and the mysterious power of the material (fig. 151).

FIG. 151 JAN VAN DEN DOBBELSTEEN
PEARL OF THE SOUTH 1997
detail of installation; ø 35 cm

The work of Jan van den Dobbelsteen has a strong conceptual tendency, and for each idea he chooses the most appropriate materials and techniques, so that his oeuvre is an amalgam of art forms. Whether this involves paintings, a monumental assignment, a ceramic work or a CD-ROM, Van den Dobbelsteen picks his subject to the bone. The physical work of art is consequently the material concentration of force, about which he says the following:

"That power which is defined as consciousness in all drawings
That power which is known as reason in all drawings
That power which exists in all drawings in a form of sleep, as hunger, as shadow
That power which exists in all paintings as energy, from the first, as forgiveness, in the form of species, as bashfulness
That power which exists in all sculptures as peace, in the form of faith, as loveliness, as fortune, as vocation,
That power which exists in all installations in the form of memory, as compassion, as fulfilment, as mother, in the form of illusion."

Birza is the artist with perhaps the most pronounced love/hate relationship toward ceramics. He works with ceramics in the same way as he does in an almost taunting type of painting, where he allows beauty and ugliness to fuse with each other. Grotesque shapes, glazed in colors that fry the retina: sometimes he treats clay as a playful medium, unemphatically and almost as an excuse not to have to paint, and other times he pounces on the material like a lion, creating images that go beyond his own imagination, as in the ceramic sculptures *REAL (My fuckin' Kangaroo is damn right! (And so is my pelican)* from 1994 (fig. 152). To him, the ceramic work is only successful "if, while you're making it, you already have the feeling that it's becoming stone."

Birza makes deliberate use of a "beautiful/ugly" combination in his paintings, ceramics and installations. This creates an opposition within his work and thereby a certain tension, a defiance of taste and an enrichment of meaning. He achieves this slightly disorienting effect in a brilliant manner with a series of painted floral still lifes, the *Power Flower Portraits* (1996-97). Each bouquet derives "its look" as much from the vase in which it is placed – ranging from pre-Columbian pottery to Ming vases, from anonymous department-store porcelain to a Greek amphora, from plastic knick-knacks to delftware – as from the make-up of the bunch of flowers or whatever is meant to pass for this.

FIG. 152 ROB BIRZA
REAL (MY FUCKIN KANGAROO IS DAMN RIGHT! AND SO IS MY PELICAN) 1994
sculptures

FIG. 152

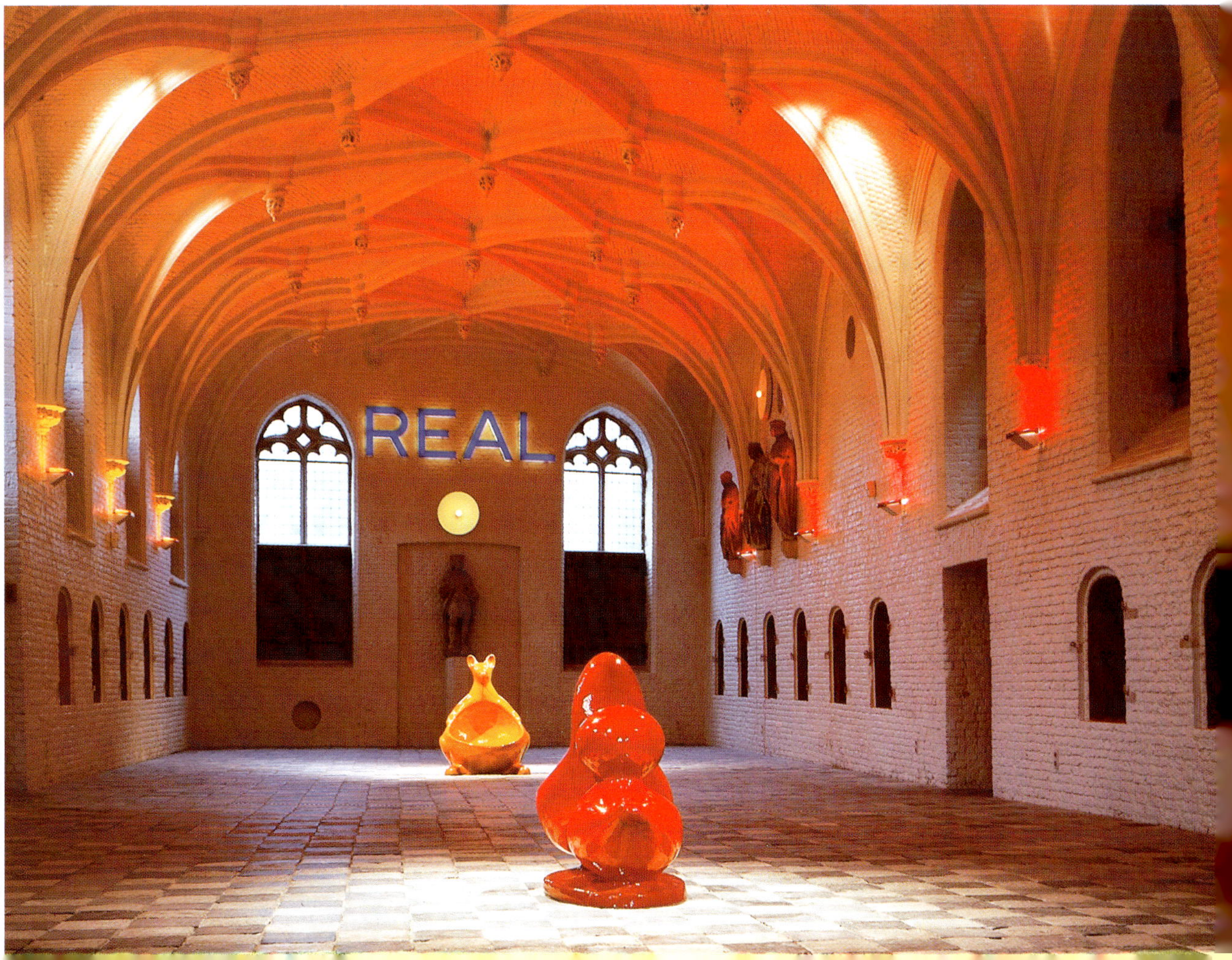

While working on this series Birza got his hands into the clay and modelled a number of vases, whose diversity is no less than that of their painted sisters. Unhampered by a lack of technical skill, he fostered his lack of inhibition toward this medium. And filled with an aversion toward the indefinable aesthetics of so much ceramic work, he made "ugliness" the instrument of his "message". "I resist aesthetics and, at the same time, I want to achieve this. It's not an objective, mostly just a condition. Aesthetics have more to do with language; this is a way to convey something... I often find ugliness more interesting than beauty:...I'm seeking a kind of vehemence; it's a certain type of 'banality', a seemingly contradictory way of telling something. 'Beautiful' is so short-lived."

FIG. 153 ROB BIRZA
POWER FLOWER
PORTRAITS (NR. 2) 1996
egg tempera on canvas; 160 x 140 cm

Though vases and flowers may have an obvious relationship, Birza uses them to the extent that they serve his painterly approach. Just as his paintings have little to do with the bouquets, his ceramics have little to do with the vases. Everything is centered around painting. This is where it all starts and where it all ends (fig. 153). He produces ceramics, builds installations and designs sets in order to ultimately "better understand what painting is." Seen as such, his ceramics are not a "jaunt", but another playful form of painting, meant to tell the same story – a story about and full of absurdities – in a different material. His ceramic-painterly combination shows how the material lends itself to the content, not as an subordinate element but as a qualifying factor – without which the work of art simply would not exist. Here the choice of material has been determined by a content-related necessity.

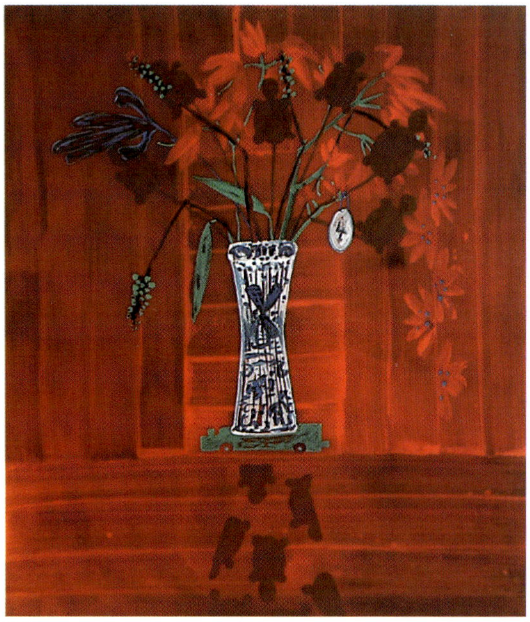

FIG. 153

"Painting is drudgery; ceramics is fun!" **Alphons Freijmuth** allows the words to slip out spontaneously. But shocked by his own frankness, he hastens to nuance this remark.

Endless modelling in clay – at school and in the sculpture department of the Amsterdamse Rijksacademie – provided the basis for working in ceramics later on. Much later, in fact. Almost apologetically, Freijmuth adds that his youthful adeptness in making spatial work stands in the way of his endeavors to create a three-dimensional illusion on a flat surface. Continual drawing activities, even now, must keep Freijmuth's skills balanced in that respect. However, despite the laborious struggle with the third dimension, painting is his true love. Thematically, he attempts to assimilate opposing styles and ideas from twentieth-century art: expressionism and constructivism, Van Gogh and Mondriaan. Obstinacy seems to be the driving force, passion the language of his work.

Even though his paintings express an authenticity, single-mindedness and directness, the grappling which is needed to produce a good and fresh work eludes the eye of the onlooker. "When you start to repeat yourself so much that the act of painting becomes a burden, ceramics can be a liberation." And so it goes. Freijmuth had the opportunity to work in clay at the right time. Familiar with the material and its sculptural potential, the ceramic objects seem to come about effortlessly in his hands, providing a tremendous impulse, also for painting. Even Picasso experienced such a liberating effect with clay. Just when he had become bogged down in a particular mode of painting, he made the acquaintance of the Ramiés at their ceramics studio in Vallauris. With heart and soul, he dedicated himself to the sculptural material, which freed him from the premeditated structures of his paintings from that time.

"With a painting, you yourself have to create the environment in which you place an object; with a sculpture, it is simply present. In ceramics the problem of the third dimension is gone; you just step out of the flat surface of the painting. That's probably why one sees painters who produce sculpture, but hardly ever sculptors who produce paintings." And with thinly veiled delight, he admits: "Ceramics has a certain playful element, which allows you to shape an idea quickly, something that isn't possible in a painting due to a certain caution."

Painting and working in ceramics now go hand in hand. In what Freijmuth refers to as "modderkoppen' (mud heads), the accent is on the sculptural quality of the material. They are unglazed or only slightly glazed. With the vases and other heads (fig. 154), sculptural and painterly elements merge in an appealing way. Now and then Freijmuth produces small quantities of ceramics. This work is like his painting: imbued with joy, anger, sadness, resignation, detachment and deceleration – the entire scope of human experience.

FIG. 154 ALPHONS FREIJMUTH
UNTITLED 1997
sculpture; 30 x 25 x 20 cm

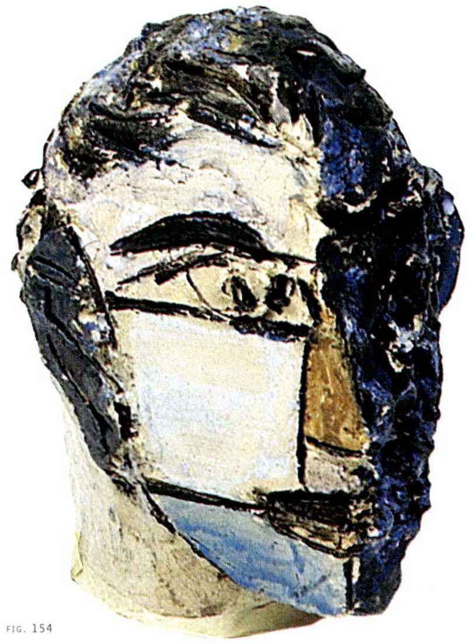

FIG. 154

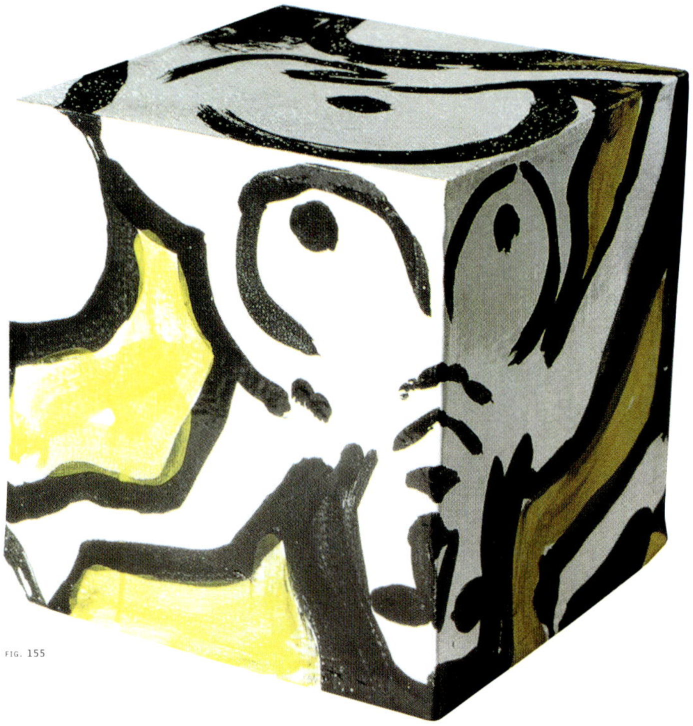

FIG. 155

FIG. 155 A.R. PENCK
WÜRFEL 1990
sculpture; 24 x 24 x 24 cm

Penck's stiff figures conquered the world long before he painted them on a ceramic surface. By 1978 he had already tried out every available visual medium. Curiosity had yet to lead him to expand his store of artistic expressive means with ceramics at the age of forty-eight. In this he received considerable encouragement from the ceramist Kattrin Kühn, who invited Penck on repeated occasions to come and work at her studio Droysen in Berlin. She made the vases, plates and objects according to his instructions.

Curiosity is generally the driving force by which Penck plunges into science, art and politics with equal ease. His insatiable hunger for knowledge and experience and his indomitable energy bring to mind those of the equally unstoppable Picasso. Both drew, painted, produced sculpture, graphic work and ceramics. "Love and death" is the predominant theme in which Penck and his illustrious predecessor enjoy free rein with respect to the painting of ceramics; in the pictorial praise of women, love and hunting both artists attempt to keep death at a distance. But there is a fundamental difference: whereas Picasso utilized the very sensuality and sculptural quality of clay to bring about a convergence of the sculptural and pictorial aspects of the image, Penck often goes right against it. A prime example of this is a series of geometric objects – spheres, pyramids and cubes – onto which he paints female nudes with an expressionistic brushstroke. The geometric form of the ceramic object contradicts the fluid lines of the bodies (fig. 155). In doing this Penck does not force conformity, however. On the contrary, the contrast between the angular ceramic object and the "round" painting is exploited by him. It gives him painterly freedom and heightens the frequently erotic character of his work. Penck's ceramic work demands to be held or – with the larger vases – to be viewed from all sides, not only so that one can see every inch of painting but also to make the very act of looking less detached.

The swan the swan
and not the plan
the bee the bee
and not the machine

the mother the mother
and not the computer
will rule over
dragons, tigers and dead bones.

Der Schwan der Schwan
und nicht der Plan
Die Biene die Biene
und nicht die Maschine
Die Mutter die Mutter
und nicht der Computer
sollen Sieger sein
über Drache, Tiger, Totenbein

ar penck

Bruce McLean had also worked in every conceivable medium by the time he first came to produce ceramics. "An invitation in 1985, from Douglas Woolf, to come to Fulham Pottery sparked off a latent interest in clay. I was invited to become part of a forgotten tradition of artists being invited to decorate pots and jugs. It was suggested to me that I might like to make some ceramic sculptures. I decided to make jugs for wine and plates for food. Objects of function and objects to be seen with and to place. I enjoy the sloshing on of the slip when I decorate the objects. No concepts ceramics here, behaving badly with yet another material. Manipulating stuff – earth, water, fire – and then to put a blue bowl and acid green through the tangerine test."

These last remarks reflect the cheerfully subversive nature that is typical of all of McLean's activities. With the work that he produced in London and, two years later, in the Netherlands, he cast a nonchalantly critical eye on "New Ceramics", a movement among ceramists who were then breaking away from the craftsmanly/aesthetic ceramic tradition (dominated by Bernard Leach) with more bold and expressive work. This is sooner a sly dig than a fierce attack.

McLean's responses are subtle, despite the strength and vitality of his work. Actually, response is hardly the word. He maneuvers on the basis of an acute awareness of the (art)world surrounding him and anticipates events and situations. In his performances this is immediately discernible due to their physical impact as live acts. In the paintings, sculptures and ceramics, the message must be drawn from within the conventions of these media. Some of his fellow "concept" artists seemed, during the early eighties, to want to assure themselves of a place in art history with the same traditional media. Not McLean, however. On the contrary, anything that smacks of a claim to timelessness is put into perspective by him; he prefers to use his work as a Trojan horse, channelling the same themes and subjects into the world in a different way than in his performances. With virtuosity and a sense of understatement, Bruce McLean continues his satire of social and artistic conventions, of bureaucracy and consumerism on paper, canvas, in stone, metal and ceramic work.

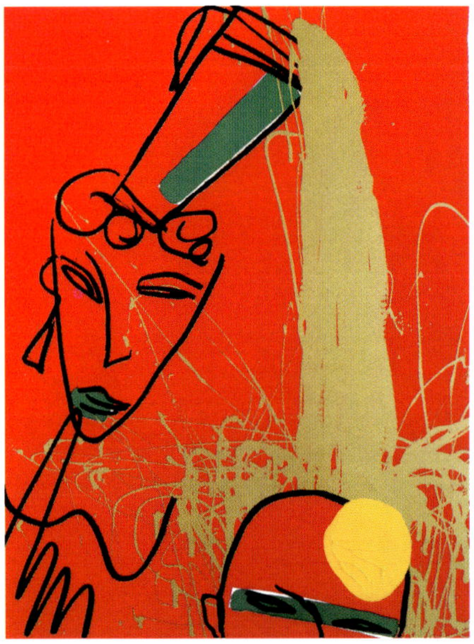
FIG. 156

FIG. 156 BRUCE MCLEAN
WHERE DO YOU STAND? 1988
screenprint with additional handworking; 120 x 92 cm

A constant factor in this is space, in which people move, behave and deal with objects. Enlarged teacups, pitchers and jugs are striking props in scores of performances, installations and paintings (fig. 156). Conversely, the facial expressions, gestures and dance movements from the performances make up the decorations, reduced to neutral iconographic marks, on the ceramic objects. In combination with the exuberant use of color on the oversized bowls, plates, pitchers and jugs, McLean plays on the entire range of human sensitivities with his ceramics.

Mel Gooding describes McLean's ceramics (in *Crafts Magazine*, June/July 1986) as follows: "Bowls, plates, amphorae-like vases and jugs become arenas of imaginative action in which McLean attacks with wit and passion certain obsessive themes – sexual love, family affection, social encounter – and in which he plays with effects impossible in any other medium: startling incandescences of fired colour, sgraffito incisions that invite the finger to trace the curving lines of his design (fig. 157). Confounding the distinction between the decorative and the fine, these are above all objects of use: the bowls demand fruit, the plates bread, the jugs wine. Art, gloriously celebratory and at once sacramental and profane, enhancing the daily ceremony, enters life through these splendid works and takes its place at the table of human conviviality."

FIG. 157 BRUCE MCLEAN
UNTITLED 1988
plate; ⌀ 32 cm

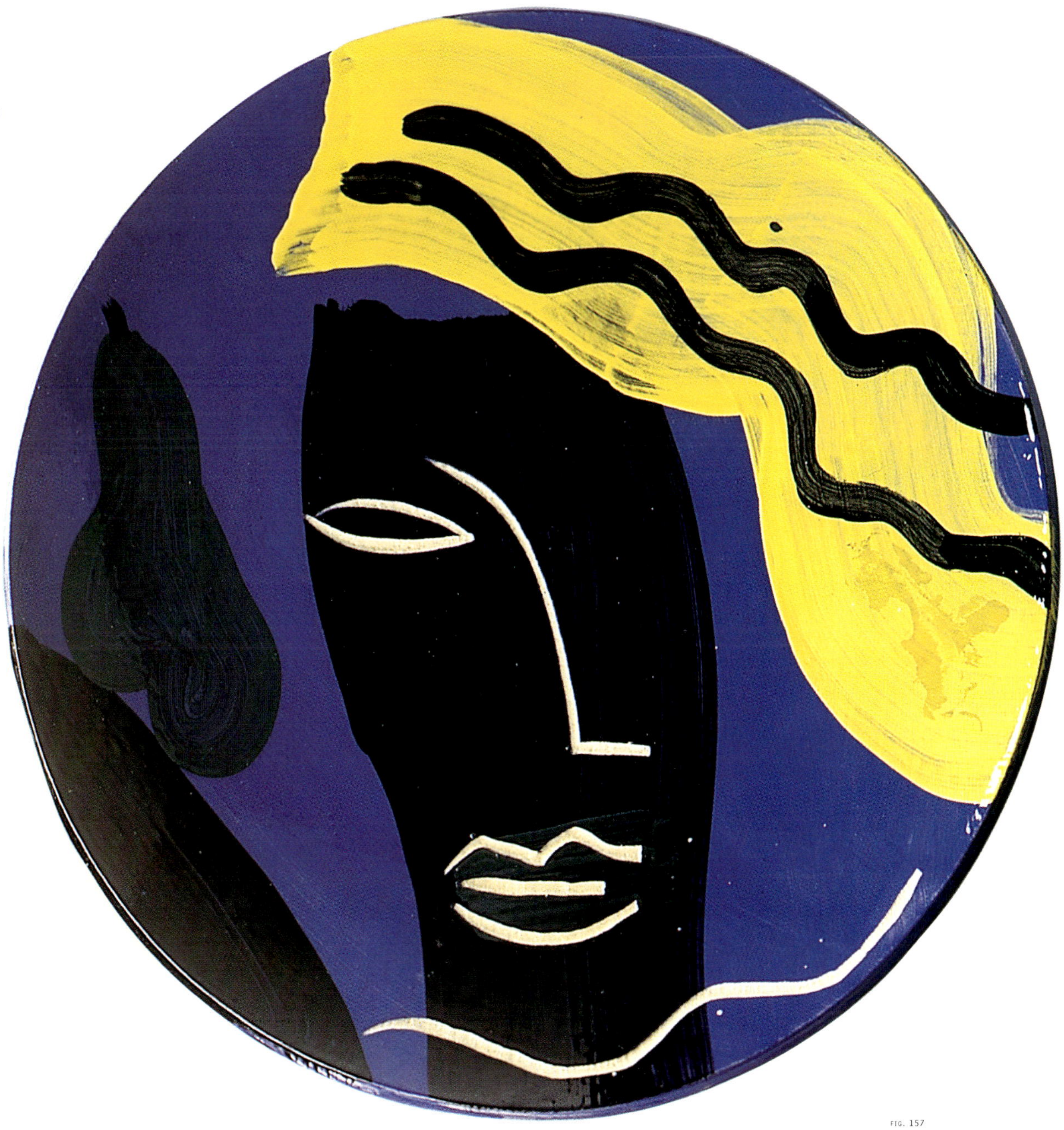

FIG. 157

EDITED BY
Yvònne G.J.M. Joris
Museum Het Kruithuis

TEXTS
Janet Koplos
Max Borka
Willemijn Stokvis
Jos Poodt

TRANSLATIONS
Ted Alkins
Beth O'Brien

PICTURE/COPY EDITORS
Wil van Gils
Thea Sterken
Museum Het Kruithuis

DESIGN
Scritto, Ghent/B

LITHOGRAPHY
Studio Pages, Brussels/B

PRINTED BY
Goff, Ghent/B

PUBLISHED BY
Het Kruithuis, Museum of Contemporary Art
Citadellaan 7, 5211 XA 's-Hertogenbosch/NL

DISTRIBUTED BY
Harry N. Abrams, Incorporated, New York

WITH THE SUPPORT OF
The Mondriaan Foundation, Amsterdam/NL

ISBN 9065 38172 4 (Het Kruithuis)
ISBN 0 8109 6369 8 (Abrams)

PHOTOGRAPY

Archives Capron, Vallauris/F (fig. 134); Archivio Fontana, Milan/I (fig. 51); Lars Bay (fig. 74); Pieter Boersma (fig. 83); Els van den Boorn, Amsterdam/NL (fig. 106); Jörg von Bruchhausen, Berlin/D (fig. 53, 54, 55); Paul H. de Bruin, Amsterdam/NL (fig. 127); Català-Roca, Barcelona/E (fig. 10); Peter Cox (fig. 123, 149, 150); Jan van den Dobbelsteen (fig. 107, 151); David Douglas Duncan, Mouans-Sartoux/F (fig. 138); Alphons Freijmuth, Amsterdam/NL (fig. 102, 103); Henk Geraedts, Tilburg/NL (fig. 120); Tom Haartsen, Schiedam/NL (fig. 89); Philippe Halsmann, New York/USA (fig. 35, p.122, p.139); Udo Hesse (fig. 99); Friedhelm Hoffmann (fig. 155); Philippe Jouarre (fig. 39); Ida Kar (fig. 25); Nico Koster, Amsterdam/NL (fig. 59); Kröller-Müller Museum, Otterlo/NL (fig. 63); Peer van der Kruis, Heeze/NL (fig. 3, 5, 7, 8, 9, 11, 12, 16, 18, 20, 21, 22, 24, 26, 29, 31, 32, 33, 36, 37, 41, 42, 43, 44, 48, 49, 50, 52, 56, 57, 60, 61, 64, 65, 66, 69, 70, 71, 72, 76, 77, 78, 80, 82, 85, 86, 87, 88, 90, 92, 94, 96, 98, 100, 101, 104, 105, 108, 112, 113, 114, 115, 117, 118, 119, 121, 122, 124, 126, 129, 130, 131, 132, 140, 141, 147, 154, 157, p. 3); Edo Kuipers (fig. 153); The Museum of Modern Art, New York/USA (fig. 1, 13, 28, 34, 38); Photo RMN Gérard Blot (fig. 46); Photo RMN Béatrice Hatala (fig. 45); Photothèque des Musées de la Ville de Paris (fig. 40); Edward Quinn, Nice/F (fig. 47); Thijs Quispel, Oosthuizen/NL (fig. 128); Alain Ramié, Vallauris/F (fig. 136); Man Ray, New York/USA (fig. 30); Henny Riemens (fig. 67, 142, 143, 144, 145, 146); Wim Riemens, Middelburg/NL (fig. 152); André Villers (fig. 133); Alfred J. Wyatt (fig. 27); Hans Zoete, Eindhoven/NL (fig. 116).

Friends of Museum Het Kruithuis

ABN/AMRO-bank, 's-Hertogenbosch
Alynia Lerou Architecten, 's-Hertogenbosch
Appèl Servicegroep, 's-Hertogenbosch
Croonen Adviseurs, 's-Hertogenbosch
CW Lease Nederland B.V., 's-Hertogenbosch
Faber Vastgoed B.V., 's-Hertogenbosch
The Greenery International B.V., 's-Hertogenbosch
Heineken Nederland B.V., 's-Hertogenbosch
Heijmans N.V., Rosmalen
Hogeschool, 's-Hertogenbosch
Huijbregts Beheer, Nieuwkuijk
ING-bank, 's-Hertogenbosch
Kamer van Koophandel & Fabrieken, 's-Hertogenbosch
De Keizer Assurantie B.V., Rotterdam
KPMG Accountants, 's-Hertogenbosch
Van Leeuwen/Van der Eerden advocaten, 's-Hertogenbosch
Uitgeverij Malmberg, 's-Hertogenbosch
Kunsthandel/Lijstenmakerij Monart, 's-Hertogenbosch
Jac. Mulders Electro B.V., Rosmalen
N.V. PNEM, 's-Hertogenbosch
PTT Telecom, 's-Hertogenbosch
Rieken & Oomen, Maastricht/'s-Hertogenbosch
Stienstra B.V. Bedrijfshuisvesting, 's-Hertogenbosch
Swinkels, Maas & Verhorevoort, 's-Hertogenbosch
Würth Nederland B.V., 's-Hertogenbosch